RADICAL EVIL

Ⓢ

Each volume of this annual series will contain original essays from leading theorists focusing on one topic of immediate cultural and political concern. While experts from a variety of fields will contribute to each volume, the avowed aim of the series is to demonstrate the fundamental psychoanalytic character of the issues raised and the solutions required. Against the narrowing and reduction of psychoanalysis to a specialized vocabulary, which so often takes place in cultural studies, the project of these volumes is to enlarge the scope of psychoanalysis by equating it, more properly, with its concepts, no matter what term designates them. From the perspective of this enlargement, our modernity – including its 'postmodern' inversion – will be shown to be more thoroughly defined by psychoanalysis than was previously thought, and the strategies for thinking our current conditions will be rigorously overhauled.

RADICAL EVIL

edited by
JOAN COPJEC

VERSO

London • New York

First published by Verso 1996
This collection © Verso 1996
Individual contributions © individual contributors 1996
All rights reserved

The right of the individual contributors to be identified as
the authors of their work has been asserted by them in
accordance with the Copyright, Designs and Patents Act 1988

Verso
UK: 6 Meard Street, London W1V 3HR
USA: 180 Varick Street, New York NY 10014–4606

Verso is the imprint of New Left Books

ISBN 1–85984–911–3
ISBN 1–85984–006–X (pbk)

British Library Cataloguing in Publication Data
A catalogue record for this book is available from the British Library

Library of Congress Cataloging-in-Publication Data
A catalog record for this book is available from the Library of Congress

Typeset by Keystroke, Jacaranda Lodge, Wolverhampton
Printed by Biddles Ltd, Guildford and King's Lynn

CONTENTS

INTRODUCTION
Evil in the Time of the Finite World

JOAN COPJEC

When we contemplate the international situation, we
cannot fail to be struck by the utter barbarity of civilized
nations that cling fast to fundamental principles they refuse
under any circumstances to abandon:

> Each separate state, so long as it has a neighboring state which it
> dares hope to conquer, strives to aggrandize itself through . . .
> conquest, and thus to attain a world-monarchy, a polity wherein all
> freedom, . . . virtue, taste, and learning, would necessarily expire.
> Yet this monster (in which laws gradually lose their force), after it
> has swallowed all its neighbors, finally dissolves of itself, and
> through rebellion and disunion breaks up into many smaller states.
> . . . The result is that the *philosophical millennium*, which hopes for a
> state of perpetual peace based on a league of peoples . . . which
> tarries for the completed improvement of the entire human race,
> is universally ridiculed as a wild fantasy.

And if we then refocus our attention on a more intimate
scale of human relations, we find numerous examples of
this same perfidious egoity, of

> a secret falsity even in the closest friendships, . . . a propensity to
> hate him to whom one is indebted, . . . a hearty well-wishing which
> yet allows the remark that 'in the misfortunes of our best friends,
> there is something which is not altogether displeasing to us.'[1]

Such sentiments, common enough today, could be
attributed to countless contemporary sources, who might be
speaking of the break-up of either Yugoslavia or the Soviet
Union, the rash of 'tell-all' books or the petty perfidies of
talk-show guests. These words, however, belong to

Immanuel Kant, who employs them in a late text, *Religion within the Limits of Reason Alone*, to acknowledge the 'insurmountable wickedness', the *radical evil* that inhabits the heart of man and which he can 'by no means wipe out' (*RL*, p. 66).

This acknowledgement will seem scandalous to those of us who see Kant as the apostle of reason and progress. It is as if in evil progress had hit a bump that threatened to expose it as mere anthropomorphic illusion, or reason had suddenly been shown to be corruptible at its core. That is, in admitting the innateness or radicality of evil, Kant could seem either to have discarded his belief in the powers of reason and the perfectibility of man and reverted instead to a belief in original sin, or to have found in these Enlightenment notions a new source of evil. It was easier for his contemporaries to take the former position, to think that Kant had in his old age returned to one of the traditional religious views against which they were then battling. To us, the latter position comes more easily; we almost spontaneously assume that Kant must have begun, in his old age, to renounce his former optimism and to fear that the Enlightenment principles he had so long preached might themselves become the doctrine of a modern-day religion, more dangerous than the kind it superseded. The difference in these reactions stems from the fact that between Kant's contemporaries and us there have intervened numerous colonialist battles and two all-out world wars which have been borne by a kind of implacable fury and devastation that could not possibly have existed during the centuries before Kant wrote and of which even he could only have had abstract glimmerings.

Let us not forget, the 'international situation' (*den aüszern Völkerzustand*) Kant contemplates is just barely formulatable as a notion at the end of the eighteenth century. The contemporary ring of his complaint is slightly off; it sounds a bit prematurely. For nations in the modern sense, republics rather than monarchies, whose very destinies depend on the will of their people, were at this time in the earliest stages of conception and formation. And thus the conflicts, the colonial and world wars, that would break out between these nations – and would give rise to the very notion of the 'international situation' – were merely an emerging possibility when Kant expressed his bleak sentiments. When these wars did in fact take place, they would be unlike any that had been fought before, more barbarous, more cruel. What would make them so different from earlier wars is that they would be waged by nations who were able to enlist the will of their people, who were for the first time free to dispose of it as they chose. It was only when war had will on its side that it acquired its limitless capacity for destruction.

The question that must immediately be asked is this: How base is will, that is, is it *fundamentally* base? What, finally, does Kant mean by the term *radical evil*?

While he most certainly means that evil is *rooted* in human will, has no existence
apart from will and cannot be eradicated from it, critics have been less sure how
far down he supposes evil to go, how far a 'secret falsity' and a 'propensity to
hat[red]' permeate human will. The question is: Does evil consume will entirely
or does it leave behind something that might positively strive toward good?

This volume was first planned to commemorate the 200th anniversary of the
publication of *Religion within the Limits of Reason Alone*,[2] and to continue to try
to sort out some of the questions raised by what is regarded by many as the
thoroughly baffling concept of evil proposed in it. It is appropriate that as we
wrote our essays, several nations were in the process of finding ways to mark the
fiftieth anniversary of the Second World War and commemorate the Holocaust.
Yet the horrible evidence of what Kant variously called the *wickedness, corruption*
and *perversity* of the human heart is, unfortunately, not encountered only in
memory, it is also met with among our current experiences. We are daily
obliged to witness fresh atrocities as ethnic and racial hatreds seek to express
themselves in the annihilation of their proponents' enemies; as nations deci-
mate themselves, breaking up into ever smaller and more fractious units; as
terrorists of every stripe blow up people and buildings in an effort to protect
their own and the rights of their 'unborn'; as multinational interests devise
more advanced forms of exploiting labour and crushing resistance; and on and
on. If Enlightenment philosophy's 'wild fantasy' of 'moral improvement' and
universal humanity, of the fostering and protection of human rights, progress
and universality is everywhere ridiculed, if the whole aureola of concepts
surrounding that of will is tarnished, this is because – some would say – these
concepts are responsible for bringing about the very disasters they pretend to
ward off. In the last two centuries will has revealed itself to be free to will its own
enslavement to fascist heroes and to 'just' causes (such as freedom, humanity,
human rights) that have demanded the torture and execution of those who
opposed them. And things keep going from bad to worse.

It would seem to be necessary, then, to take another look at the notions of
will, progress, freedom and universal rights that emerged in tandem with the
notion of radical evil. The first thing to be considered is the often forwarded
proposal that Kant could not face squarely his own discovery of the radicality of
evil; he could not admit that it ultimately extends beyond the corruption of all
our moral maxims (the imperatives that command us to act disinterestedly, for
the good) – which is what he conceded – to a corruption of the will itself. That
is, some critics have claimed, if we take Kant's thinking where it refuses to go,
we will find that radical evil is worse than he was prepared to admit, that it is,
in fact, *diabolical* or *absolute*.[3] By this they mean that will is capable not simply of

opposing the moral law, but of making this opposition the very motive of our actions. If this were so, we would be capable of doing evil simply for the sake of doing evil, not merely for the sake of some profit to ourselves. Kant firmly and expressly denied to man this decidedly Romantic capability. One such denial is expressed in the following way: 'Man (even the most wicked) does not, under any maxim whatsoever, repudiate the moral law in the manner of a rebel (renouncing obedience to it)' (*RL*, p. 31). Some assume, however, that the horror Kant felt at such a possibility caused him to retreat into simple and questionable reassertions of the 'fact' of will; they treat his insistence on the essential *goodness* of will as merely a defensive gesture designed to protect him from the shuddering thought of a diabolical evil or a malign reason that aimed at pure destruction. This implies, of course, that after his confrontation with evil, Kant's belief in human perfectibility and the goodness of will was maintained in blatant contradiction to his own arguments. I will propose, however, that the best way to understand the status of Kant's belief in the essential goodness of will is not to begin by looking askance at the seeming contumaciousness of his claim regarding its self-evidence, but by pausing to reflect on the obstinacy of his assertions regarding the self-evidence of evil. This, as I have been suggesting, is what is really odd and not merely because it seems to be out of step with the new-found optimism of the philosophical age whose figurehead he was and out of line with the cherished convictions he held in common with educators that the world moves in a *positive* direction, from bad to better. When Kant immediately concedes that moral goodness cannot be deduced from experience, which only provides proof of the *badness* of man, we have to wonder at the readiness with which he accepts the fact of our wickedness.

We go only part way to understanding what he is up to when we note that in *Religion within the Limits of Reason Alone*, Kant's purpose is to contest previous accounts of evil, which could only grasp it as a negative phenomenon. In his earlier writings, even Kant held to the long-standing religious or metaphysical view that considered evil to be nothing in itself, but merely the *lack* or deficit of something.[4] In this view, disease, disaster, political and social injustice and suffering of every sort were treated either as illusions fomented by the limitations of our merely mortal understanding, or as actual, but temporary, conditions attributable to the limitations of human will by earthly passions or by human freedom through original sin. By imputing evil to mortal defect or privation, as that which interfered with the full appearance of the Good, the various solutions to the problem of evil were designed to leave both the Good and God unscathed and thus, ultimately, justified.

But in *Religion within the Limits of Reason Alone*, evil no longer has only this shadowy, insubstantial existence; it no longer has less reality than good does.

Instead evil appears as a positive fact, firmly rooted in reality. At this point it ceases to be a religious or metaphysical problem and becomes, for the first time, a political, moral and pedagogical problem. This conceptual 'revolution' is brought about by detaching evil from human finitude (conceived as simply the limitations imposed by our mortal nature) and attaching it to human freedom (or to our immortal aspirations). Kant's underlying question is historically posed. He does not ask himself how evil is possible, he asks, rather, how evil is possible given the fact of freedom. He wants to understand how it happened that men who had recently won their freedom, who no longer needed to bow to external pressures, chose to calculate in terms of these pressures, that is, chose to act immorally. That is to say, Kant sees evil as uniquely the product of a free humanity, and it is this which is new in his thought.

But once having made the point that Kant's innovation was to link evil to human freedom, we are forced to acknowledge that the evidence of evil is not as simple as the constant consensual complaints against it would imply. For if evil is defined as a positive act freely carried out, then empirical evidence alone is no longer sufficient to identify it. We can only conclude that an act is evil on the basis of an *unobservable* condition: that it was governed by the free adoption of a bad maxim. Before Kant, it was possible to conceive the battle between good and evil as taking place between will and sensuous motives. It was thought that our mortal nature made us susceptible to worldly temptations that promised us pleasure and flattered our pride, and that our will, or moral nature, provided us with the only power we had to combat these temptations. One acted for ill out of a weakness or deficiency of will whose default allowed external, sensible incentives to control one's actions. Kant argued, however, that no external incentive, no pure animal interest, could in and of itself – that is, could in the absence of will – govern the actions of men. Will does not combat sensuous motives, it determines the rules of our actions. The battle between good and evil is thus redefined as taking place between the adoption of two possible types of rules: good or bad; disinterested (that is, based only on moral law) or self-interested (based on self-regard). If we act badly, out of self-interest, this is because we have *chosen* to be influenced by external concerns, we have incorporated a particular pathological desire into a maxim, allowed it rather than the moral law to become the motive of our action. In Lacanian terms, we must always desire to be lured by a particular desire. In the absence of this second-level desire, we are completely indifferent to even the most highly prized object.

One of the consequences of this redefinition of evil is that it burdens us with full responsibility for our actions; we are no longer able to exonerate ourselves by claiming to be victims of our passions and thus of external circumstances.

Lately, we have been taught to refuse this position as politically naive, since it seems to isolate and elevate us above the entire set of our social circumstances, to disregard our embeddedness in historical time. Yet this dismissive reading of the Kantian position has not only sacrificed the astuteness of its historical insights, it has also stoked the fires of our modern misanthropy.

To counter this historicist prejudice and restore Kant's argument to its proper political power, one needs first of all to note the profound dissymmetry in the outcome of the moral battle, as Kant describes it. Rather than weighting things toward the triumph of the autonomous will over a selfish investment in external circumstances, as critics of his supposed naivety might lead one to suspect, he surprises us by observing *only* a bad outcome. Evil self-interest trumps moral righteousness every time, as the evidence inescapably shows. What Kant's rigorism forces us to confront is not simply the occasional or partial combination of self-interested and purely moral motives, but the very subordination of moral, universal law to the imperatives of self-regard. He locates in man a profound malignity that causes him to be bad even when he is good; that is, even as we heed the moral law, we do so, according to Kant, for self-interested reasons. If we perform some virtuous act, it is to impress others with our virtue; if we decline to tell a lie, it is because we are afraid we might be caught in it, and so on. Moreover, Kant argues, this is not simply true of some of us, some of the time, but is universally true of all of us, without exception. 'The ultimate subjective ground of all maxims . . . is entwined with and, as it were, rooted in humanity itself' (*RL*, pp. 27–8). Radical evil, 'the foul taint in our race' (*RL*, p. 34), is everywhere and always evident in the fact that man devotes his will to the pursuit of egoistic gain. Far from transcending the network of his social circumstances, he enmires himself in them, harmonizes with his social surroundings by seeking his own desire in the desire of others and his value in their admiring or admonishing eyes.

In order to mock this propensity of man, Kant, in *The Critique of Practical Reason*, quoted a satirical poem in which a couple each wish for the ruin of the other. The sentiment and phrasing of this poem recall François I's account of his battle against Charles: 'Oh marvelous harmony; what I want, he wants, too. What my brother Charles wants [Milan], I want, too.' There is no mistaking this sentiment, for it is the common motif of all-out and perpetual war that initiates modern struggles for 'pure prestige', in which individual subjects and nations seek the absolute elimination of their rivals. Yet what has been obscured by contemporary thought is the fact that this relativization of our desire is no less an incitement to war when we decide not, as in the case of François I, to define our wants as the *same* as our brother's, but as irreducibly *different* from his. The celebration of the plurality of cultures and hence the relativity of our desires is, in Kant's terms, no less an indication of the wickedness and corruption of the human heart than is the coveting of all our brother holds dear. That is, 'to each his own desire' is no less dangerous a sentiment than 'what I want, he wants, too'. For cultural relativists also adopt a heteronomous definition of desire that supposes it to be determined by the desires of other members of one's own culture. Relativism simply foregrounds the banal truth of every such heteronomous definition of desire: it inevitably encounters an obstacle in the form of another who refuses to prize what we value, who refuses to recognize our worth. These two seemingly opposed positions are also similar in that they both negate the possibility of an autonomous will – one that is not dependent on others – and of ethics itself, in so far as they make what is historically present and true the sole standard of what should be, dissolve 'ought' in the medium of a historical 'is'.

Guilt

But how can we, from a Kantian position, condemn historicism's heteronomous definition of will and desire when Kant himself seems to be incapable of safe-guarding his own notion of autonomy? Doesn't the concept of radical evil represent the collapse of the very distinction between an autonomous and a heteronomous will? Doesn't 'the foul taint of our race' consist precisely in the fact that our will *cannot* determine itself by itself, but must instead seek motivation in some extraneous content, that desire is *never* our own, but always another's?

To be honest, these are not the only questions Kant's position raises at this point. My own description of the dissymmetry between good and bad outcomes has blundered through an aporia in Kant's thought without bothering to expose it. You will remember that it was his fundamental argument that the principle of evil is not to be found in man's animal or sensible nature, which obliged Kant to discredit simple observation as evidence of moral wrongdoing. In order to condemn an act as bad, one would have to conclude that it was performed in accordance with a bad maxim; and in order to reach this conclusion, one would have to look beyond outer appearances to fathom the depths of another's or own's own heart. And yet, as Kant himself insists, this is impossible; one cannot with certainty acquire 'knowledge of the basis of [others'] maxims . . . or of their purity' (*RL*, p. 57). If freedom shields the human heart from observation, makes us inscrutable, it would seem that what Kant *should* have argued is that we can never know whether a particular act is guided by a good or a bad maxim. But, as we have seen, he concludes instead that all our maxims are bad and he condemns all our acts as '*always* . . . defective . . . *always* inadequate' (*RL*, p. 60;

Kant's emphasis). How does one account for the harshness of his judgement, the certainty with which he regards the fact of evil? What makes Kant so sure not only that we always *transgress* the moral law, but also that we are conscious of these transgressions and that we *loathe* them? For, as I have already noted, in distinguishing radical from diabolical evil, Kant argues that the latter is impossible for man, who never elevates his transgression into a universal law, but rather regards his own act as a culpable and loathsome exception to it.

This inexplicable profession of certainty in a place where we expected only uncertainty has resonance for readers of Freud, who will discern similarities between the philosopher's argument and the psychoanalyst's description of the superego. Freud, too, regarded moral conscience as 'sure of itself', as requiring no confirmation and no justification for the condemnation it heaps upon us. A sense of guilt, he says, is 'as self-evident as its origins are unknown'.[5] Common to Freud and Kant is the unexpected assertion not only that moral conscience is always certain, but that it is, moreover, certain of only one thing: its guilt. And in the arguments of both, this guilty conscience seems to have been allowed to usurp the entire territory of moral action in that it condemns *all* our acts as bad, even and especially those performed by the most virtuous among us. Saving his strongest denunciations for those acts that outwardly appear to be the most moral, Kant responds exactly like Freud's superego, which is most remorseless in its condemnation of precisely those who are the most conscientious about fulfilling their moral duty.

Why should this be so? Everyone who would wish to maintain the possibility of a Romantic refusal of the law, a *diabolical* evil that would subvert its power, insists on misunderstanding this point, which has to do with the nature of the law. To clarify what is at issue here, let us examine a statement I just made: moral conscience is certain of only one thing: its *guilt*. Is this actually true? Doesn't Kant – and Freud, for that matter – also say that moral conscience is certain of – can neither mistake nor escape – the clear and imperative voice of conscience, which bids us obey the *moral law*? Yes, but there is no contradiction here. When Kant says, for example, that 'there is no man so depraved but that he feels upon transgressing the internal law a resistance within himself and an abhorrence of himself' (*RL*, p. 31), he is not arguing that man is conscious of two separate and opposing phenomena: the moral law and its infraction. Rather, he is arguing that our only consciousness of the law is our consciousness of our transgression of it. Our guilt is all we know of the law. This is how Gilles Deleuze, for example, describes Kant's innovation in the conception of moral law:

> Kant, by establishing THE LAW as an ultimate ground or principle, added an essential
> dimension to modern thought: the object of the law is by definition unknowable and

elusive. . . . Clearly THE LAW, as defined by its pure form, without substance or object of any determination whatsoever, is such that no one knows nor can know what it is. It operates without making itself known. It defines a realm of transgression where one is already guilty, and where one oversteps the bounds without knowing what they are.[6]

The moral law is, in Kant, purely formal, empty of content; and the voice of conscience, while indubitable, utters neither prescription nor proscription; it says *nothing* to us because it speaks to us in our singularity, as free and autonomous subjects. Addressed to us alone, the voice is that which cannot be exhausted in any phenomenalized language. For whatever message is imparted completely by language is *transmissable* to others.

And addressed to us as free yet finite subjects (affected by sensibility), the voice of conscience reveals not only the autonomy of our will – the fact that we can freely determine our actions without regard to creature interests – but also that we are free to choose *whether* to be free or to bow to these interests. As is well known, Kant indicates this double aspect of human will by using two different words for it: *Wille*, when he refers to its legislative capacity, and *Willkür*, to refer to the choice of freedom it gives itself. It would be a mistake, however, to hypostasize this distinction by speaking of two different kinds of will. The function of the distinction is to expose the self-limiting nature of human will, the internal impediment that divides it from itself. This internal non-coincidence of human will with itself prevents man from identifying in any straightforward way with his own autonomy. Our moral experience reveals to us not our freedom so much as our failure to be sufficiently free; or, better, our capacity for freedom is suggested to us only through our moral chastisements. Reversing the historicist error – which completely absorbs 'ought' into 'is', effectively eliminating the former – Kant absorbs 'is' (the nature of human will, which is to be free) into 'ought'. The only way we know that we *can* act freely – that is, that we *are* free – is through the voice of conscience, which tells us that we *ought* to free ourselves from our slavery to external motives. In Lacan's translation, the status of the subject becomes, with Kant, ethical rather than ontological; the subject can only be supposed on the basis of moral conscience. This is also what Kant means when he claims that the moral law never presents itself as such, has no content other than this negative experience of our failure to comply with it. Guilt, our sure sense that we have transgressed the law, is the only phenomenal form in which the law makes itself known to us.

The liberal reading of Kant – which has him identify man directly with his freedom and with an unalienated, undivided will – apparently ignores all the textual evidence of will's internal division in order to fabricate a voluntarist version of this philosophy. *Religion within the Limits of Reason Alone* must be almost totally overlooked in this case. But other more recent interpretations of this neglected text, purportedly more 'progressive', offer a different misreading of Kant. Deconstructively intent on pinpointing his blind spots, these are the readings that attribute his refusal to grant man devilish powers to a lack of intellectual nerve. It is now possible to see where this critique goes wrong. In order to elevate resistance to the law into a maxim, it would be necessary to phenomenalize the law, but, as we have seen, the moral law resists phenomenalization. In fact, it is this very resistance that is responsible for the radicality (or ineradicableness) of evil in the first place. To say that we always obey the moral law for immoral, self-interested reasons is to say that the moral law cannot be formulated as a maxim. The attempt to think diabolical evil turns out to be another attempt to deny will's self-alienation, to make of will a pure, positivized force; this reading, then, offers a voluntarist alternative to Kant. But since the fault in human will cannot be repaired, it is apparent that this alternative wrongly credits man with a power for pure destruction, that is, with a power in the first instance to destroy himself, to annihilate his own freedom.[7] In another vocabulary, one could say that the death drive is never encountered directly, in an unalloyed form.

In sum, the concept of radical evil successfully avoids the seductions of voluntarism *and* historicism by acknowledging, in the first case, that human desire is constitutively dependent on others and human will can only realize itself in a content that alienates it from itself, and, in the second, by linking our propensity to evil to guilt. The phenomenon of guilt is our proof that the subject is free, that it exceeds the historical content in which alone it realizes itself. While necessary, all such content is nevertheless necessarily inadequate. This does not mean that the excess of the subject is anterior or exterior to the content that inadequately contains it, but that historical content's inadequacy or mute inability to justify itself – in short, its very historicity – *is* this excess, *is* the subject. From this perspective we could say that the wedge between 'is' and 'ought' – between the actual, phenomenal or historical forms of the subject and the moral law that frees it from them – is driven through the heart of historical fact, separating it from its ultimate justification for being. Because things could always be otherwise, the subject *is*. Historicists take a contrary view, arguing that it is because things could always be otherwise, because history is always undoing what is, that the subject is *not*.

Law and Punishment

There are, however, other accounts of the historical consequences of the emptying out of moral law besides Kant's. According to these, a law with which we are constitutively unable to comply binds us not to our own freedom, but to a punishing enslavement to an all-powerful law. Adolph Eichmann might be thought to provide the proof of this contention, for he conflated his respect for Hitler and obedience to the leader's orders with his 'Kantian' respect for moral law. And Deleuze gives a troubling inflection to his discussion of the relation between the empty, indeterminate moral law and its phenomenalization in transgressions when, citing the work of Kafka, he shifts his attention from the law itself to 'the extreme specificity of the punishments' incurred by its transgression. Suddenly the notion of the empty law is historically concretized for us in scenes of totalitarian bureaucratic terror in which unwitting citizens are charged with transgressions against vague and obscure laws without being allowed either to confront their accusers or clarify the nature of their crimes. This is Foucault's picture of panoptic power, in which the law withdraws only to make itself manifest in the prisoners whom it exposes and defines by their deviations from some supposed norm, by their faults and failures, their general subjection to regimes of scrutiny and punishment. The implication, once again, is that Enlightenment notions of moral law, freedom and will created the inevitable conditions for a voluntary yet infrangible servitude.

How, despite his privileging of guilt as the abiding core of moral experience, does Kant escape this charge? And, to return to an earlier point, how does the guilty subject Kant constructs avoid falling prey to the escalating and unending punishments of the superego, so memorably described by Freud? Although he conceived *guilt* as infinite (our transgressions of the law being endless), Kant was careful to add that *punishment* need not be (*RL*, p. 66). In fact, he explicitly counsels us on how to escape the cruel tortures of the superego or, as he says, 'the accuser within us', which is 'more likely to propose a judgment of condemnation' (*RL*, p. 70). 'More likely than who?' we can't help asking. To what other judge can we appeal? Kant's warning is surprising. Since the autonomy of the subject depends on a refusal to cede moral decisions to external authorities or influences, we might have expected this internal accuser to be hailed as the instance of judgement on which the subject ought to rely. But Kant says 'no'; this judge is also to be mistrusted. On what basis does a dismissal of these intimate accusations become conceivable? How is it possible to avoid the paradoxical cycle of guilt and punishment that results from listening to the internal voice of conscience?

In order to answer these questions, it will be helpful to understand first how the paradoxical logic of the superego *does* follow (though not, as I will argue, unavoidably) from the notions of the autonomous subject and the empty moral law. For it cannot be doubted that a kind of servitude has historically been consequent on these notions. If Kant's definition of a positive or radical evil has so far accorded very little with our intuitive sense of what it means to speak of *modern* evil or to claim that an unprecedented wickedness has been introduced into the world, here we finally arrive on more familiar ground. We come face to face with the colonialist taste for empire, the Nazi lust for genocide, and casuistry of the bloodiest kind. For if these modern phenomena do not have their source directly in the perversion of our maxims (in radical evil) or in the experience of guilt that accompanies this perversion, they are founded in a particular *response* to this perversion and guilt.

Subordinating the moral law to laws of self-interest, we deliver ourselves to our animal interests and to the principles of predation that govern them. Yet if Kant is correct, if as humans we freely choose to obey our sensible inclinations, then some evidence of our freedom or of our capacity to resist these inclinations must betray itself in our actions. If, despite the constancy of our choice of evil or the inextirpableness of our self-regard, we rightfully believe ourselves to be free and thus capable of moral action, then we should expect to find some trace of the surplus of our being beyond mere mortality in our own actions, which would thereby demonstrate their irreducibility to mere animal behaviour.

Salò (1975), Pier Paolo Pasolini's film about Italian fascism, provides some clues of where to look for this surplus. In one sequence, that of the most beautiful ass contest, the libertines survey a sea of bare bottoms in order to choose the one most pleasing to them. The monotonous anonymity (to our eyes, at least) of row on row of this single exposed body part helps to establish the parallel Pasolini wants to draw between these sadistic sodomites and Italy's fascist leaders. For these nude, anonymous and vulnerable bodies recall to mind prisoners in concentration camps, except for the fact that those disposable bodies were always half-starved or dead and rotting. The comely young bodies in the film are well-fed, well-formed and in some fantasmatic sense indestructible. As the contest proceeds, two of the philosophically inclined libertines conduct a short disquisition on the subject of this comparison, the first solemnly opining: 'The act of the sodomite is the most absolute, in the mortality implied, for the human race.' To which the second answers, 'There's something still more monstrous: the act of the executioner.' 'True, but the sodomite's act can be repeated thousands of times,' the first rejoins. The second will not be outdone: 'A way can be found to repeat the executioner's.' He need not specify what the executioner's way entails; we know that it is accomplished through the execution of another victim, and another and another, ad infinitum. Six million and more. Where the allies and cohorts of Hitler pursued the ever-receding 'final solution' by exterminating an infinite series of victims, the sadistic libertine endlessly tortures the same victim, who miraculously refuses to die or even display on his beautiful body the signs of torture. 'Don't you know', one libertine asks the boy with the most beautiful ass, 'that we'd want to kill you a thousand times to the limits of eternity, if eternity has any?' It does not, neither for the sadistic sodomite nor for the Nazi and fascist executioners, at least not one that is reachable by them.

For libertine and executioner alike, what Kant referred to as the 'totality of this series of approximations carried on without end' (*RL*, fn. p. 61) always lies asymptotically beyond their grasp; though the severity of the tortures escalates, the act of torture remains 'defective', 'inadequate', unable to complete itself through the extraction of a sufficient dose of pain. In each case, the futility of the torturer's act is attributable to the resistance of the victim. The body of the libertine's victim resists through the persistence of its beautiful form, which escapes any deformation. The bodies of the executioner's victims, on the other hand, resist through their very formlessness. Philippe Lacoue-Labarthe and Jean-Luc Nancy, in an essay entitled 'The Nazi Myth', uncover the fantasy of the Jew constructed by National Socialism, according to which:

> The Jew has no *Seelengestalt*, therefore no *Rassengestalt*: his form is formless. He is the man of the universal abstract, as opposed to the man of singular, concrete identity. Thus Rosenberg takes care to point out that the Jew is not the 'antipode' of the German, but his 'contradiction,' by which he no doubt very clumsily means to say that the Jew is not an opposite *type*, but the very absence of type, a danger present in all bastardizations, which are all parasitic.[8]

Having no form, culture or nation of his own, parasitic on those of others, the Jew arrayed in borrowed forms avoids detection. In other words, one could never be sure one had tracked down the last one. The extermination of the Jewish race then fantasmatically presents itself as a task that stretches out through a limitless eternity, and the 'Jewish plot' presents itself not only as secret but eternal as well, without beginning or end. But if the victims are indestructible, the wills of their torturers are no less so; they seem to toughen, to assert themselves more insistently in their attempts to triumph over such impossible obstacles.

Once again, the nagging question arises: Is *this* the will Kant was so intent on defending? I think we can see now not only that it is not, but why it is not. As I have already pointed out, Kant describes human will as alienated from itself by an *internal* fracture. But the executioner experiences this impediment to his will as coming from the victim's resistance; only an enemy other opposes the torturer's unalienated will, checking its otherwise absolute power. Freud used the term *projection* to describe the mechanism by which what is internal to the subject comes to be viewed as imposed from outside, but he was not satisfied that the term adequately described all that was involved in this process. I will therefore suggest another term by which we might explain that response to *radical evil* – or the internal fracture of human will – which produces the phenomenon of *modern evil.*

That which is missing from the notion of *projection* is supplied, I will argue, by the notion of *subreption.* Through subreption, a supersensible idea, that is, one which can never be experienced, is falsely represented as if it were a possible object of experience. One of the things the concept of radical evil tells us is that human freedom and immortality are supersensible ideas. To repeat the argument: while it uncovers the experience of guilt that makes it necessary to *suppose* our freedom (or our ability to act without regard for our merely mortal being), radical evil also reveals that this guilt is *all we experience* of freedom and immortality. Almost as soon as they were invented, however, these supersensible ideas were erased as such and misrepresented as sensible phenomena.

How does this subreption come about? What does it mean to speak of a *sensible* definition of human freedom and the immortality of the soul? It would seem that if these supersensible ideas were denied, the subject would become totally assimilated to its mortality, reduced to its natural unfreedom and finitude. But this is not what happens; as we said, the fact that the subject *is* free reveals itself in a certain surplus: of fantasy. That is to say, while through subreption the subject is assimilated to its concrete, historically defined particularities (the 'blood and soil' of National Socialism, for example), its freedom and immortality return in the fantasy of *progress to infinity* (to which National Socialists were not the only ones wholly to commit themselves). Within this fantasy, subjective finitude and failure are effaced by the promises of progress. Death is indefinitely postponed and the checks on the power of human will are denied any ultimate victory. It should be easy to see how this fantasmatic notion of infinite progress sustains the individual fantasies of both the sadistic libertines and the executioners, who hold on to a sensible definition of themselves without surrendering their freedom or immortality. Their fantasies allow them to dream of the 'enjoyment of ever-increasing pleasures' and a 'freedom from evils' (*RL,* p. 61).

The Superego and Teleological Judgement

Once again, this argument is bound to introduce confusion. How can Kant, one of the prime proponents of progress and the perfectibility of man, come to stand for the very opposition to them? The confusion arises from a failure to distinguish between different concepts of progress. Infinite progress is *not* the one for which Kant reserved his approbation, as *Religion within the Limits of Reason Alone* makes clear. What causes his disdain for that conception of progress is undoubtedly the fact that it is produced through subreption. This is how he states his objection: '[C]onduct itself [defined] as a continual and endless advance from a deficient to a better good, ever remains defective' (*RL*, p. 60). Why is this so? Because, as he explains a few lines earlier,

> the distance separating the good which we ought to effect in ourselves from the evil whence we advance is infinite, and the act itself, of conforming our course of life to . . . the law, is impossible of execution in any given time.

In other words, whatever dreams the fantasy of infinite progress encourages, the fact remains that its definition of the subject as 'ever only a *becoming*' (my emphasis) assimilates us to 'our failure ever wholly to be what we have in mind to become' (*RL*, fn. p. 61). The notion of progress to infinity anchors us to our mortality, to a temporality that ensures our failure from moment to moment, to an infinity of failure, therefore, and an infinity of punishments.

When Kant urges us to turn a deaf ear to the 'accuser within us', who would pronounce on us too severe a verdict, he is attempting to prevent our getting caught up in the belief in a progression to infinity. But the connection between this particular belief and this severe judgement is perhaps not altogether clear in Kant; it awaits Freud and psychoanalysis to elucidate it. I have already made the point that the internal judge to which Kant refers is strictly equivalent to the superego that, as Freud describes it, heaps blame in proportion to the diligence of our moral efforts, demands greater sacrifices the more we sacrifice. It is only by placing Freud's description alongside Kant's warnings against our modern faith in infinite progress that we begin to see how the infamous paradoxes of the superego relate to the paradoxes of Zeno, thus lending the latter a political cast. Zeno's paradoxes were designed to ridicule the philosophy of Becoming, while the paradoxes of the superego demonstrate that the more we define ourselves as *mere* becoming, the more we place ourselves in the service of a cruel and punishing law of sacrifice, or, as Lacan says, a 'dark God':

> There is something profoundly masked in the critique of the history that we have experienced. This, re-enacting the most monstrous and supposedly superseded forms of the holocaust, is the drama of Nazism . . . which only goes to show that the offering to obscure gods of an object of sacrifice is something to which few subjects can resist succumbing, as if under some monstrous spell. . . . [T]he sacrifice signifies that, in the object of our desires, we try to find evidence for the presence of the desire of this Other that I call here *the dark God*.[9]

Lacan's suggestion that enslavement to this cruel law of sacrifice is *not* the equivalent of an unconditional obedience of moral law follows Kant's lead.

That the voice of conscience is heard to demand the sacrifice of enjoyment indicates the extent to which we have subscribed to the historical fantasy of infinite progress, which turns out in Kant's reading to be nothing but a fantasy of infinite deferral. While on the one hand this fantasy seems to allow us to defer our own death infinitely, on the other hand, experience has shown, it binds us to death by reducing life to the struggle against it. And while the fantasy seems to hold out a promise of infinite pleasure, it in fact requires us always to tether our pleasure to this promise. In short, the historical subreption that attempted to redefine our ethical vocation as the pursuit of happiness and the cherishing of well-being, or physical life, has brought us the most unimaginable horrors and an undeniable 'contempt for life'.[10] The eugenic schemes of National Socialism are only the most obvious display of the paradoxical effects of the subreption that has placed us in the thrall of our internal judge.

This leads us to observe one final paradox. While appearing to force on us an acknowledgement of our guilt – the moment to moment inadequacy of all our acts, which causes our deeds to remain infinitely unachieved – this subreptive fantasy of progress ingeniously uses our guilt as a ruse to absolve it, that is, to acquit us of our real crime. It is Freud who provides us with the only account we have of the crime of which we are each guilty: the murder of the primal father, described in *Totem and Taboo*. As a result of this murder, fear and obedience are retroactively installed in us, causing us to respect a father with whom we are unable to identify and a law to which we are unable to conform. The murder places both the father and his law out of reach.

But if Freud supplied the account of this primordial crime, Kant supplied an explanation of its primordiality which should have protected *Totem and Taboo* from the ludicrous anthropological misreadings by which it was dismissed. The primal murder does not take place in some temporal past, but in a noumenal moment, which is not the same as saying that it occurs *outside* time. Unlike original sin, which implies that man simply inherits guilt for a sin committed before his birth, the murder of the primal father implies that each man accomplishes the murder himself, though not in historical time.

The crime is, therefore, not a possible object of experience. Yet the historicist subreption treats it as though it were, turning the murder into an as yet unrealized deed. This has the effect of both exonerating us of the murder and making us guilty of its nonaccomplishment. That is, it places us under the jurisdiction of our internal accuser, which condemns severely every failure of will to realize itself. It is this that lends our comportment toward the enemies who would impede us its note of execration.

Is the ultimate message of Kant, then, simply, 'Acknowledge your real guilt!' or, in psychoanalytic terms, 'Assume your castration!'? Are we to be saved from one harsh judge only to be delivered to another, more inescapable? The answer appears to be 'yes', for Kant does indeed assert the necessity of submitting ourselves to another, a final judge or a 'teleological judgment'.

A reference to a final judgement would seem to cancel any possibility of conceiving the freedom of will or the perfectibility of man, to undermine Kant's whole project. In fact, Kant builds his moral theory on a firm opposition to finalism. A moral or free act is one that is not directed by any end; it is absolutely unconditioned and therefore does good only for the sake of doing good. And yet, he argues, while no end can serve as the *basis* of a free act, it is unreasonable to think that no consequences issue from it, that there is no *terminus* of our actions. This notion of an end spares reason the absurdity of attempting to imagine an ethics that would be indifferent to any goal.

The source of the distinction I am trying to draw between the notion of infinite progress and the notion of progress proposed by Kant lies precisely in this terminus or end: absent in the former, it is indispensable in the latter. The question is: How does Kant prevent this end from being reabsorbed by will into a determinant of action? How, in other words, does he preserve the distinction between basis and terminus that is needed to keep progress from becoming destiny? The answer: he makes the end indeterminate.

The currently much-maligned notion of Kantian universalism has to be understood in this way. The universal defines the terminus of moral action; it is the goal toward which actions are directed and without which the decision to act would be irresolvably stymied. In this era of relativism and deconstruction,[11] when ethical thought has shrivelled under the force of theoretical common-places such as 'We can never know in advance or fully control the effects of our acts' or 'What is right for us may not be right for someone else', Kant's universalism is a most welcome corrective. What it says, in effect, is 'Be reasonable! Be practical!' Of course we can't control the future or see into someone else's heart, but what practical sense would it make to undertake any action if we did not conceive it as having some end or consequence, as operating causally in the world? Yet to say that the goal of ethics is to ensure that justice is extended to all, universally, is not to prejudge or prescribe any particular act. For such a goal does not define the universal from which no one is to be excluded by supplying it with any *content*. Empty of content, this end remains external to our acts and does not inhabit them; the end is not collapsed into its means, nor the future into the present of action. The goal of universal inclusion does not define what we must do. It would be wrong, however, to assume that the *requirement* of this final end is itself empty, that it adds nothing to the notion of ethics. Without it there would be no way of acknowledging that our acts are not merely random behaviour, that they are always executed with purpose, always result in some end.

We could summarize by saying that, contrary to current doxa, the Kantian universal is neither an underlying principle that informs individual beings nor a superior instance that subsumes our particularity; it is, rather, the focal point of our actions. Far from dissolving particularity, it is the essential means of sustaining it. Moreover, as the final end of all moral acts, this notion grounds ethics in practical reality without reducing the question of what we ought to do to the question of what is currently acceptable, without resorting to relativism.

Let us return to the related topic of teleological judgement with which I introduced this discussion of universalism. It is to this final judgement, rather than that of our inner accuser, that we are advised to present ourselves. The radicality of human evil, the fact that all our acts are defective, is reinforced by the notion of infinite progress. As a result, we are susceptible to the condemnations of our inner judge. Without negating the fact of radical evil, the final judgement, through the gift of grace, makes up for it. This gift, or 'surplus . . . over the profit of [our] good works' allows all our defective actions to be judged as a completed whole. Although, from moment to moment, we seem to be hopelessly ill-willed, we are, by the grace of the final judgement, granted a 'good disposition', or moral nature, and this disposition 'stands' in the place of the totality of this series of approximations carried on without end; makes up for [our] failure . . . ever wholly to be able to be what we have in mind to become' (*RL*, fn. p. 60).

Instead of a notion of infinite progress, of a mortality that is simply deferred and pleasure indefinitely renounced, Kant puts at the centre of his ethics a surplus that makes us not the *instruments* of the future, but its *beneficiaries*. He credits us with a being that we, radically evil, can never deserve, yet he credits it to us, nevertheless, 'exactly as if we were already in possession of it' (*RL*, p. 70). In one of those Möbius-strip turns characteristic of his philosophy, Kant makes the voice of conscience testify not only to our failures, but also to the bounty that is ours despite ourselves. While, as a result of our primordial crime, the moral law has withdrawn itself from the phenomenal world and conformity to it has thus become impossible, 'the bare idea of conformity [becomes] a stronger incentive for the will than all the incentives [of] . . . personal gain' (*RL*, p. 56).

Before dismissing this argument as theological vacuousness, it would be helpful to reconsider the rise, throughout the world, of religious fundamentalism. Although this phenomenon is commonly viewed as a reaction *against* modernity, such that the electronic aggression and media savoir-faire of this growing fringe are seen as somehow incompatible with its fundamentalist message, there is in fact no lack of sympathy between a certain belief in progress and religious dogmatism. The more we hold on to a certain notion of science, the more we secure the Kingdom of Heaven. Having no *natural* limit, in the sense that it is procedurally obliged to seek the causes of causes, the conditions of conditions, without end, reason/science is structurally predisposed to the fantasy of infinite progress and thus disciplinarily devoted to its own failure. The ratcheting up of self-punishments follows on this. Ironically, then, the attempt to seize life from the perspective of our sensible existence uproots us from life and leads to an indefinite postponement of gratification. It makes self-contempt the only *rational* result of any self-estimate. In a world such as this, salvation can only be conceived as coming from *outside*, beyond reason – and so it increasingly is.

The Ends of Man

The convocation to a final judgement is designed to dismantle the cruel machinery that sustains such religious dogmatism. Kant's convoking gesture is purely *formal* – since the final judge to which he would have us address ourselves is without attributes, including the ordinarily expected ones, such as omnipotence and omniscience – but it is not *empty*. It is indispensable to the grounding of reason in the world, to conceiving the practical employment of reason. As rational beings, we find it impossible to act in the world without a reason for doing so, without purpose. Teleological judgement allows us to pose this ultimate question regarding our actions, 'What is my purpose?'

Lacan has made a fair translation of this question, one that emphasizes its teleological complexity: '*Che vuoi?*' (What do you want of me?). Like Kant's, this question is posed to a final judge, whom Lacan calls the big Other. And also like Kant's, this final judge is determinate, that is, it is totally without attributes, barred. No answer is returned, then, in response to our question; yet despite this, it is not useless to pose it. First because, as Kant underlined, by defining the harmony of reason and nature as the goal of one's actions, the question gives reason a practical scope. To ask 'What do you want of me?' is to ask 'What are the consequences of my actions?'. The favour or gift of the Other's non-reply will be too easily interpreted as meaning that these consequences cannot be known in time, since time alters them endlessly. This misses the more fundamental point. In so far as we address it to an Other, any specific question also carries a bid for recognition. To ask 'What is my purpose?' is also to ask 'What am I worth?'. Thus, the Other's refusal to answer is not to be construed simply as *the absence of a final judgement*, but rather as *the delivery of an indefinite judgement*: 'Your purpose, your worth, is not reducible to the consequences of your actions. You are more than you do.' From the final judge, the subject learns not *what* it is, but *that* it is external to itself.

But it might be better to turn this observation around. What is teleological judgement, what makes it possible, if not the fact that the subject exceeds itself? This means that the subject *includes* as part of what it is this reference or appeal to a final judge, to a point from which the subject can be viewed. This reference maintains the subject's singularity outside all the deeds and misdeeds offered for review. The reference prevents the subject from being 'exhausted' or 'used up' by its deeds and misdeeds, that is, from becoming the *instrument of purpose.*

Kant's optimism about progress or the perfectibility of man must be understood against the background of this explanation. It is not in the good works or clever inventions of man that Kant placed his faith (these could never provide sufficient evidence to satisfy him of man's virtuousness), but in his moral being, his capacity to act unconditionally. Kant is well aware, since he himself demonstrated it to us, that this capacity can never be independently realized, it exists only in its failure of realization. We must, therefore, take him to be saying that the perfectibility of man lies not in the future (which has no chance of ever arriving), but in the present, in the incorporation into the present of the final judgement. It is only by including within itself this limit or final point that the subject avoids reducing itself to its own inextirpable inadequacies, its own ineradicable evil.

Human freedom makes radical evil a structural inescapability. But radical evil contributes to the historical phenomenon, modern evil, only on one condition: the elimination of the perspective of the final judgement. When this limit is no longer included within the subject as part of its definition and is instead infinitely deferred, placed outside it, modern evil results. That is, when the subject is no longer conceived as that which exceeds itself, as that which is the same despite all its divisions, and is reduced to mere becoming or deferred being, then it becomes subject, for all the reasons I have given, to a harsher judgement and a cruel, insatiable judge. To this 'dark God' no question of purpose is posed, rather an offering is tendered: 'Use me!' The greatest post-Enlightenment danger has turned out to be not our capacity to make reason an instrument of our will, but reason's capacity to make instruments of us. For once we are enlisted into the service of our obscene accuser, there is nothing that we will not sacrifice to it.

Let us hope that as the 'philosophical millennium' draws to a close, the 'wild fantasy' of 'the completed improvement of the entire human race' does not become another object of sacrifice. This would be the bleakest fall-out of infinite progress.

The Essays

Kant's legacy is unmistakable in all the essays that follow, for each of them treats evil as a modern political problem, one that cannot be divorced from the question of human freedom. This is not to say that Kant's theory is always the focus of the essays. Machiavelli, who placed evil at the heart of modern political theory, and Schelling, who made Kant's notion of radical evil the centre of his philosophy, are the subjects of two of the essays. The Holocaust, the single most agreed upon example of modern evil, is, understandably, either a focus or reference point of several of the essays: one examines the claim of Adolph Eichmann that in unconditionally obeying the Führer he was, like any moral man, simply doing his duty; another proposes that the Nazi death camps' project of *physical* annihilation makes a post-Auschwitz theory of the 'physiology of evil' necessary; a third explores the various and often conflicting strands of the politics of memory by which postwar Germany has attempted to reattach and/or leave behind its Nazi past. Regicide and hate speech are two other phenomena that also come under scrutiny, the former for the way it unsettles Kant's theory, the latter for the way it unsettles our notions of free speech and rights.

This bare description of their topics, however, can give little sense of the real complexity of these essays, which acknowledges not only the gravity of the issues raised by the question of evil, but also the fact that the question is doubled. The theory of evil has to be examined alongside the phenomenon since, in a sense peculiar to evil, the thinking about it, the fascination with it, is part of what is new in the phenomenon. Our examination is further evidence of this fascination.

Notes

1. Immanuel Kant, *Religion within the Limits of Reason Alone* (*RL*), trans. Theodore M. Greene and Hoyt H. Hudson (New York: Harper and Row 1960), pp. 28–9.
2. *Religion within the Limits of Reason Alone* was first published in 1793; the idea for the current volume was first conceived in 1992.
3. Jean-Luc Nancy, in his informative and intelligent book, *The Experience of Freedom*, trans. Bridget McDonald (Stanford, Calif.: Stanford University Press 1993), makes this argument. Jacques Derrida refers in a footnote in *Given Time 1: Counterfeit Money*, trans. Peggy Kamuf (Chicago: Chicago University Press 1994) to a 'satanic *cruelty* that Kant does not want to acknowledge', p. 166. Slavoj Žižek, a colleague with whom I usually agree, has referred in several places to Kant's inability to admit the fact of diabolical evil. In fact, I seem to be going against the contemporary tide on this issue.
4. The source of my information regarding the history of the concept of evil and Kant's relationship to it comes from Olivier Reboul's indispensable book, *Kant et le problème du mal* (Montréal: Presses de l'Université de Montréal 1971).
5. Sigmund Freud, *Totem and Taboo*, trans. A. A. Brill (New York: Random House 1946), p. 90.

6. Gilles Deleuze, *Coldness and Cruelty* (New York: Zone Books 1991), p. 83.

7. After this essay was completed, an essay by Judith Butler, 'Conscience Doth Make Subjects of Us All', appeared in *Yale French Studies*, vol. 88, 1995, in which she proposes that we turn away from or refuse the law 'in order to expose [it] as less powerful than it seems', p. 25. While she is discussing Althusser rather than Kant's notion, it is still not clear to me what the political gain would be in opposing a law that enables us to take our distance from positive, social laws. Nor is it clear how this 'turning away' is to take place.

8. Philippe Lacoue-Labarthe and Jean-Luc Nancy, 'The Nazi Myth', *Critical Inquiry*, vol. 16, no. 2, Winter 1990, p. 307.

9. Jacques Lacan, *The Four Fundamental Concepts of Psycho-Analysis*, trans. Alan Sheridan, ed. Jacques-Alain Miller (London: Hogarth Press and the Institute of Psycho-Analysis 1977), p. 275.

10. In his excellent book, *L'éthique: Essai sur la conscience du Mal* (Paris: Hatier 1993), Alain Badiou foregrounds the relation between an ethics founded on the pursuit of happiness and this modern contempt for life.

11. I do not mean to conflate relativism and deconstruction; the former seems to me trivial, while the latter does not. Nevertheless, as I argued in my essay, 'Sex and the Euthanasia of Reason', in *Supposing the Subject* (London and New York: Verso Press 1994), I believe deconstruction's position on the subject is mistaken.

1 SELFHOOD AS SUCH IS SPIRIT

F.W.J. Schelling on the Origins of Evil

SLAVOJ ŽIŽEK

How should one begin an essay on Schelling? Perhaps the most appropriate way is by focusing on the problem of Beginning itself, the crucial problem of German Idealism. The 'materialist' contribution of Schelling is best epitomized by his fundamental thesis, according to which, to put it bluntly, the true Beginning is not at the beginning: there is something that precedes the Beginning itself – a rotary motion whose vicious cycle is broken, in a gesture analogous to the cutting of the Gordian knot, by the Beginning proper, that is, the primordial act of decision. The beginning of all beginnings – the mother of all beginnings, as one would say today – is, of course, 'at the beginning was the Word' from the Gospel according to St John. Prior to this, there was nothing, that is, there was only the void of divine eternity. According to Schelling, however, 'eternity' is not a nondescript bulk – a lot of things take place in it. Prior to the Word there is the chaotic-psychotic universe of blind drives, of their rotary motion, of their undifferentiated pulsating, and the Beginning occurs when the Word is pronounced which represses, rejects into the eternal Past, this self-enclosed circuit of drives. In short, at the Beginning proper stands a resolution, an act of decision which, by way of differentiating between past and present, resolves the unbearable tension of the rotary motion of drives: the true Beginning is the passage from the 'closed' rotary motion to 'open' progress, from drive to desire, or, in Lacanian terms,

1

from the real to the symbolic. One is tempted to evoke here 'The Sole Solution', a thoroughly Schellingian science-fiction story by Eric Frank Russell which describes the inner feelings of somebody filled with doubt, someone who turns around in a futile circle and cannot reach a decision, who makes all kinds of plans which are then immediately aborted. Finally, he makes up his mind and says, 'Let there be light!' In short, throughout the story, what we take for the groaning of some confused neurotic turns out to be the hesitation of God immediately before the act of creation. The beginning thus occurs when one 'finds the word' that breaks the deadlock, the vicious cycle, of empty and confused ruminations.

The crux, the turning point, in the history of the Absolute is thus the divine act of *Ent-Scheidung*, or resolution, which, by rejecting the vortex of drives, their 'mad dance' into the darkness of the eternal past, establishes the universe of temporal progression dominated by *logos*-light-desire. But how does this act relate to *human* history? The relationship between the divine 'ages of the world' and human history is that of repetition. First, the rotary motion of contraction and expansion, the 'divine madness', is released by the intervention of the divine Word, that is, the act of creation; then, because of man's fall, this shift from the timeless-eternal rotary motion to the progressive temporal line has to repeat itself within human history. Human history itself is thus divided into two great epochs, the pagan epoch of rotary motion (the eternal 'return of the same', the circular rise and fall of great pagan civilizations, clearly stands under the sign of a pre-symbolic vortex of drives which sooner or later reduces to dust every progressive formation) and the Christian epoch of linear teleological progress (the continuous approach to the ideal of freedom regulated by the divine Logos which, finally, in Christ's Revelation, gets the upper hand over the destructive vortex of drives).

In so far as the same shift from the domination of rotary motion to the domination of linear progress is repeated within Christian history itself in the guise of the passage from the medieval societies of the circular 'return of the same' to the modern capitalist societies of incessant progress and expansion, one is tempted, in a 'reductionist', historico-materialist vein, to anchor Schelling's mega-narrative of the divine 'ages of the world' to a very precise and constrained ontic event: the passage from the traditional, premodern community to modern capitalist society. That is to say, what Schelling proposes is a narrative of the ages of the Absolute itself; this narrative, the most anti-Lyotardian, the largest possible, offers itself as the ideal testing ground for Fredric Jameson's provocative idea that all narratives are ultimately variations on the same theme, that of the passage from the closed organic community to modern capitalist society. Every narrative tries to explain how things got out of joint, how the old 'authentic' ties disintegrated, how the organic balance of the circular movement that characterizes traditional societies was transformed into the modern, 'alienated', unbalanced individualist society in which we live. Is the Schellingian passage from rotary motion to linear progress not this same story of the emergence of modern capitalist society elevated (or inflated) to the level of the Absolute?

How is the emergence of the Word connected to the pulsating 'rotation' in God, that is, to the interchange of expansion and contraction, externalization and internalization? How, precisely, does the Word discharge the tension of the rotary motion? How does it mediate the antagonism between the contractive and the expansive force? The Word is a contraction in the guise of its very opposite, an expansion, that is, in pronouncing a word, the subject contracts his being outside himself, he coagulates the core of his being in an external sign. In the (verbal) sign I, as it were, find myself outside myself, I posit my unity outside myself, in a signifier which represents me:

> It seems universal that every creature which cannot contain itself or draw itself together in its own fullness, draws itself together outside itself, whence, for example, the elevated miracle of the formation of the word in the mouth belongs, which is a true creation of the full inside when it can no longer remain in itself.[1]

The formation of the Word is thus the exact opposite of the primordial contraction/abjection by means of which, according to the Stuttgart Seminars, God expels – casts out, rejects out of Himself – His real side, the vortex of drives, and thus constitutes Himself in his Ideality, as a free subject. The primordial rejection is an act of supreme egotism, since in it God 'gets rid of the shit in Himself' in order to purify and keep for Himself the precious spiritual essence of His being; whereas in the formation of the Word, He articulates outside Himself, that is, He discloses, (sur)renders, this very ideal-spiritual essence of His being. In this precise sense, the formation of the Word is the supreme act and the paradigmatic case of creation: *creation* means that I reveal, hand over to the Other, the innermost essence of my being. The problem, of course, is that this second contraction, this original act of creation, this 'draw[ing] together outside itself', is ultimately always unfitting, contingent: it betrays the subject, it represents him inadequately. Here, Schelling already announces the Lacanian problematic of the *vel*, of a forced choice which is constitutive of the emergence of the subject. The subject either persists in himself, in his purity, as the void of pure $, and thereby loses himself in empty expansion; or he gets out of himself, externalizes himself, by way of 'contracting' or 'putting on' a signifying feature, and thereby alienates himself, that is, he ceases to be what he is:

the subject can never grasp itself *as* what it is, for precisely in attracting itself [*sich-Anziehen*] it *becomes* an other; this is the basic contradiction, we can say, the misfortune in all being – for either it *leaves* itself, then it is as nothing, or it attracts-contracts itself, then it is an other and not identical with itself. No longer uninhibited by being as before, but that which has inhibited itself with being, it itself feels this being as alien [*zugezogenes*] and thus contingent.[2]

Therein resides Schelling's reformulation of the classical question 'Why is there something rather than nothing?': in the primordial *vel*, the subject has to decide between 'nothing' (the unground/abyss of freedom that lacks all objective being, in the Lacanian matheme, pure $) and 'something', but always irreducibly in the sense of 'something extra, something additional, something foreign, put on, in a certain respect something contingent'.[3] The dilemma, therefore, is

> either it remains still (remains *as* it is, thus pure subject), then there is no life and it is itself as nothing, or it *wants* itself, then it becomes an other, something not the same as itself, *sui dissimile*. It admittedly wants itself *as* such, but precisely this is impossible in an *immediate* way; in the very wanting itself it already becomes an other and distorts itself.[4]

Everything thus revolves around the primordial act by means of which 'nothing' becomes 'something', and Schelling's entire philosophical revolution is contained, condensed, in the assertion that this act, which precedes and grounds every necessity, is in itself *radically contingent* – for that very reason, it cannot be deduced or inferred, but only retroactively presupposed. This act involves a primordial, radical and irreducible alienation, a distortion of the original balance, a kind of constitutive 'out of jointedness': 'This whole construction therefore begins with the emergence of the first contingency – which is not identical with itself – it begins with a *dissonance*, and *must* begin this way.'[5] In order to emphasize the nonspontaneous, 'artificial', 'corrupted' character of this act, Schelling plays on the multiple meanings of the German verb *Anziehen*: being attracted, drawn to something; contracting a disease; putting on clothing; acting in a false, pretentious way. Apropos of this last feature, Schelling directly evokes what was later (by Jon Elster) conceptualized as 'states that are essentially by-products':

> There are certain moral and other qualities that one only has precisely to the extent that one does not have them, as the German language splendidly expresses it to the extent to which one does not put on [*sich anzieht*] those qualities. E.g., true charm is only possible precisely if it does not know about itself, whereas a person who knows of his charm, who puts it on, immediately stops being charming, and if he conducts himself *as* being charming will instead become the opposite.[6]

The implications of this theory are as radical as they are far-reaching: the fake is original, that is, every positive feature, every 'something' that we are, is ultimately 'put on'. At this point, one might be tempted to oppose Schelling to Hegel, that is, to the Hegelian logical necessity of the immanent self-deployment of the absolute Idea. But before yielding to this commonplace contrast, it would be worth pausing to consider the fact that Hegel develops a homologous *vel* in his *Phenomenology of Spirit*, apropos of the Beautiful Soul and the act. The choice that confronts the subject here is between inactivity and an act that is by definition contingent, branded with a merely subjective content. This contingency of the act disturbs the balance of the (social) substance in which the subject is embedded; the reaction of the substance thereby set in motion inexorably leads to the failure of the subject's enterprise.

The true critical-materialist supplement to Schelling is to be sought elsewhere: in Marx who, in his dialectics of the commodity-form, also starts from the need of the abstract-universal value to embody itself in a contingent use-value, to 'put on' a use-value dress, or to appear in its form. As Marx is quick to add, however, *at least two* use-values (commodities) are needed if a value is to express itself, so that the use-value of the first commodity gives body to the value of the second commodity. And Lacan's definition of the signifier as that which 'represents the subject for another signifier' ultimately amounts to the same assertion of an irreducible duality. If a subject is to be represented by a signifier, there must be a minimal chain of two signifiers, one of which represents the subject for the other.

The crucial point not to be missed here is that, in so far as we are dealing with a *subject*, the 'contraction' in question is no longer the primordial contraction by means of which the original Freedom catches being and thereby gets caught in the rotary motion of contraction and expansion, but the contraction of the subject outside himself, in an external sign, which resolves the tension, the 'inner dispute', of contraction and expansion. The paradox of the Word is therefore that its emergence resolves the tension of the pre-symbolic antagonism, but at a price: the Word, the contraction of the self outside the self, involves an irretrievable externalization-alienation. With the emergence of the Word, we pass from *antagonism* to Hegelian *contradiction* between S and S_1, between the subject and its inadequate symbolic representation. This 'contingency' of the contraction in the Word points towards what in structuralist terms is called 'the arbitrary nature of the signifier'. Schelling asserts the irreducible gap between the subject and a signifier the subject has to 'contract' if he is to acquire (symbolic) existence: the subject as S is never adequately represented in a signifier. This, 'contradiction' between the subject and his (necessarily, constitutively inadequate) symbolic representation provides the context for Schelling's 'Lacanian' formulation according to which God-Absolute becomes inexpressible at the very moment He expresses Himself, that is, pronounces a Word. Prior to his symbolic externalization, the subject cannot be said to be 'inexpressible' since the medium of expression itself is not yet given, or, to invoke Lacan's precise formulation, desire is *inarticulable* precisely in so far as it is *articulated* in a signifying chain.

In short, by means of the Word, the subject finally *finds* himself, comes to himself. He is no longer a mere obscure longing for himself since, in the Word, he directly attains himself, posits himself as such. The price for this, however, is the irretrievable *loss* of the subject's self-identity. The verbal sign that stands for the subject, that is, in which the subject posits himself as self-identical, bears the mark of an irreducible dissonance, it never 'fits' the subject. This para-doxical necessity – by which the act of returning to oneself, of finding oneself, immediately, in one's very actualization, assumes the form of its opposite, of the radical loss of self-identity – displays the structure of what Lacan calls 'symbolic castration'. This castration involved in the passage to the Word can also be formulated as the redoubling, the splitting, of an element into itself and its place in the structure. Apropos of the Word, Schelling refers to the medieval logic in which *reduplicatio* designated the operation by means of which a term was no longer conceived *simpliciter* but posited *as such*: *reduplicatio* points towards the minimal, constitutive gap that forever separates an element from its re-marking in the symbolic network. With regard to this point in Schelling, Wolfran Hogrebe invokes the difference between an element and its place in an anonymous structure.[7] Because of this 'structure of castration', the Spirit is supernatural or extranatural, although it grew out of nature: nature has an ineradicable tendency to 'speak itself out', it is caught in the search for a speaker (*die Suche nach dem Sprecher*) whose Word would posit it as such; this speaker, however, can only be an entity which is itself not natural, not part of nature, but nature's Other. Or, to put it in a slightly different way, nature is searching for itself, it strives for itself, but it can only 'find itself', attain itself, *outside itself*, in a medium which is itself not natural. The moment nature becomes *ein Aussprechliches* (something that can be spoken of in meaningful propositions), it ceases to be the *Aussprechendes* (that which is speaking):[8] the speaking agency is the Spirit as $, the substanceless void of non-nature, the distance of nature towards itself. In short, the fundamental paradox of symbolization – the paradox the term *symbolic castration* aims at recapturing – is that nature can attain itself, its self-identity, only at the price of a radical decentring: it can only find itself in a medium outside itself. A father becomes a father as such, the bearer of symbolic authority, only in so far as he assumes his 'castration', the difference between himself in the immediate reality of his being and the place in the symbolic structure which guarantees his authority. The father's authority is radically decentred with regard to his being as a flesh-and-blood person, that is, it is the anonymous structure of the symbolic Law which speaks through him.

This paradox, of course, can also be formulated in terms of the Hegelian opposition of In- and For-itself: in so far as an object is In-itself, it is not yet fully itself, it has not yet found itself, achieved its self-identity; however, it can only become For-itself via a decentring *reduplicatio*. That is, the price of achieving full self-identity is that the object in question is no longer just itself but is itself *plus* a supplementary re-mark through which alone self-identity can be accomplished. The opposition In-itself/For-itself thus involves the paradoxical logic of a failed encounter, of the splitting of identity into a 'not yet' and a 'no longer'. In order to elucidate this point, suffice it to recall the Derridean problematic of the gift:[9] the moment a gift is recognized by the other as such, as gift, it is no longer a pure gift but is already caught in the logic of exchange. A gift is always in between, either not yet a gift – a gift only In-itself – or no longer a gift, since this recognition (its positing as a gift For-itself as such) causes it to lose its status as gift. The same goes for the 'invention' of something new: in order to be fully actualized as invention, the act of invention has to be acknowledged as such by the field of existing knowledge, integrated into it, recognized as invention – but the moment this occurs, invention is no longer pure invention but becomes part of established knowledge.

Schelling's fundamental problem is the possibility of human freedom. He resolves it by arguing that without the abyss of primordial freedom, which precedes the vortex of the real, it would not be possible to account for the emergence of human freedom in the heart of the realm of natural necessity. The chain of natural necessity can be torn asunder, the light of freedom can break out of the vicious circle of natural drives and illuminate the obscure Ground of being, only if natural necessity itself is not an original fact but results from the contraction of the primordial abyss of Freedom, of a Willing which wills nothing. That is, it is only because this primordial Freedom, by means of its contraction, gets entrapped in the vicious circle of its own self-imposed chains, that man is able to sever these chains and regain himself. In other words, human freedom is actual, not just an illusion that is due to our ignorance of the necessity that effectively governs our lives. And man is no mere epiphenomenon of the universe, but a 'being of the Centre', a being in whom the abyss of primordial Freedom breaks through in the midst of the created universe. In this way, Schelling is able to think of human freedom as actual *and* man as a finite, mortal being, subordinated to the Absolute. That is, he is able to avoid both extremes:

the notion of man as an epiphenomenon whose freedom is an illusion grounded in his ignorance, as well as the false elevation of man to the subject of all being, with no Absolute above him.

In Schelling's philosophy of identity, freedom is still conceived in the classical idealist way: as the capacity of the Absolute to deploy its content, to actualize its potential, according to its inherent necessity, unconstrained by any external impediment. But from this notion of the Absolute as Identity, it is not possible to provide a satisfactory solution to the key problem of how the infinite Absolute passes to the finite multitude of temporal entities. It is only when Schelling breaks away from his philosophy of identity with its specification of freedom as the 'concrete' freedom of a living person, that he can solve the problem of creation, that is, of the 'descent from the infinite to the finite'. The emergence of the finite is now grounded in an antagonism which dwells within God himself. The passage from the infinite to the finite, from eternity to the temporal reality of finite entities, is no longer characterized as the fall or descent from the Absolute. The creation of the universe of finite temporal entities is, on the contrary, conceived as an ascent; it designates the process by means of which God endeavours to 'find Himself', to regain his mind by curing Himself of the rotary motion of drives, of His 'divine madness'. This, then, is how Schelling solves the problem of the 'fall' of eternity into time: this 'fall' is actually not a fall at all but a *Beginning* in the precise sense of a relief from an unbearable tension, a resolution; that is, it is an act which resolves an acute, debilitating deadlock. By positing the finite-temporal reality, God breaks out of the vicious circle of drives, He accomplishes the passage from the drive's self-enclosed pulsating, which can never stabilize itself into firm reality, to the actual world of differentiated objects, from pre-symbolic antagonism to symbolic difference.[10]

Here, in this attempt to reconcile 'system' and 'freedom', resides Schelling's unique place in the history of philosophy. Man is a subordinated moment of the Absolute, a link in the 'great chain of being'; he emerges from nature and nature remains forever the Ground of his being, yet he is simultaneously a free being which, as such, is self-centred, an end in itself, directly rejoining the Absolute. How, precisely, are we to think these two sides together? Schelling resorts here to his key notion of powers (*Potenzen*). In the hierarchically ordered 'great chain of being', the same structural-formal relationship repeats itself in different powers. What is *gravitation* for inert matter (the striving to rejoin the outside centre of gravity) is *melancholy* for man as a finite, mortal being separated from the Absolute and longing to rejoin it; a plant is to an animal what woman is to man and so on. The crucial point not to be missed here is the *self-relating* character of this repetition: when a given relationship between two poles (between A and B, the ideal and the real pole) is raised to a higher power, one of the two poles is posited as the form, the neutral medium, of the new, higher polarity. The polarity of plant and animal, for example, has as its neutral medium *life* (that is, the domain of life is structured along the polar axis of vegetable and animal life); life raised to a higher power is *animal life*, and within the animal domain, the polarity of plant and animal is repeated in the guise of the polarity of female and male. It is because of this self-referentiality that we are not dealing here with the same form repeating itself in different material domains, but with an incessant interchange between form and content: part of the content of a lower level becomes the formal principle of a higher level. We can see now why Schelling uses the term 'enchainment' (*Verkettung*) in order to designate the hierarchical succession of polarities. These polarities are literally 'enchained' in so far as one pole of the lower level becomes the global, formal principle encompassing both poles of the higher level. In short, this enchainment of powers displays the structure of *mise-en-abyme*.

What, then, do we get at the two extremes of this process of self-relating elevation to a higher and higher power? At the lowest end, of course, we have *das Ding*, the ineffable real of the Thing, and at the opposite end, the substanceless void of $\$$, the pure subject. What again and again sets in motion this process in which one and the same polarity reappears in different 'powers' is the fact that, at any given level, in any given 'power', the subordination of the real under the ideal pole (of darkness under light, of female under male) never takes place without a remainder which, of course, is the Lacanian object *a*. This reference to Lacan enables us to interpret the Schellingian polar tension of A and B as the minimal signifying dyad of S_1 and S_2, while the 'impossible' relationship between $\$$ and *a* ($\$ - a$) designates the strict correlation between the remainder that eludes the signifying couple and the subject. For Lacan (as well as for Schelling) the subject as $\$$ is not a thing or a state of things but an *event* that occurs when the symbolic enchainment fails in its attempt to absorb without remainder the real of the Thing. In short, the repetition of the dyad A:B in ever new 'powers' is *stricto sensu* the symbolic repetition that constitutes a signifying chain. And, in so far as the relationship A:B invokes sexual difference (between masculine and feminine principles; in Schelling, the sexual connotation of A:B is explicit), its repetition in higher and higher powers bears witness to the fact that 'there is no sexual relationship', since every formulation of A:B entails-produces a remainder which, of course, is the object *a* as a-sexual.

How does this repetition of the antagonistic 'impossible' relationship between A and B lead to the emergence of man? According to Schelling, man's position is radically problematic, marked by a maximum gap between possibility and actuality. With respect to his place in the enchainment of powers, man is *in potentia* the crown of creation, yet his actuality is that of a shattering fall, so that Schelling even characterizes the appearance of man as a 'blockage in development'. In man, the development (the increase of powers) is destined finally to reach a turning point and bring about a crucial reversal in the relationship between A and B: the predominance of A (the ideal, spiritual principle of expansion) over B (the real, bodily principle of contraction). That is to say, in nature, the relationship A:B stands under the power of B: Spirit gradually reveals itself, yet it remains constrained by the inertia of Matter, enveloped in it. In man, on the contrary, B should subordinate itself to A: Spirit should get the upper hand and rule directly, while the corporeal should rid itself of inertia and transform itself into an ethereal, transparent medium of the shining of the Spirit. It is thus easy to imagine the chain of development as a continuous progression from lower (inorganic) to higher (organic) forms of nature, and finally to man. Yet with man, the 'crown of creation', an unexpected complication arises. Instead of a simple shift from B to A as the predominant principle, B itself, the contractive principle, profits from the illuminating power of A to gain full awareness of itself. It comes to light, is posited as such, emancipates itself and asserts itself as the egotistic evil Spirit; this is, in fact, the 'fall'.

Therein resides the paradox of man: if the progression of nature were to continue unperturbed in man, a new angelic entity would appear and dwell in the power of A, an entity for whom matter would lose its inertia and turn into a transparent medium of A. Because of his fall, however, man is, instead, a radically split entity. On the one hand, he lacks a proper place, is unable to find a home in nature, becomes a stranger on earth, and his terrestrial life is a series of horrors; on the other hand, the true world, the world of spirits, appears to him as a spectral, unattainable beyond, as the ultimate enigma, the radical uncertainty of what will happen after death. Instead of a subordination of natural life to spiritual life, man's terrestrial existence is characterized by the separation of the two lives by the barrier of death, so that one succeeds the other; for man, the true life can only be imagined in the guise of an *afterlife*. In short, Schelling provides here one of the most forceful formulations of the paradigmatic modern notion of man's radical, constitutive, *displacement*, his lack of a proper place.

The paradox is therefore that, contrary to what one is led to expect, Spirit and Matter are harmoniously coordinated in nature, whereas the fall of man perverts their proper relationship and entails their irreducible discord. The true stumbling block to the idealization of the real is not in nature but in man; it is with man that the hierarchical scale of progression, of intensification of powers, stumbles. Nature is a picture of the harmonious progression of life forms, whereas the universe of man, of human history, offers the sad spectacle of a degenerate, poisoned nature, caught in a vicious cycle: man's world is full of ruins.

Significantly, teleological descriptions, as a rule, refer to the purposefulness of nature. It is easy to present nature as a purposeful totality in which every organism unknowingly serves some higher end. Human history is, on the contrary, replete with horrors and misfortunes, with enterprises gone awry, with senseless suffering and destruction. In short the ultimate paradox of teleology is that whereas in nature, which acts blindly, as a purposeless mechanism, we easily discover purpose, in human history, where man acts consciously to pursue clear goals, we find a meaningless expenditure of human potential.[11] Man hampers the free circulation of nature, he is a kind of embolism in the upward flow of natural energies, and, as Schelling puts it with his unique naivety, it is as if nature possesses an obscure presentiment of this fact and takes its revenge by bringing upon man natural catastrophies, earthquakes, droughts, floods.

The first task of a materialist reading of Schelling, of course, is to demonstrate how nonhuman nature appears as a meaningful, harmonious, purposeful totality *only from the standpoint of man as the locus of senseless destruction and purposeless expenditure of forces*: the point from which everything appears meaningful must itself be the point of the suspension of meaning. The second task of such a reading is to acknowledge fully *the structural necessity of the 'stagnation' of natural progress in man*: this stagnation is not an unfortunate accident, since *the 'egotistic' perversion of the Spirit is constitutive of spirituality*:

> That principle which is raised from the ground of nature, and by which man is divided from God, is man's selfhood, but this becomes *spirit* because of its unity with the ideal principle. Selfhood as such is spirit; or man as selfish, particular being (divided from God) is spirit; it is precisely this combination which constitutes the personality. But by being spirit, selfhood is raised from the creaturely to the super-creaturely; it is will beholding itself in complete freedom, no longer the instrument of the universal will creating in nature, but above and outside all nature. Spirit is above light, just as in nature it raises itself above the unity of light and the dark principle. Thus by being spirit, selfhood is free from both principles.[12]

In man as a living, actual spirit, selfhood – which, in an animal, is merely a blind egotistic striving – comes to light. By means of this self-illumination, I become aware of myself, I 'posit' my self in the radical exclusion of all otherness. That which, in me, resists the blissful submergence in the Good is therefore not my inert biological nature, but the very kernel of my *spiritual* selfhood, the awareness that, beyond all particular physical and psychical features, I am a unique *person*, an absolutely singular point of spiritual self-reference. In this precise sense, 'selfhood as such is spirit': the Spirit in its actuality is the contraction of Light itself *against* nature ('above and outside all nature'). In other words, if man were to dwell in the Good, he would have to renounce that very unity which makes him an individual person and submerge himself in the universal medium of Light. This contraction of the Light itself (of the spiritual principle of love) into a concrete living person is unthinkable for the standard idealism which is able to deal only with the impersonal kingdom of Ideas, never with the *actual, personal existence* of the ideal principle.

This 'egotistic' perversion of Spirit, which is inherent to the very notion of actually existing Spirit, forms the core of Schelling's conception of Evil, at which he arrived by means of a radicalization of the notion of 'radical Evil' developed by Kant in *Religion within the Limits of Reason Alone*. Schelling's starting point is a repudiation of the traditional philosophical *topos* according to which the possibility of Evil is grounded in man's finitude, in his deficiency with respect to divine perfection, that is, in the fact that he is split between the material and the spiritual world. Schelling literally turns this *topos* inside out and asserts that the root of Evil, on the contrary, lies in man's *perfection*, his advantage over other finite creatures, and, on the other hand, in a certain split in *God Himself*. That is to say, the central tenet of *The Treatise on Freedom* is that, if one is to account for the possibility of Evil, one has to presuppose a split of the Absolute itself into God in so far as He fully exists and the obscure, impenetrable Ground of His Existence. With the speculative audacity characteristic of his mode of thinking, Schelling locates the split which opens up the possibility of Evil in God Himself. This distinction between God's Existence and its Ground, between the Absolute in so far as it fully exists, in so far as it is posited as such, illuminated by the Light of Reason, and the Absolute as obscure longing (*Sehnsucht*) which strives for something outside itself without possessing a clear notion of what it actually strives for, means that God is not fully 'Himself' – that there is something in God which isn't God.

In *The Treatise on Freedom*, this relationship between the obscure Will of the Ground and the illuminated, effectively existing Will, is not yet thought through, so that Schelling's position is here strictly speaking contradictory. That is to say, his answer to the question 'What does the obscure Will aspire to?' is: it strives for illumination, it yearns for the Word to be pronounced. If, however, the obscure Will of the Ground itself aspires to *logos*, in what precise sense is it then *opposed* to it? His later text, *Weltalter*, resolves this contradiction by qualifying the first Will as the divine *Selbstheit*, as the contractive force which actively opposes the Light of Reason and thereby serves as the necessary ground of the latter's expansion. However, already in the *Treatise*, Schelling's position is more subtle than it may first appear: this obscure, impenetrable side of God, the Ground of His Existence, is *not* to be conceived as a positive Base, the true foundation of Being, with Reason as its parasitic accident. The Ground is in itself ontologically hindered, hampered; its status is in a radical sense *pre-ontological*: it only 'is' under erasure, in the mode of its own withdrawal. The only true Substance is the Spirit, that is, God in His actual Existence, and *Grund* is ultimately a name for God's self-deferral, for that elusive X which lacks any proper ontological consistency, yet on account of which God is never fully Himself, cannot ever attain full self-identity. God needs this foreign body in His heart since without this minimum of contractive force He wouldn't be 'Himself'. What, paradoxically, forever prevents God from attaining full self-identity is the very impenetrable kernel of his *Selbstheit*.

This tension in the midst of the Absolute itself is therefore far more enigmatic than it may appear, since it is thoroughly incompatible with the oppositions that define the space of traditional ontology. The opposition between Ground and Existence does not overlap with the opposition between mere possibility and actuality (if this were the case, Ground couldn't corrode from within the self-identity of actual Existence); nor is it simply a new name for the duality of the Real and the Ideal in Schelling's early philosophy, that is, for the symmetrical polarity of two ontological principles (the Ground is 'less' than Existence, it lacks full ontological consistency); and it definitely doesn't imply that Ground is in any way the 'true substance' or the 'foundation' of Reason. The enigma resides in the fact that Ground is ontologically non-accomplished, 'less' than Existence, but it is precisely as such that it corrodes from within the consistency of the ontological edifice of Existence. In other words, Schelling first opposes Existence (the fully actual God) and the mere Ground of Existence (the blind striving that lacks actuality) as the Perfect and the Imperfect, and then goes on to treat the two as complementary and to conceive the true completeness as the unity of the two, as if the Perfect itself needed the Imperfect in order to assert itself. *This is why there is Evil in the world: because of the perverse need of the Perfect for the Imperfect*, as if the intersection of the Perfect and the Imperfect were more perfect than the Perfect itself.

How, then, is the emergence of Evil related to this distinction between Ground and Existence? Schelling's basic definition of Evil as the *Verkehrung* (perversion, or, rather, distorting inversion) of the proper relationship between Ground and Existence is misleading in so far as it leaves open the door for two traditional misconceptions against which his entire argument is directed: the notion of Evil as the split itself (between Existence and Ground, between the Infinite and the Finite), that is, as the fall of the Finite from the Infinite (in contrast to Good as the unity of the Finite and the Infinite); and the notion of Evil as the assertion of the Ground to the detriment of Existence, of the Finite to the detriment of the Infinite, that is, the predominance of Ground over Existence (in contrast to Good as the predominance of Existence over Ground, of Reason over obscure drives).

Schelling's thesis is much more subtle: both Good and Evil are modes of the *unity* of Ground and Existence; however, *in the case of Evil, this unity is false, inverted.* In what sense? Suffice it to recall today's ecological crisis: its possibility is opened by man's split nature, that is, by the fact that man is simultaneously a living organism (and, as such, part of nature) and a spiritual entity (and, as such, elevated above nature). If man were to be only one of the two, the crisis could not occur. As part of nature, man would be an organism living in symbiosis with his environs, a predator exploiting other animals and plants; yet, because he is a part of nature, he would be included in its circuit and unable to pose a fundamental threat to it. As a spiritual being, man would entertain towards nature a relationship of contemplative comprehension with no need to intervene actively in it for the purpose of material exploitation. What renders man's existence so explosive is *the combination of the two features*: in man's striving to dominate nature, to put it to work for his purposes, 'normal' animal egotism – the attitude of a natural, living organism engaged in the struggle for survival in hostile environs – is 'self-illuminated', posited as such, raised to the power of Spirit and thereby exacerbated, universalized into a propensity for absolute domination which no longer serves the end of survival but turns into an end in itself.[13] Therein resides the true 'perversion' of Evil: in it, the 'normal' animal egotism is 'spiritualized', it expresses itself in the medium of Word. We are thus no longer dealing with an obscure drive, but with a Will which, finally, 'found itself'.

We can see, now, how far we are from the traditional notion of lack, privation or imperfection as the ground of Evil. As Schelling points out, 'the simple consideration that man, the most perfect of all visible creatures, is alone capable of evil, shows that the ground of evil could by no means lie in defect or privation'.[14] Evil does not reside in finitude as such, in its deficiency with regard to the infinite God – it can only emerge in a finite creature which again rejoins the Infinite, that is, when the unity of the Finite and the Infinite is re-established in man as a finite but free being.

The problem of Evil could then be restated in the following way: how is the *false* unity of Ground and Existence possible? The first thing to emphasize here is the elementary dialectical point that man is the *unity* of Ground and Existence precisely in so far as it is only in him that their *difference* is finally explicated, posited as such: only man is aware of being split between the obscure vortex of natural drives and the spiritual bliss of *logos*, that is, his psychic life is the battle-ground of two principles or Wills, whereas in nature, the Light of Existence remains implicit, contained in the Ground.[15] Man is the only creature that can elevate itself to this duality and sustain it: he is the highest paradox of *universal singularity* – the point of utmost contraction, the all-exclusive One of self-consciousness, *and* the embracing All, that is, a singular being (the vanishing point of *cogito*) who is able to comprehend/mirror the entire universe. In God prior to Creation, the two principles are still in a state of indifference. In the realm of nature, the second principle – A, the Spirit – can only appear under the domination or through the power of B (as the implicit, secret spiritual content of nature), which, again, means that their difference is not yet posited as such, that the two cannot yet come up against each other. When, however, with the emergence of man, the two principles – Existence and its Ground – are posited in their distinction, they are not merely opposed to each other: *their unity also has to be posited*, that is, each of them is in the same breath posited as united with its opposite, as its opposite's inherent constituent. In other words, from the previous *indifference* of the two principles we pass to their *unity* – and it is here that we encounter freedom as the freedom for Good and Evil, since this unity can take two shapes, the shape of the true or of the perverted unity. On the one hand, nature can spiritualize itself, it can turn into the medium of Spirit's self-manifestation; on the other hand, with the emergence of the Word, the obscure principle of Ground and Selfhood – which up till now acted as an anonymous, impersonal, blind force – can become spiritualized, illuminated, it can become a Person aware of itself. At this point we are dealing with an Evil which, in full awareness of itself, *wills itself as Evil*, which is not merely indifference towards the Good but an active striving for Evil.[16]

The domain of ideologico-political struggle exemplifies perfectly the way in which 'Evil' is not particularity as such but its false, 'perverted' unity with the universal: not 'egotism' as such but egotism in the guise of its opposite. When a political agent (the Party, for example) claims to represent the universal interest of the State or Nation, in contrast to its opponents who, of course, are reproached with pursuing only narrow, power-seeking goals, it thereby structures the discursive space so that every attack on it – on this particular political agent – is *eo ipso* an attack on the Nation itself. 'Evil' in its most elementary form is just such a short-circuit between the particular and the universal, a presumption that my words and deeds are directly the words and deeds of the big Other (the Nation, Culture, the State, God), a presumption that inverts the proper relationship between the particular and the universal. When I proclaim myself the immediate 'functionary of Humanity' (or the Nation or Culture), I thereby effectively accomplish the exact opposite of what I claim to do. That is, I degrade the universal dimension to which I refer (Humanity, the Nation, the State) to the level of my own particularity, since it is my own particular point-of-view which decides on the content of Humanity. I am thereby caught in the infernal cycle of 'the more one proclaims one's purity, the more dirty one becomes': the more I refer to the universal in order to legitimize my acts, the more I effectively debase it to a mere means of my self-assertion.[17]

We can see now why, according to Schelling, the status of the philosophy of nature is introductory or, more precisely, preparatory: only in man, in whom both principles are finally posited as such, do things become real; in man, for the first time, everything – the fate of the entire universe, the success or failure of Creation – is truly at stake. Schelling is here radically anthropocentric: all of nature, the universe as such, was created in order to serve as the setting for man's ethical struggle, for the battle between Good and Evil.[18] Consequently, Schelling can claim that God loves and wills nature, the universe, the entire Creation, only on behalf of man and in man. In this way, Schelling can also account for the strange feeling we have when we encounter an evil deed of enormous dimensions. It is as if this deed concerns not only human beings but the entire universe, as if, in it and through it, the universe has gone awry, has been perverted or derailed (see, for example, the scenes of frenzied nature – earthquakes, the solar eclipse – that accompanied the Crucifixion). In this precise sense, man is for Schelling the 'being of the Centre'. Perhaps a reference to a specific Hitchcockian procedure can be of some help here. In a series of Hitchcock's films, we are sometimes given a shot which, because of its relation to the preceding shots, appears to be subjective; but then, while the camera remains immobile, the very subject whose point-of-view this shot was supposed to render enters; that is, he *enters his own picture/frame*, as it were. This is what the 'centrality' of man is about: man has in a sense 'his own centre in himself', unlike natural-material objects whose 'centre of gravity' is located outside themselves (which is precisely why matter is subordinated to the force of gravitation).[19]

The unavoidable conclusion of *The Treatise on Freedom* is therefore that God, in so far as He is Himself engaged in the process of Creation, becomes God only through man's free choice of Him. It is not difficult to discern here the echoes of the old theosophical idea sustained, among others, by Meister Eckhart, that God Himself is born through man. Man gives birth to the living God within himself, that is, man accomplishes the passage of the impersonal, anonymous divinity into the personal God. This, of course, charges man with the burden of a terrible responsibility: the fate of the entire universe and, ultimately, of God Himself depends on his acts. Every human victory over Evil, every emergence of a community of believers contributes to the formation of the mystical body of God Himself, and vice versa: man's choice of Evil asserts God's *Selbstheit*, His contractive force. Schelling, in fact, defines Hell as the 'consuming fire of the divine egotism'. Here Schelling subscribes to the revolutionary messianic theology whose most outspoken representative within Marxism is Walter Benjamin (see his *Theses on the Philosophy of History*). According to this tradition, history is an 'open' process, a succession of empty signs, of traces that point towards the eschatological moment to come in which all accounts will be settled, all (symbolic) debts will be compensated, all signs will acquire their full meaning. The arrival of this moment is not guaranteed in advance, but depends, rather, on our freedom. The outcome of the struggle for freedom will determine the meaning of the past itself: it is the struggle that decides what truly happened. We can see that only a thin, barely perceptible line separates this messianic, revolutionary logic from the most extreme fatalism according to which every-thing has already happened and things, in their temporal process of becoming, merely become what they always already were. The past itself is not fixed, but 'will have been'; through the deliverance to come, *it will become what it always already was.*

What, then, is the Fall of Man? When man emerges as self-consciousness, he posits himself as a self-centred being, as a subject who reduces all other entities to the medium of his self-assertion, to mere objects to be appropriated and exploited. The unthinkable paradox for this self-centred attitude is that my self-consciousness is not simply mine, is not simply the consciousness of myself as subject, for as self-consciousness I am always already decentred, a medium in which a transcendent Object (the Absolute) attains consciousness, becomes aware of itself. It is not possible for me to comprehend this Object since it transcends me; I can only apprehend its dimensions through an ecstatic yielding. The price the active-appropriative consciousness pays for its false pretence to be its own centre is that the world it inhabits necessarily assumes the appearance of a foreign, hostile, superior power indifferent to its plight. We encounter here an exemplary case of what Hegel calls 'reflective determination': in my perception of objective reality as the Kingdom of Satan, as the place of misery and sorrow, I perceive my own egotistic, self-centred attitude towards this same reality in an objectivized, reified form. Or, in Lacanian terms, I receive my own message in inverted form. Therein resides the crucial political sting of Schelling: the more individuals experience themselves as responsible and self-motivated subjects, the more the State opposes itself to them in the guise of a foreign, hostile agency that frustrates their projects, that is, the more they are unable to recognize them-selves, their own spiritual substance, in the State. In a utopian perspective (utopian, since false pride is inherent in man), the State would be surmounted by a religious community devoted to an ecstatic relationship to a transcendent Other. This ecstatic relationship is the highest freedom available to man according to Schelling, who distinguishes three levels of freedom:

1. The common notion of freedom conceives it as the freedom to choose, to decide by pondering the pros and cons, disregarding any external coercion.

For dessert I've chosen apple rather than cherry pie because I like apple pie better, not because I was forced to do so by some authority (parents, peers). This is the level on which utilitarianism works. Man obeys a calculus of felicity, it claims. But if this were all, man would behave like the proverbial Buridan's donkey, who starved to death between two piles of hay.

2. The next, higher level of freedom is therefore the level of the fathomless, groundless decision, based not on positive reasons but only in itself. The paradigmatic example of this is the primordial act by means of which I choose my eternal character. Such an act horrifies persons with weak wills. What confronts one here is the possibility of an act that would not be supported by any arguments for or against it. A free person, in this sense, is not one who, yielding to 'pathological' temptations, forsakes his duty, but one who, with an 'irrational' obstinacy, follows his own path even if it clearly runs against his material interests. (Recall Orson Welles's favourite story about the scorpion who stung the frog on whose back he rode crossing the river; the scorpion, of course, knew that, as a consequence of his act, he would drown.) This is also the level of Evil as spiritual, demoniac, diabolical will. As Schelling argues, it is incomparably more spiritual, remote from sensual *Genuß*, than is the Good.[20] The Good always involves a harmonious unity of the sensual and the spiritual; it is a Spirit that penetrates and illuminates nature from within and, without forcing itself upon nature, renders it ethereal and overcomes its inertia. In contrast to this, diabolical Evil is a pale, bloodless, fanatical spiritualism that despises sensuality and is bent on violently dominating and exploiting it. This diabolical spiritualism, a perversion of true spirituality, is the obscure Ground that has 'attained itself', its selfhood; that is, it has reached the Light and posited itself as such.[21]

3. This second level of freedom as groundless decision is, however, not yet the highest; one surpasses it when one submerges oneself in the primordial abyss (*Ungrund*) of the Absolute, in the primordial Will that wills nothing. In this state activity and passivity harmoniously overlap. (The paradigmatic example of this, of course, is the mystical experience of love.) Against this background, Schelling gives a specific twist to the distinction between *Vernunft* and *Verstand*, Reason and Understanding, which plays a crucial role in German Idealism: '*Vernunft* is nothing but *Verstand* in its subordination to the highest, the soul.'[22] *Verstand* is the intellect as the active power of seizing and deciding by means of which man asserts himself as a fully autonomous subject; but man reaches beyond this when he turns his very subjectivity into the predicate of an ever higher power (in the mathematical sense of the term), that

is, when he, as it were, yields to the Other, 'depersonalizes' his most intense activity and performs it as if some other, higher Power were acting through him, using him as its medium. An example would be an artist who, in the highest frenzy of creativity, experiences himself as a medium through which some more substantial, impersonal Power expresses itself.

This tripartite categorization of freedom is founded upon the distinction between the abyss of pure Freedom and God as Entity (*Seiendes*) who is no longer *freedom itself* but *is free*. Pure Freedom is, in other words, not a personal God, but an impersonal Deity (*Gottheit*). Freedom can only become a predicate if we are already dealing with the duality of Existence and its Ground. God as actual person who is free must possess a contracted ground of his being that is not directly accessible but can only be inferred from his activity, as its reclusive, withdrawing base. Reality as such (inclusive of the psychic reality of a person) involves contraction: without contraction, it bursts asunder in unconstrained expansion. Hogrebe's exegesis is, again, clarifying: Schelling's crucial problem, he argues, concerns the 'impossible' relationship between subject and predicate. What takes place in the passage from freedom as subject to freedom as predicate (that is, to an entity that is not freedom itself but is a free being) is the 'disciplining' of freedom. The transformation of freedom into a predicate renders it bearable, neutralizes its traumatic impact since, as long as freedom remains its own subject and not a predicate, it can only effectuate itself in the guise of a destructive vortex that devours every determinate content, a fire that dissolves every fixed shape.

In the last pages of his book on Schelling, Jean-François Marquet provides a clear outline of the enigma of freedom with which Schelling is trying to cope.[23] Schelling interprets Parmenides's 'thinking and being are the same' as the unity of *Das-Sein* and *Was-Sein*: everything that *is* must be *something*, it has to possess a *notion* that renders it *thinkable* in its *Was-Sein*, in what it is. What is at stake here is precisely the notion, not a mere name. As Schelling points out, however, when we are dealing with a person, the relationship between notion and name is the inverse of the one that obtains for a thing. The notion of a thing provides some minimal information about it, tells me what this thing is, whereas its eventual name tells me nothing. In the case of a person, on the contrary, I cannot say that I really know someone when I know that she exists and what she is (her positive features); I effectively know a person only when I conceive both her existence (the fact that she exists) and her notion (what she is) as the two predicates of an I, of the person as such, of the unfathomable kernel of her freedom. What I have to know about someone in order to claim that I know her is not merely *what* she is but above all *who* she is, what she wants as a free being.[24] True freedom means not only that I am not fully determined by my surroundings, but also that I am not fully determined by *myself* (by my own notion, by what I am, by my positive features): a person relates freely both to her existence and to her notion, that is, she is not fully determined by them but can transcend them (she can put her existence at risk and can transform the bundle of features that make up her identity). The fact that another person is for me originally an enigma, an abyss beyond her positive features, accounts for the key role of symbolic *obligation* or *debt*, for the desperate attempt to bind the Other in a network of intersubjective relations. Since I cannot directly take hold of the Other, of the abyss that forms the elusive centre of her being, I can only hold her to her word. Schelling simply took seriously and literally the fact that God, as absolute Other, is also a free person and as such, He also can become free only by taking some distance from the Ground of His being, by relating freely to this Ground, by not being wholly determined by it. The paradox (sacrilegious from the orthodox point of view, of course) is that this free relationship towards the Ground presupposes a dependency on it. God's Light, the creative emanation of His *logos*, is, as Schelling puts it, a 'regulated madness' that draws its energy from the vortex of drives, just as a human person is truly free not by opposing his drives but by adroitly exploiting their energy, by regulating their madness.

Paradoxical as it may sound, by means of this specific notion of freedom as the subject's free relating to her existence and notion, Schelling became the first to delineate the contours of a *materialist* notion of the subject. In standard (idealist and materialist) versions of the philosophical opposition between subject and object, materiality is always on the side of the object. The object is dense, impenetrable and inert, whereas the subject is the transparency of the Thought to itself. Within this horizon, the only way to assert a materialist position is by demonstrating that the subject is always already an object (this procedure is homologous to the Derridean strategy of demonstrating that the voice is always already a writing, it always contains some material trace that introduces a minimum of self-deferral, of noncoincidence with itself). In clear contrast to this standard view, the materialist notion of the subject outlined by Schelling (but also by Hegel, in his deservedly famous description of the struggle for recognition between the master and the slave) focuses on the fundamental impenetrability, the inert density, that defines our encounter with another subject and distinguishes it from our encounter with an ordinary object. Again, paradoxical as it may sound, ordinary objects are in this precise sense *less* material than another subjects, since objects lack the opacity characteristic of the Other's desire. An ordinary material object is in the end always transparent, since it lacks the enigma that would render it effectively opaque. This original violence of the Other – which is constitutive of what Heidegger called *Mit-Sein*, of our relating to another human being – is what gets completely lost in the Habermasian notion of the free space of intersubjective dialogue. Perhaps even Heidegger's otherwise exemplary analysis of *Mit-Sein* in *Sein und Zeit* passes too quickly over this traumatic dimension.[25]

One of the fundamental motifs of Schelling's thought is the original ex-stasis (*Ausser-sich-gesetzt-werden*) of the Spirit. The predicative activity of Understanding is founded on a pre-predicative reference to a 'constitutive outside'; the Spirit is constitutively 'outside itself': a kind of umbilical cord connects it to a traumatic kernel that is simultaneously its condition of possibility (the well from which the Spirit draws its resources) and its condition of impossibility (the abyss whose all-destructive vortex continuously threatens to swallow the Spirit). In the best tradition of the Hegelian pun, Schelling reactivates here the literal meaning of being 'out of one's mind', the standard expression for a state of madness. The constitutive 'madness' of the human mind resides in the fact that it is originally 'out of its mind', ex-static with regard to itself. In this way, Schelling provides a persuasive answer to the Kantian criticism that his ruminations about the Absolute involve a regression to pre-critical metaphysics, that is, an illegitimate foray into the noumenal domain, a forbidden leap from the mere notion of God to His actual existence. From Schelling's standpoint, the terms of the traditional problem of the ontological proof of God had to be inverted: what is truly problematic is not God's existence but his notion. Since the Spirit itself is originally not 'within itself' but 'outside itself', the true question is not how we can move from the notion of God to the actual existence of God, but the exact opposite. What comes first, what is always already here, is the experience of a 'senseless', pre-predicative, pre-semantic existence, and the true problem for philosophy is how to accomplish the passage from this senseless existence to Reason, to explain how our universe got caught in the web of Reason in the first place.

This view gives rise to a series of postmodern associations: Reason can only thrive on a foreign, 'irrational' Ground of the rotary motion of drives from which it draws its life force, but it simultaneously has to maintain a proper distance towards this Ground. If it gets too close to the vortex of drives, it runs the danger of losing its identity and going mad:

> Following the eternal act of self-revelation, all is rule, order, and form in the world as we now see it. But the ruleless still lies in the ground as if it could break through once again, and nowhere does it appear as though order and form were original, but rather as if something initially ruleless had been brought to order. This is the incomprehensible basis of reality in things, the indivisible remainder, that which with the greatest exertion cannot be resolved in the understanding, but rather remains eternally in the

ground. From this non-understanding is born understanding in the true sense. Without this preceding darkness there is no reality of the creature; the gloom is its necessary inheritance.[26]

This Ground is similar to the figure of woman in David Lynch's films: a traumatic Thing, the point of simultaneous attraction and repulsion, that stands for the vortex of life itself threatening to draw us into its depressive abyss. And does this pre-predicative vortex of the real not resemble the Lacanian notion of *jouissance?* Does Schelling himself not determine the real (*das Reale*) as the circular movement of 'irrational' (that is, pre-logical, pre-symbolic) drives which find satisfaction in the very 'meaningless' repetition of their circular path? For Schelling (as well as for Lacan) this real is the limit, the ultimate obstacle which destines every semantic idealism, every attempt to deploy the Absolute as a self-enclosed matrix generating all possible significations of Being to failure. For both Schelling and Lacan, the most radical version of this semantic idealism is, of course, Hegel's system, which is therefore the principal target of their critiques: the symbolic order can never achieve its full completion and close its circle because its very constitution involves a point at which meaning stumbles against its own boundary and suspends itself in enjoy-meant (*jouissense*).

Appealing as it may sound to our postmodern receptivity, such a reading is nonetheless off the mark: it falls short of the *Grundoperation* of German Idealism common to Schelling and Hegel, since it fails to bring the duality Reason/ Ground to the point of self-reference. What has to fall is the last barrier that separates Reason from its 'irrational' Ground: the most difficult task, the greatest effort, of philosophical speculation is to bring to light the *madness* (*Wahnsinn*) *of the very gesture of instituting the domain of Sinn.* Every organization of sense, every universal conceptual scheme by means of which we attempt to comprehend reality, is in itself – at its most fundamental, for structural and not merely contingent reasons – biased, out of balance, crazy, minimally paranoiac (as early Lacan would have put it): its imposition disturbs the 'natural order of things' and throws the universe off balance. In other words, there is no neutral universality: every universality, every attempt to obtain a global comprehension or intelligible all, bears the indelible mark of the pathological exclusiveness of One, that is, it hinges on the partiality of its position of enunciation.[27] So, again, it is not sufficient to say that no conceptual structure is perfectly neutral, that it fails to comprehend reality in a truly impartial way; the point is rather that the status of this bias is *a priori*, structural. We are dealing here with the inherent constituent of the emergence of a formal structure: in short, with the *condition of the structure's consistency*. Without this exclusive base in One, without this partiality and distortion sustained by a minimum of egotism, the structure disintegrates, loses its consistency in a dispersed plurality. When we repeat after Schelling that every order arises on the base of and has its roots in a general disorder, we are therefore not making the usual relativist point that man's ordering activity is limited to local attempts to introduce a minimum of order into the wide ocean of primordial chaos, to attempts which are, as such, ultimately doomed to failure. Our point is rather that the very imposition of an order is an act of supreme violence; *order is a violent imposition that throws the universe out of joint.*[28] Disorder is the condition of possibility of order not only in the sense that the very notion of order is only conceivable against the background of general disorder, that is, as a series of local attempts to limit the disorder, but in the sense that *the highest disorder, the highest violation of 'natural balance', is the very imposition of a (biased) order.*

We are thus back at our starting point. 'Unconscious' is not primarily the real in its opposition to the ideal; in its most radical dimension, 'unconscious' is rather the very act of decision/differentiation by means of which the ideal establishes itself in its opposition to the real and imposes its order onto the real, the act by means of which the present differs from the past. That is, it is the act by means of which the rotary motion of drives is repressed into the eternal past. Is this not clearly indicated in Schelling's 'formula of the world' (*Weltformel*) from *Weltalter III* (p. 688)?

$$\left(\frac{A^3}{A^2 = (A=B)} \right) B$$

The ever increasing sublation (*Aufhebung*) of the real (B) in the ideal (A), the progressive subordination of the real to the ideal, relies on the exception of a B which, as the excluded ground of the process of sublation, guarantees its consistency. This supplementary B which brackets or enframes the progressive sublation of B by A provides a minimal definition of *dialectical materialism*: the fundamental materialist thesis is that a universal can only become 'For-itself', be 'posited as such', in so far as a kind of umblical cord links it to a particular element whose official status is merely one of the species of the universal. In other words, the elementary idealist illusion resides in the belief in the possibility of a purely neutral universal, of a universal that is not anchored to a particular material *locus* (or, with regard to language, the belief in a pure enunciated that does not involve a particular/partial subjective position of enunciation). Hogrebe is thus fully justified in supplementing Hegel's '*Das Wahre is das Ganze*' by restating it thus: '*Das Wahre ist so das Ganze bis auf Eins, dafuer steht das B neben dem Klammerausdruck*' (The True is the Whole up to One, which is why B stands outside the brackets).[29]

Isn't Hegel aware of this, however, on another level? Isn't this, precisely, the point of his theory of the monarch: in order to actualize itself as the structure of the universal-rational mediation of all particular social content, the State has to be enclosed, grounded in an 'irrational' exception, that is, in the monarch who introduces an element of contingent personal whimsy and egotism and who, as such, clearly embodies the power of B? The condition of possibility of reason is the condition of its impossibility, or, as Lacan would have put it, 'il y a de l'Un' (there's One): a consistent rational structure has to be anchored to an 'irrational' exception, a One which, in its very capacity as exception, guarantees the structure's consistency. For that reason – and, again, everything hinges on this point – repression is always *double*: not only is the real repressed – mediated, sublated, domesticated – by the ideal, pressed into the service of the ideal, but the ideal order itself emerges only in so far as its own 'madness' – the violent act of its imposition, or, in Kierkegaardian terms, its own becoming – is repressed. In short, the obscure Ground is not merely the basis, the background, of the Light of Reason, but primarily the dark spot in the very gesture that gives rise to light as opposed to darkness.

It is as if Schelling is here caught in a radical ambiguity: again and again he succumbs to a temptation and reduces the 'madness' of the self-relating act by which the obscure Ground imposes itself onto the network of Reason, to the *external* relationship of Reason with the obscure Ground from which it draws its life force, yet towards which it has to maintain a proper distance. In the pages of *Weltalter III* which irradiate an almost horrifying poetic power (pp. 713–14), Schelling struggles to demonstrate how man's finitude, the split between Ground and Reason, condemns him to *Wahnsinn*: that which creeps in and inserts itself between the natural *Un-Sinn*, the senseless fact of physical existence, and the Divine, blissful *Sinn*, is *Wahn-Sinn* (madness, or, literally, the delirious sense, the sense which goes astray and roams around). These pages instantly recall the famous fragment from Hegel's *Jenaer Realphilosophie* on the pure Self as the pre-symbolic 'night of the world' in which horrifying apparitions haunt the mind ('here shoots a bloody head – there another white ghastly apparition'), awaiting the dawn of the Word to dispel them. *Sinn*, the true spiritual freedom, appears to man only in a flash, in the guise of a traumatic encounter whose sudden dazzle throws him off the rails. Man is anchored to his egotistic Ground to such an extent that he cannot endure the direct sight of the light of *Sinn*, but can only imitate sense, under the constant threat of slipping back into the rotary motion of Ground. (This is Schelling's way of asserting the fundamentally *hysterical* nature of human subjectivity: the hysterical – feminine – subject merely imitates morality, the symbolic order, and so on, she merely 'puts on [*anziehen*]' morality without effectively identifying with it.) Is it, however, enough to concede that this *Wahn-Sinn* is the eternal, constitutive, supplement of *Sinn*, the Ground from which *Sinn* draws its life force, the source of the perpetual renewal and discovery of new horizons of *Sinn*? Is not the notion that man's *Wahn-Sinn* inserts itself between the natural *Un-Sinn* and the divine *Sinn* deficient and misleading, in so far as it renders invisible the *wahnsinnig*, 'crazy', nature of the very gesture by means of which *Sinn* emerges out of *Un-Sinn*? It is insufficient to assert that Reason is nothing but 'regulated madness', for *the very gesture of regulating madness is in itself mad*. Or, to put it in yet another way, it is insufficient to assert that Reason discerns the islands of necessity in the sea of chaos, for the very gesture of instituting necessity is in itself radically contingent.

Schelling's *Weltformel* thus enables us to demarcate what separates dialectical materialism from idealism: the assertion that the progressive movement of sublation-mediation of B by A is itself framed by B – that it can only occur in so far as it has a foothold in B – is what provides the minimal definition of dialectical materialism. In other words, the full sublation of B in A, the accomplished spiritualization of matter by which matter would finally lose its inert-impenetrable character and turn into an ethereal medium of A, is nothing but an idealist fantasy. In a way, Hegel was already aware of this, which is why he denounced the idea of another ethereal, spiritualized matter as an empty notion of Understanding.

One should, however, be wary of a dangerous trap which lurks here: if we simply assert that A is always framed by B, do we not expose ourselves to the danger of espousing a version of *Lebensphilosophie* according to which Reason is always 'at the service of passion'? And, accordingly, does our claim that there is no neutral universality, that every scheme of Reason is a partial, violent imposition, not point towards Nietzschean perspectivism? This is clearly not Schelling's position. To put it in a somewhat simplified way, his main point is precisely that B is not everything: the vortex of the real is not the ultimate fact, since it is preceded by the abyss of pure freedom as the absolute indifference of A and B. Schelling's point is therefore *not* that A is ultimately bound to serve B; it rather resides in the irreducible gap between pure freedom and every symbolic scheme of Reason, every determinate symbolic representation of the subject in A, in the ideal medium. The leap from S (pure freedom) to A is only possible *via* a detour through B, in the medium of B, or, in other words, it is radically contingent. If the subject (S) is to represent/express itself in A, it has to rely on B, on a contracted element that eludes idealization. In Lacanian terms: there is no symbolic representation without fantasy. That is, the subject (S) is constitutively split between S_1 and a; it can only represent itself in S_1, in a signifier, in so far as the phantasmic consistency of the signifying network is guaranteed by a reference to object a.

Notes

1. F.W.J. Schelling, *Die Weltalter*, ed. Manfred Schroeter (Munich: Biederstein 1946), pp. 56–7; quoted from Andrew Bowie, *Schelling and Modern European Philosophy* (New York and London: Routledge 1993), p. 115.
2. F.W.J. Schelling, *On the History of Modern Philosophy* (Cambridge: Cambridge University Press 1994), p. 115.
3. Ibid.
4. Ibid., p. 116.
5. Ibid.
6. Ibid., p. 115.
7. See Wolfran Hogrebe, *Praedikation und Genesis* (Frankfurt: Suhrkamp 1989), pp. 102–3.
8. F.W.J. Schelling, *Die Weltalter*, p. 629.
9. See Jacques Derrida, *Given Time I: Counterfeit Money* (Chicago and London: University of Chicago Press 1992).
10. An exemplary case of how one achieves full actuality only by means of a 'fall' into temporal reality is Brünnhilde's decision to renounce, for the sake of love, her divine immortality and become an ordinary mortal woman, in Wagner's *Walküre*. What appears as a detraction (the deficiency of terrestrial existence, inhabiting a world of mortality and lack) is effectively an advantage, that is, the only way fully to realize one's desire. Brünnhilde's 'fall' is also the only way she can experience a full-blooded passion that is inaccessible to gods in their bloodless, ethereal existence. And does this not bring us to Schelling's most audacious thought: God Himself is in a sense 'less actual', 'less effective [*wirklich*]', than man? One should not confound this with the usual claim of atheism: Schelling's point is not that there is no God, that God is merely a product of human imagination. There definitely are gods, yet, as Lacan would have put it, they 'belong to the (pre-symbolic) real', that is, in themselves, they are not yet explicated, posited as such. Only in man does God become *wirklich*, actual.
11. The structure is here, of course, more complex. In accordance with Schelling's notion of beginning as the opposite of the process that follows it, the beginning of history is necessarily the fall, and the history of humankind is the teleological process of the gradual rise from the depth of this primordial catastrophe which occurs in three main stages: the pagan era, the Christian era, and the reconciliation to come. Schelling locates his own philosophy in this process, at the very doorstep of the third era, as the announcement of a total politico-spiritual transmutation by means of which humanity will redeem itself and God will fully reveal Himself. However, this outcome is by no means assured: new disasters lurk in the atmosphere all the time, threatening to blot out all progress and throw us back into the initial barbarity.
12. F.W.J. Schelling, 'Philosophical Investigations into the Essence of Human Freedom and Related Matters', in *Philosophy of German Idealism*, ed. Ernst Behler (New York: Continuum 1987), p. 242.
13. We rely here on Vittorio Hoesle, *Praktische Philosophie in der modernen Welt* (Munich: Beck 1992), pp. 166–97.
14. Schelling, 'Philosophical Investigations', p. 245.
15. In his *Treatise on Freedom*, Schelling even goes a step further and claims that true Evil can only emerge in the wake of Christianity as revealed Truth. In the pagan universe, Wisdom comes 'from below', it originates in the obscure, unfathomable depths. That is, pagan civilizations are 'natural formations,' caught in a cycle of corruption and generation, while Christian Wisdom comes 'from above,' it originates in the eternal Light exempted from the circuit of drives. And it is only in contrast to this Light, against its background, that Evil can assert itself as such. The decadence and horrors of the late Roman empire bear witness to an Evil that aggressively asserts itself as such, in a gesture of defiance against the revealed Truth.
16. In the domain of social life, for example, the supreme case of the false, perverted unity is the *State*: as a true forerunner of Marx, Schelling consistently denounces the

State as inherently evil, since it is a false, mechanical, coercive, external unity of the people, a unity imposed from above, not an organic unity that would spring 'from below'.

17. The clearest example of this, of course, was the good old totalitarian Communist Party, which claimed to stand directly for the liberation of all of humanity (in contrast to all other political agents who stood for narrow class interests). Thus, any attack on the Party equalled the attack on all that was progressive in the history of humankind.

18. Heidegger's procedure in *Sein und Zeit* is in this respect the very opposite of Schelling's. Schelling (and, among others who follow in his steps, Otto Weininger) proposes an 'ethical' reading of ontology (the very fact of reality, the fact that the universe exists, involves an ethical decision, it is a proof that, in God, Good got the upper hand over Evil, expansion over contraction), whereas Heidegger is in the habit of taking a category whose 'ethical' connotation in our common language is indelible (guilt [*Schuld*], the opposition between 'authentic' and 'inauthentic' existence) and then depriving it of this connotation. That is, he offers it as a neutral description of man's ontological predicament (*Schuld* as the designation of the fact that, due to his finitude, man has to opt for a limited set of possibilities, sacrificing all others, etc.). This denial of the 'ethical' connotation, of course, provides an exemplary case of the Freudian *Verneinung*: the whole power of Heidegger's argument relies on the fact that the denied ethical dimension maintains its underground efficiency.

19. Hoesle (in his *Praktische Philosophie in der modernen Welt*, p. 44) provides an extremely ingenious solution to the contradiction between Kant's thesis, taken over by Schelling, according to which the world was created in order to become the battleground for the moral conflict between Good and Evil, the conflict whose happy outcome, the final victory of the Good, is guaranteed by God as the necessary postulate of pure reason, and today's threat of humanity's self-destruction by means of a nuclear or ecological catastrophe: *the necessary existence of extraterrestrial intelligence*. That is to say, if the possibility of this catastrophe is serious, doesn't this render the universe meaningless and thus expose the impotence (or, even worse, perversity) of God's act of creation? The only solution is to take seriously and literally Kant's repeated insistence that the moral imperative holds not only for humans but for all other finite rational beings which perhaps, unbeknownst to us, exist on other planets, and to draw the conclusion that these ETs which will prolong the battle for morality in the event of humanity's self-destruction *have to exist*. The way to avoid this conclusion is to abandon its key premise, absolute determinism: according to Hoesle, God is all powerful, He foresaw everything, including humanity's (eventual) self-destruction. In this case, of course, the creation of the universe and of humanity with the full foreknowledge of its future self-destruction is a meaningless, perverse act. Schelling, on the contrary, remains radically anthropocentric: man's fate is open, he *can* – but will not necessarily – sink into self-destruction and thus bring about the regression of the universe to the rotary motion prior to *Ent-Scheidung*. What is therefore at stake in man's struggle for the Good is the fate of God Himself, the success or failure of His act of creation.

20. F.W.J. Schelling, *Saemtliche Werke (SW)*, ed. K.F.A. Schelling (Stuttgart: Cotta 1856–61), vol. VII, p. 468.

21. For a proper understanding of Schelling's claim that Evil is *das reinste Geistige*, much more spiritual than Good, a reference to the Lacanian formula of symbolic castration (−*phi*: enjoyment; *phi* is permitted, but only in so far as it incorporates the 'minus' of castration, that is, in so far as it is domesticated, 'phallicized', submitted to the paternal metaphor) might be of some help. As was pointed out by Jacques-Alain Miller, it is possible for the two elements of the formula, − and *phi*, to separate, to part from each other, so that we obtain, on the one side, the pure (−) the symbolic bereft of the life-substance of enjoyment and thus rendered sterile, that is, the radical erasure of enjoyment, and, on the other side, *phi*, the enjoyment which is, as it were, set loose and freely wanders around outside the symbolic. The price of separation, of course, is that this enjoyment is no longer experienced as healthy, liberating and satisfying, but

becomes something putrid, damp, and oppressive. Suffice it to recall Lenin's incisive description of the spiritual state of Russia after the crackdown of the revolution of 1905: an atmosphere of pure, mystical spirituality, of the violent denial of corporeality, accompanied by an obsession with pornography and sexual perversion. The lesson here is that so-called healthy sexuality, far from being a natural state of things which only occasionally gets perturbed, hinges on a fragile balance, on a combination of two elements (– and *phi*), which can at any moment disintegrate into its two components.

22. Schelling, *SW,* vol. VII, p. 472.
23. Jean-François Marquet, *Liberté et existence. Etude sur la formation de la philosophie de Schelling* (Paris: Gallimard 1973), pp. 569–70.
24. One should relate all this to Lacan's reading of the Freudian notion of *Vorstellungs-Repraesentanz*: not simply 'a representation that acts as a representative of the organic drive', but 'a (signifier-)representative of the (missing) representation'. A person's name is a *Vorstellungs-Repraesentanz*: what it aims at, what it encircles without signifying it, is precisely that abyss in another person which eludes representation. And incidentally, all this also enables us to discern the Kantian background of psychoanalysis: not only the rather obvious point that the drive *qua* Thing-in-itself is accessible only via its psychic *Vorstellungen*, but, above all, the not-so-obvious fact that the Kantian *Ding* is in its most fundamental dimension another subject, not a physical object.
25. At a different level, the same traumatic dimension is obfuscated by the Althusserian concept of interpellation also: when Althusser defines interpellation as the subject's constitutive (mis)recognition in the Other's call, that is, as the act of identification with the big Other, he thereby circumvents the intermediate, transitory but necessary moment of 'interpellation prior to identification' in which the subject is confronted with the opaque call of the Other to whom no discernible meaning can be attributed and which, therefore, precludes any possibility of identification; see chapter 3 of Slavoj Žižek, *Metastases of Enjoyment* (London: Verso 1994).
26. F.W.J. Schelling, 'Philosophical Investigations', pp. 238–9. Thus Schelling's determination of the *object* as the indivisible remainder is Lacanian *avant la lettre,* in so far as it runs counter to the *doxa* of the indivisible *subject* (the individual, his/her indivisible unity, in contrast to the object that can be divided *ad infinitum*). According to Lacan, the subject is not only divisible, but effectively *divided*: it is the product of the operation of signifying division, whereas the object is the indivisible remainder, the fallout, of this same operation. Lacan's matheme of fantasy which figures this link of the subject to the object (S – a) is therefore a formula that designates the encounter of two radically heterogenous entities: S *qua* the void of the distance between the signifiers in a chain, and the inert remainder of the real which resists symbolization. The Lacanian matheme is therefore the very opposite of the inherent deployment of the notional content: it figures a properly inconceivable collision of two elements whose nature is radically heterogeneous.
27. This thesis, according to which a universal is always marked by some stain of particularity, is never truly neutral, but always implies a particular point of view from which the all is disclosed (every universal notion of philosophy always involves the position of a particular philosophy, for example), is, of course, merely another way of asserting that every master-signifier (S_1) is branded, stigmatized by *a*, by the absolute particularity of an objectal leftover. An exemplary case of this One which sustains the All of universality is provided by a quick glance at any manual of philosophy. Every universal, all-encompassing notion of philosophy is rooted in a particular philosophy. There is no neutral notion of philosophy to be divided into analytical philosophy, hermeneutic philosophy, etc.; every particular philosophy encompasses itself and (its view on) all other philosophies. Or, as Hegel put it in his *Lessons on the History of Philosophy*, every epochal philosophy is in a way the whole of philosophy, it is not a subdivision of the whole but this whole itself apprehended in a specific modality. What we have here is thus not a simple reduction of the universal to the particular, but rather a kind of *surplus* of the Universal. No single universal encompasses all

particular content, since each particular has *its own* universal, that is, it contains a specific perspective on the entire field. If, then, Evil resides in the 'contracted' subjective position involved in our allegedly neutral view on the entire universal field, how are we to step out of it? The point, of course, is that the reference to universality is unavoidable, since it is inherent to speech as such: the moment we speak, a kind of universal dimension is always involved. So the thing to do is not to claim or openly admit that we only speak from our particular position (this assertion already involves a view of totality within which our particular position is located), but to admit the irreducible plurality of the universals themselves. The discord is already at the level of the universal, so that the only true self-restraint is to admit the particularity of one's own universal.

28. Does Wagner's *Ring* not bear witness to a similar foreboding? Wotan's universe of *logos*, of symbolic contracts and laws, is founded upon a primordial breach and is as such destined to fall to ruins.

29. Hogrebe, *Praedikation und Genesis*, p. 112.

2 IT MAKES US WRONG
Kant and Radical Evil[1]

JACOB ROGOZINSKI

'*Es gibt Böse.*' There is evil. Irrecusable, unjustifiable, the fact
of evil is imposed upon us. It will have always been given to
us, ready to be deciphered, in the stories of history, in the
messages of poetry and myth: 'That the world "lieth in evil"',
writes Kant, 'is a plaint as old as history, old even as the older
art, poetry; indeed as old as that oldest of all fictions, the
religion of priestcraft.'[2] We must understand these claims
– that there is evil, that man can be said to be evil – as
indisputable facts: 'That such a corrupt propensity must
indeed be rooted in man need not be formally proved in
view of the multitude of crying examples which experience *of
the actions* of men put before our eyes' (*RL*, p. 28). It is a
property of finite reason, receptive even in its spontaneity,
that its point of departure is given to it in experience as a
fact. Reason cannot construct this point but must receive it,
be affected by it, and so be obliged by its irreducible facticity.
The opening hand that it is dealt (*sa donne inaugurale*) is not
left to deduction, but rather experienced in the ethical
sentiment of respect, in the aesthetic sentiment of the
sublime, in the historical sign of enthusiasm and in the
complaint that the world dwells in evil. Kant also invites us
to listen again to that 'long and melancholy litany of
accusations brought against humanity'. The muffled cries of
the vanquished and the dead forward their complaint to us
and demand justice. They call for a tribunal which can grant
them a hearing and render judgement on the damage that

has been done. The fact of evil needs to be considered in light of this complaint. But are we yet competent to respond to such a request? With the diminishment of faith in a just God and the waning of belief in the immortality of the soul or in the dogma of original sin, the question of evil seems to have been gradually emptied of meaning until it disappears almost entirely from the horizon of our culture. But it is possible that the tradition of Western philosophy has already had a hand in the eclipse of evil in so far as it, from its origin, unfolds as *ontodicity*, by dedicating itself to the absolution of being. If 'God is not the cause of evil', if the essence of all that exists is good or if our world could only come into existence because it is the best possible world, then evil finds itself banished to the borders of being, denounced as absence, as a deficiency of being, as part of the shadow which throws the lustre of being into relief. And so long as evil is nothing, our faults will only be defaults (*causa deficiens*), a deprivation or a lack which, rather than accusing our wise Creator, only exposes our limits and imperfections as finite creatures. Instead of disappearing with the advent of modernity, ontodicity endures in the metaphysics of the modern and, by modifying its appearance, extends its domain. Once human subjectivity claims a central position for itself in being (*l'étant*), the task of philosophy will be consecrated to the absolution of man. It will attempt to acquit him, to disimplicate him, by denying his free will or, on the contrary, by purifying that will, by exalting it 'beyond good and evil'. Kant's work holds a privileged position in this passage from theodicy to anthropodicity. Without recapitulating his conception of history here, we can remember that Kant's practical philosophy, which identifies freedom with autonomy, pure practical reason with 'good will', can only recuse the possibility of a 'freedom to do evil', of a will that is fundamentally bad. No previous philosophy went so far in its celebration of the reasonable purity of human free will. We can understand, then, the indignant surprise with which his contemporaries read the essay 'On the Radical Evil in Human Nature' (*RL*, pp. 15–39): this 1792 text abruptly introduced the idea that a 'tendency toward evil' was inherent in human nature. This was a scandalous thesis, one which seemed to contradict all of Kant's previous work and one that most of his interpreters attempted to obscure.[3] But they did not understand that something seemingly 'archaic' in Kant's thought could be of more concern to us than his very 'modern' theory of knowledge, and that a conception judged absurd and retrograde by a contemporary of Voltaire and Goethe could come into sharper focus in a time illuminated by the troubled light emanating from the abjection of Auschwitz or the Kolmya.[4]

What those distant claims require from us is, as we've said, a court capable of hearing their complaints, the authority of a judge. But how can we establish an appropriate jurisdiction – how shall we judge the fault – if the wrong is not susceptible of imputation or if it is impossible to hold it against someone? To

whom shall we attribute this wrong if it is not an act of freedom that proceeds
from a will that is at fault? If we intend to do justice to this complaint, we will first
have to interrogate that dominant tendency of our modernity that exonerates
human subjectivity and blames evil on history, on society, on unconscious drives
or on the laws of heredity. In this context, it is not enough for us to say that there
is evil: we must recognize that this evil is our doing and that we will have to
answer for it to the Law. In Kantian terms, we could say that when I judge that
evil is 'my fault', this judgement puts into question my status as an ethical subject.
It incriminates the act of freedom, the 'choice of an intelligible character', in
which I decided to institute the 'highest maxim', an act which will determine
the choice of all my derivative maxims and, consequently, all the acts which 'I'
commit as an empirical self in this phenomenal world. If we have come to be
in a state of fault, it is because we were already bad and we had freely decided
to become so. As long as we recognize an inaugural act committed by a free
will at the very root of the fault, the simple requirements of judgement entail
that we retrace a fault which is 'sensible, empirical, occurring in time' to a transcendental fault that would have been its foundation, then to a structure of a
priori faultiness that would be something like the pure noumenon of the fault.
Which means that it is possible '*a priori* to infer from several evil acts done with
consciousness of their evil, or from one such act, an underlying evil maxim; and
further, from this maxim to infer the presence in the agent of an underlying
common ground, itself a maxim, of all particular morally-evil maxims' (*RL*,
p. 16). This enigmatic *Grund des Bösen*, this evil principle which has 'corrupted at
the root the underlying ground of all our maxims', is precisely what Kant calls
radical evil. Sometimes he refers to it as the irremissible debt of an *ursprüngliche
Schuld* (*RL*, p. 86); sometimes it is the twisting of a curve, a tortuous nodosity
embedded in the heart of that 'wood of which man is made', one which brings
the ethical demand for rectitude into default: 'Can one expect something
perfectly straight to be framed out of such crooked wood?'[5] This metaphor,
previously deployed in *The Ideal of a Universal History* (1784), will occur again in
Reflections on Education, The Doctrine of Virtue and *The Doctrine of Right.* It frequently
appears wherever Kant introduces the topic of opening a new path to thought
and wherever he interrogates the conditions of possibility for such an opening,
whenever he endeavours to delimit the criteria for judgement, that is, to legislate
what is just and unjust, proper and improper, right and wrong. It is as if the motif
of the curve signified a fundamental aporia, as if it symbolically figured the risk
of a perpetually menacing failure which it would be necessary to designate each
and every time so as to hold it more firmly at bay. And perhaps we should
discover in this project to thwart or to frame this twisting which exceeds all
framing, this desire to square a knot of the impossible, to disappear the twisted

fold of a primordial wrong, something specific to Kantianism.[6] Examine the effect of a proper name in a linguistic system: the German translation of the phrase 'to square off' (équarrir) is kanten. In this sense, for Kant, the business of thought would be the rectification of and the compensation for this wrong. But the hypothesis of radical evil seems to suggest that the wrong is irreparable. Thus the most troublesome of all facts – that there is evil – returns to us in the enigma of a wrong that will always have been destined for us. 'Destined' not in the sense of a destiny, since it could no longer be imputed to us, but in the sense of a faulty destination present from the beginning, of an initial being-wrong given to thought since the send-off of its there is. 'Es gibt Böse, es gibt Krümmung': there is evil, there is wrong, it makes us wrong (ça nous donne tort).

According to Kant, we must think of this gift as radical, that is, as absolutely originary, 'in this sense, that it [evil] is posited as the ground antecedent to every use of freedom in experience . . . and is thus conceived of as present in man at birth' (RL, p. 17). Temporal succession only concerns the natural connection of phenomena, not the things in themselves, and has no purchase on the intelligible character which, as a law of transcendental causality, is situated beyond time. And this allows us precisely to 'save freedom': for if 'past time is no longer under my control', and if I were entirely immersed in the flux of becoming that is carrying off the world of phenomena, I would allow myself to be caught up in the infinite causal chain of necessity, and my freedom would be worth little more than that of a turn-jack or one of Vaucanson's marionettes. If it is to be imputed to me, the faultiness of my fault must transcend all temporal determination: it must be posited as an 'act preceding all acts', as the primordial decision of an inaugural hand that I am dealt (une donne inaugurale) in which my being is at stake, which engages me in my being forever. The radicalness of radical evil would therefore seem to indicate that it is so deeply rooted in my freedom that 'it cannot be eradicated' (RL, p. 27); that this manner of being bad, adherence to which corrodes the flesh of my being, distorts each of my acts and stigmatizes them. From the beginning, it will have made us wrong (donné tort), and this gift (don) is irrevocable. But if this is the state of things, if this destination is so hardened and congealed that our fate has always already been sealed, is it still within our power to compensate for that wrong? Can the redemptive return of the Bekehrung which duty prescribes for us deliver us from it? How shall we judge an inexpiable fault, and suffer for it, if judgement no longer authorizes the possibility of a pardon? The doctrine of radical evil traps itself in an aporia: the wrong should give itself in time, it should bind us hopelessly to the chain of phenomena, but if it gives itself outside of time, it predestines us for all eternity. Unless this aporia is the result of an overly restrictive determination of the atemporality of the noumena. The Critique of Pure Reason insists on the unchanging permanence of the character of the intelligible in which 'nothing happens' and there is 'neither before nor after'.[7] Classically, this results in a definition of the atemporal as a function of phenomenal temporality, as an act of negative abstraction which, in representing the atemporal as an eternal present, maintains the beyond-time within the influence of time. If we want to avoid eternalizing wrong and retain some hope of its remission, we would need to extract it from its maintenance in the present, to understand that the fault springs up suddenly from a completely different temporality, from a noumenal *durée* which exceeds the *Jetzt-Zeit* of the phenomenal world to the same extent as its internal inversion.[8] No matter how far back its memory runs, the self only encounters the linear enchainment of present moments which have succeeded one another. But not a single one of these moments could have opened itself to the event of the fault because that moment supposes both that there is an instituting act of free decision and that 'at the time [in the point of time, the *Zeitpunkte*] I act I am never free'.[9] Nonetheless, for my assertion to be imputable to me, it is every bit as necessary that it be within my power and that I be 'susceptible of, and subjected to, imputableness in the very moment of that action [*in dem Augenblicke der Handlung*] just as much as though ... [I] had stepped out of a state of innocence into evil' (*RL*, p. 36). Thus at every instant the continuous interlocking of points in time, whose order of succession forges the chain of maintenance, crosses the gap in the *Augenblicke* where time rips itself open to deliver the possible. The furtive flapping of a caesura, a syncopation of necessity, that wink of time which opens on the abyss of noumenal duration, liberates the perspective of this entirely other temporality, the time of the Other, whose affection invests the noumenal ego as the subject of ethics. From the moment that the 'it judges me' emerges across the *Abgrund* of duration, I discover myself, trapped by the instant, as subject to fault, as *sub judice*.

The double dealing (*double donne*) of temporality: at the crossroads of time a glance at the trap reveals a sudden clearing in which my faulty weakness and the promise of a redemptive *Bekehrung* intertwine. *It will have been necessary*: this is the time of chance, the day of forgiveness on which, in one transfiguring instant, the Kantian good news announces itself: that return is still possible, that he can even now rescue us from our maintenance in the eternal present, can acquit the past, disencumber the future and give us all time. That radical evil, which should have made us wrong, is not radical enough to stigmatize us forever. And at this moment, in a clap of thunder, we see the full magnitude of the scandal of the fault: at any instant we could have redeemed ourselves, but we failed to do so. The very moment which should have delivered us redoubles our wrong and points to our guilt. Nor does Kant hesitate to recognize some truth in the Biblical story of the Fall which, if we stop projecting it into a mythic past, can account for our surrender, ceaselessly reiterated in the waning of an instant: 'from this it is clear that we daily act in the same way, and that therefore "in Adam all have sinned" and still sin' (*RL*, p. 37). Hell, for Kant, is nothing other than that declivitous infinity of the moment in which our future is discovered to be an endless relapse, an '*incalculable misery*' (*RL*, p. 63). How we could each time consent to our undoing, why we ceaselessly allow ourselves to abandon all hope, these are the most difficult questions the human animal poses to the philosopher. Doubtless we must renounce our attempt to think the origin of wrong, whose 'basis of an explanation remain[s] ever hidden in darkness' (*RL*, p. 52). To explain freedom, Fichte says, would be to destroy it, and what is radical evil if not that senseless decision of freedom which is freely renounced at every instant? Consequently, if the provenance of evil remains incomprehensible, if it refers us back to that enigma of a *serf-arbitre*, a voluntary servitude, to what extent can our actions be clearly attributed to us? According to which criteria can we arrive at an exact determination of our merits and our faults?

But perhaps we must give up the possibility of ruling on good and evil from the vantage point of a *determining* judge whose criteria and rules would already be given. Since we are only concerned with the phenomenon of the fault grasped in its empirical particularity, and must extend it to the universal faultiness at its foundation, our judicial faculty here would be reflective and not determining. This point is suggested by the *Critique of Pure Reason*, in which Kant remarks that the 'character of the thing-in-itself', which is to say, of the free subject, 'can never in truth immediately be known, but is indicated to us [given, *angegeben*] by its empirical character'. It is again a question of a given, but one that is *Angabe* in the sense that an informer 'gives up' a guilty party and testifies against him. By designating itself as the effect of a free act, the empirical fault is a symbolic informant, an index which denounces to the critical judge the faulty freedom of the intelligible character as if it were the cause of evil, as if wrong came from that side. We would no longer have the right to say that there is evil, but only that we must judge *as if* it made us wrong (*ça nous donnait tort*). Nonetheless it would be possible that this reflective imputation, far from facilitating the task of the judge, could finally render all ethical judgement impossible. In so far as they are not schema but symbols, indirect and analogical figurations of the unfigurable, the accusatory traces which his actions leave in the world of phenomena will never be enough to incriminate the ethical subject. In the final account,

> the real morality of actions, their merit or their guilt, even that of our own conduct, thus remain[s] entirely hidden from us. Our imputations can refer only to their empirical character. How much of this character is ascribable to the pure effect of freedom, how

much to mere nature, that is, to faults of temperament . . . can never be determined; and upon it therefore no perfectly just judgement can be passed. (*CPR*, p. 475)

But the critical judge is not only confronted with the opacity of the intelligible character, with an undecidable confusion of free causality and necessity. Kant remarks that, in researching the principle of our actions, moral investigation 'everywhere comes upon the dear self, which is always there'.[10] And that 'secret impulse of self-love', by 'falsely appearing as the idea of duty', seems capable of devouring or parodying the ethical obligation, of simulating the sovereign · evidence of the Law (*FM*, p. 23). The *Anthropology* will analyse this potential for dissimulation, this narcissistic mimesis, through which 'egotism expands without resistance, if not openly . . . at least in secret . . . under the cover of an apparent abnegation and pretense of respect.' So successful is its dissimulation that any demarcation between the two characters is thereafter tinged with an anxiety-producing signification: it will seem as if an invisible force were at work, entrenched behind the opacity of the intelligible character, which takes malign pleasure in confusing trails and fraudulently falsifying all marks so that it can erase any indices of its wrong and prohibit even the possibility of judgement. In this case, our inability to judge would not essentially result from our finitude and the limits it imposes on our moral discernment, but from the wrong that, in an instant, slips away: it 'resides in radical evil . . . which (inasmuch as it puts out of tune [*verstimmt*] the moral capacity to judge . . . renders wholly uncertain both internal and external attribution of responsibility)' (*RL*, p. 34). 'There is wrong' means that radical evil resides in its dissimulation, that being-wrong is twisted being, the falsity or the feint, the *Unlauterkeit*, the tortuous impurity of bad faith. And, in Kant, this above all designates the 'tendency to deceive oneself in the interpretation of the moral law. . . . Accordingly, the Bible . . . denominates the author of evil (who is within us) as the liar from the beginning, and thus characterizes man with respect to what seems to be the chief ground of evil in him' (*RL*, p. 37).

Under these conditions, it would seem that all criteria for judgement fail, and that we were incapable not only of understanding but even of discerning good and evil. In this vein, the *Critique of Practical Reason* had already explicitly condemned the practice of traditional moral philosophers who pretend to determine a priori what is good and to 'derive moral laws from the concept of the good'. What they don't see is that this concept, taken in itself and hypostatized, remains indeterminable from a rational point of view and therefore doesn't allow for the foundation of practical obligation. Against this dogmatic moralism, and the scepticism its failure inevitably engenders, Kant calls for a *Copernican revolution in ethics*: it is not 'the concept of the good as an object of the moral law [that] determines the latter and makes it possible, but rather the reverse, i.e., that the moral law is that which first defines the concept of the good' (CRp, p. 66).[11] This perspectival shift reintroduces a criterion for judgement that should permit us to pronounce rationally on good and evil: an action can be judged good from the point of view of the Law, that is, if it conforms to the prescription of the Law. Far from hypostatizing evil, Kant would invite us to define it in relation to the Law, as its always possible transgression, as that resistance or that transgression whose possibility the Law 'reveals by itself and, after a fashion, in itself'.[12] Inasmuch as human reason doesn't give itself the Law, but is organized in response to the Law's call, ethical decisions finally amount to letting oneself *be obliged*, to opening oneself unreservedly to that imperative vocation which provokes and also *alters*. What is evil, then, if not precisely that reserve, that withdrawal (*repli*) which keeps me within myself and at every instant turns me away from that opening? The curve of wrong figures that twist in a faulty will which folds back on itself and no longer wants to be only itself? Secluded in its ipseity, refusing to submit itself to the obligation of autonomy, how can it but fall into the trap of that worst of all masters, of the principal heteronomy, self-love? Once it declares itself a categorical imperative, the Law invests my freedom, deploys it and redresses its curve to deliver me from my seclusion in the cloister of the proper. 'Ordinary good and evil here show themselves as the difference between two modes of being. Good is now the being in the unconditional opening . . . , bad is the being which closes itself off from the native facticity of that place in which man receives.'[13] But does this suggest that we will henceforth dispose of a determining criteria which would permit us to define a priori the concepts of good and evil? Or that we will be able to deduce from them, with certainty, our duties and our prohibitions? There are formulations which would allow us to believe this, and there are those who have not failed to exploit those formulations so as to interpret Kantian ethics as a dogmatic moralism. But we must not forget that the Law, as a 'fact of pure reason', remains, for Kant, inaccessible to our finite understanding. And that he warns us against precisely that dogmatic naivety, that 'mysticism of practical reason' which, in trying to present moral concepts directly to intuition, 'makes a schema out of that which can only serve as a symbol'. Which is to say that the imperative prescription of the Law stands apart from the 'typical' prescriptions in which it is dispensed, and it can only arrive at self-figuration in an indirect, analogical mode through the bias of symbols, those ambiguous traces which it leaves for us to decipher. Practical judgement, far from being reduced to the 'schematic' application of a re-established universal determination, is at every turn played out in a singular set of givens – a single deal of the cards (*donne*) – in the testimony of an experience in which what is unpresentable in the Law is

presented aesthetically when I am invested by the Law with the affect that Kant
calls the sentiment of respect. And this pure respect for the Law 'only applies
to persons', that is, it only makes sense for a man whose 'example holds a law
before me which strikes down my self-conceit' (*CRp*, p. 79). The appeal of the
Law, which transfixes my freedom with respect, addresses me from the simple
presence of 'the man I see there before me', from the alterity of a face that would
give itself like the flesh of the Law. Only in abandoning myself to this proof do
I discover myself in my own finitude as being-wrong in view of the Law, and the
reception of an infinite strangeness is what makes me wrong.

What, accordingly, is radical evil if not the final effort of my self, recoiled
(*repli*) back upon its duplicity, which, simulating respect, parodying duty, refuses
to appear in front of the Law, which fails to respect, and fails the call? It is that
feigned opening, that metaphysical experience of defiguration which Kant
designates by the name of *lie*. In the lie, a man 'throws away and . . . annihilates
his dignity as a man'. That is, his ability to receive the Law: the liar 'is a mere
deceptive appearance of a man, not a man himself'.[14] In the bad fold (*pli*)
of that transcendental appearance in which appearances are distorted from
the moment of their apparition, the social bond is knotted and broken, 'all
such rights as are founded in contracts become null, void, and infirm'. Caught
in this universal falsity, the Law itself becomes 'uncertain and empty'.[15] When
the respect due to one's given word is betrayed and loses all credibility, the
being-together of men confesses its failure and any promise, any contract, any
agreement about rules is denounced even before it is expounded. If it is true that
in language games, the rules of the game 'do not carry within themselves their
own legitimation, but are the object of a contract, explicit or not between players'
and 'if there are no rules, there is no game',[16] then radical evil, which cancels all
the rules, signifies that we cannot *really* play at that particular game. That we all
cheat all the time and that there is no 'beautifully played trick' that doesn't
retain in its beauty the mark of this originary violence. What is questionable
about the social bond, the aporia of the political, is that no rule holds unless it
abides by a metarule that organizes all games: it is necessary that there be a Law
above their laws, preserved from their agon, capable of vesting each player with
the imperative commandment: 'Do not invoke the name of the Law in vain.'
Or, more soberly, 'respect the Promise'. If this final recourse fails, if the guardian
of the Law himself indulges in a lie, wrong triumphs and it is appropriate that
we lose all hope. When Kant declares that radical evil has 'corrupted the
foundations of all our maxims', or, in a symbolic mode, that the 'original Liar' is
the Prince of this world, we must consider the possibility that the destiny of man,
his *Bestimmung*, has always been falsified by the discord of a primordial
Verstimmung. That human existence occurs entirely in the retreat of the Law and

in the errancy of its disfiguration. The complaint that the 'world dwells in evil' might mean that being-in-the-world is being-wrong.

Does this mean that there is no pardon available in this world? That in it we are falling ceaselessly at every moment and on every side? Could there be no clearing, no single fixed, guaranteed point that resists hyperbolic evil and permits us to undo the double grip of wrong? For even if it wrongs us (*ça nous donne tort*) on all sides, is it not necessary that there be something that, beyond the wrong, could have made possible the enigma of its donation? There *must* be such a space if I can judge myself to be at fault, that is, if there was a moment in which I experienced in the sentiment of respect that it judges me to be at fault. And even if wrong were the secret name of being, even if it must have made being itself wrong, it would nevertheless have been necessary for this wrong to be discerned above and beyond this being which it incriminates, because the appeal of the Law is that *it is necessary*. And because I do not myself address this missive, because my practical reason does not give itself the Law but gives itself to the Law, we can be confident that the proposition *the Law is necessary, there is Law* is required before I have understood it or expressed it, and even before I have taken in the sentiment of respect. But can this Law, estranged as it is from the world, escape from that which serves as the law of the world? Unless it takes refuge in the ecstasy of a silent transcendence where it would fail its own call, the Law is obliged to engrave its trace in the world it exceeds. It owes itself to my respect. It is the Law's own luck that man was found in the gap of duration ready to receive it and take charge of the precious deposit entrusted to his keeping. In this sense, its destination depends on our good will. But if it is at man's discretion that the Law is dispensed, can it remain invulnerable to the attacks of radical evil? No doubt the it-judges-me, which constantly invests my will, is ordered by a set of givens (*une donne*) more originary than the lie of origins. The *Doctrine of Virtue* will insist on the radicality of this *gewissen*, on this sort of originary practical apperception which returns to haunt the conscience of man at fault and transfixes it with remorse (compare *MM*, pp. 225–7). But is this murmuring that obsesses me truly the sublime voice of my judge? How can we judge the provenance of a voice? How shall we decide the destination of a deposit 'whose owner has died without having left instructions on this matter'? Is it really the credible messenger of the Lords of the Castle? Of the appeal of the Law only a distant echo is retained in my heart of hearts, only those symbolic marks of remorse and guilt which figure at a distance the figurelessness of the Law. Consequently these stigmata of fault, which are only representatives by proxy, the lieutenants of the It Is Necessary, puppets of its state control, abandon themselves without restraint to the game of supplements and dissimulations, distortions and dissonances, to the delirium of a generalized

Verstimmung in which the epiphany of the Face is disfigured and stiffens in a grimace. In these troubled regions, to which Kant occasionally compares the road to hell, any criteria for judgement would now seem to slip away without hope of recovery. Thus Kant notices the 'paralysis' of our reason that is completely incapable of discerning the divine from the diabolic origin of an imperative calling, as exemplified by 'the command delivered to Abraham to slaughter his own son like a sheep' (*RL*, p. 175). Even if the prescription bids us 'do a good act which in itself we already recognize as duty', even there 'this criterion fails', for the Evil spirit 'often disguises [*verstellt*] himself, they say, as an angel of light' (*RL*, p. 82).

Not only will we never know which is the side of wrong and which the side of Law, but it is possible that we will no longer even come to recognize or distinguish the sublime voice of duty from the impure voice of the oracle.[17] Nevertheless, a moment arrives, a crossroads, which compels us to choose and, confronted with the risk of absolute injustice, to decide each time between wrong and Law. The entire interest of the subject of practical reason lies in his being obliged to confront his own radical limit – even its terror – symbolized, with the pathos of the exemplary cases Kant offers us, by the Grand Inquisitor (*RL*, p. 174), by the assassins who track down my friend, by the tyrant who threatens me with 'the same sudden death' unless I make a 'false deposition' (*CRp*, p. 30). Or even by that senseless vocation that summons me, at the risk of breaking the covenant, to sacrifice my son, the only guarantee of that covenant, there and then on the mountain of Moria. The summation, in which the indescribable wrong that saturates all prescription and the address that follows the failure of the It Is Necessary accuse each other, results in a cross of obligation: that we must be obliged to decide among undecidables. We are obliged to decide even though the 'choice of the highest maxim' is at stake, even though our reason fails, though the symbols slip away, though the prescriptive voice – in its very calling – betrays itself, reveals the wrong which degrades and confuses it, and must avow the secret connivance which has always linked it to its double. With this perversion of the imperative – this *Verstellung* of its *Darstellung*, this *Verstimmung* of its *Stimme* – pure practical reason comes up against its limit, the instable boundary of a parergon that exposes it to the gravest of dangers. For the worst injustice is this confusion of the tongues of good and evil, this panic of a deregulated reason which founders in the labyrinth of its simulacra and makes us, as a note in the *Critique of Judgement* furtively envisions, 'consider the ethical law itself as a simple illusion of our reason'.[18]

But a reason that is able to go so far astray, a reason so falsified and mendacious, would be radically bad; it would be radical evil. And it is at this point, as if in a sudden recoil from the abyss of the Law, that Kant decides to stop short and absolve once and for all the reasonable will. At the very moment he exposes his doctrine to radical evil, he insists that 'neither can the ground of this evil be placed in a *corruption* of the morally legislative reason – as if reason could destroy the authority of the very law which is its own, or deny the obligation arising therefrom; this is absolutely impossible'. Accordingly, 'man (even the most wicked) does not ... repudiate the moral law in the manner of a rebel (renouncing obedience to it). The law, rather, forces itself upon him irresistibly by virtue of his moral predisposition' (*RL*, pp. 30–31). Kant now returns to a previous position, one found in the *Critique of Practical Reason*, which affirmed the irrecusable evidence of the Law and implicitly refused to admit even the possibility of its failure or dissimulation. Our reason could not be perverted to the point at which it would no longer be able to distinguish between the sublime voice of the Law and its hellish caricature. Or rather, the pure calling of duty distinguishes itself and solicits our respect by the grace of its orthophony, by the singular clarity of its intonation. By the same token, wrong denounces itself, its twisted and incredible inflection never fails to provoke laughter or disgust. If there were a conflict between the two principles,

> were the voice of reason with respect to the will not so distinct, so irrepressible, and so clearly audible even to the commonest man, it would drive morality to ruin. ... Suppose that you had an acquaintance who ... were to attempt to justify himself before you for having borne false witness. ... And suppose that he then affirmed, in all seriousness, that he had thereby fulfilled a true human duty – you would either laugh in his face or shrink from him in disgust. (*CRp*, p. 36)

Ethical law would have no difficulty assimilating itself to our reason: no discussion would be necessary; it would be a fact. It is even, according to Kant, the 'unique fact of pure reason', and we know that he will rely on this single fact, on the minuscule note of a tonal accent, on the grain or the timbre of a silent assonance, to deduce the 'objective reality' of freedom and to confer a certain degree of reality on all the Ideas of reason, including the immortality of the soul and the existence of God. The 'keystone of any edifice' rests on this fragile *factum rationis*. This occurs as though, having acquitted the reasonable will, Kant believes himself authorized to submit the enigmatic gift of the Law to the apodictic certainty of a principle of reason, to consider it as a fact of reason in the sense that reason would be made into Law, that reason would make itself Law. By making Law its business, pure reason 'to that extent proclaims itself to be primordially legislative (the donor of the Law): *sic volo, sic jubeo*' (*CRp*). And the originary passivity of the it-judges-me allows itself to be arraigned in the free and voluntary edict of an I judge: the Law retracts into the Self. But if it is true that practical reason gives itself Law and that it grasps Law immediately in the clarity of its autoenunciation, then evil is nothing. From the vantage of this fixed and assured fulcrum, the first evidence of *Ego volo*, the shadows of the *Unlauterkeit* are dispersed and the evil genius of radical wrong evaporates like a bad dream. If our reasonable will (*volonté*) is henceforth completely acquitted, in this pure will (*vouloir*), which necessarily wills the Law and gives it to itself without ever being wrong, the choice of evil cannot come from that autonomous legislative will (*Wille*), but only from a contingent decision made by our free choice (*Willkür*). And this decision will be occasioned less by an active and voluntary failure than by a flaw in the will, a lack of moral force. In this case, evil could no longer be understood as a 'negative quantity', as a bad will which could choose to resist a good will: it could only be the degree zero of morality, the sign of our pathological 'fragility', our inability to resist sense-based inclinations.

When he expels evil from the intelligible world, when he casts it out beyond the borders of practical reason, Kant falls back into ancient errors of ontodicity. But he nonetheless finds himself obliged to transgress these limits whenever he tries to think the unthinkable fact – that there is evil – in all its radicality. Because of these transgressions, his work after 1792 appears to oscillate between two incompatible orientations, and he finds himself forced to deny this *ontological equivocation* and to patch the tear that his work aggravates. To the extent that it participates in the ontodictic tradition, Kant's practical philosophy reduces our wrongs to passing infringements: the subject at fault, although he recognizes the universal import of the categorical imperative, nonetheless claims a particular exemption for himself.[19] Even as he transgresses the prescription, the guilty subject confesses his appartenance, and, to borrow St Augustine's terms, in his resistance he only demonstrates that 'there is no place in which one completely escapes' the Law. But it is in the interests of reason that we are forbidden to consider that reason could cease to be identified with Law, could cease to be arraigned within its sovereign jurisdiction. That the Law, if finally released from its guardianship of the principle of reason, could retreat into its bottomless donation and abandon us to the distress of the undecidable. Once the identities of the Law, reason and will have been broken we would no longer be able to absolve a priori the rational will, and would have to admit its troubling potential to revolt against the Law, to decide freely to oppose it, to opt for evil, without thereby ceasing to be reason and will. Insanity would be the work of pure reason and evil would again become a negative quantity, a *Wiederstrebung* rising up from the deepest structures of being. We would be faced with the impossible itself, with the abyss of Kantianism: with a 'reason exempt from the moral law, a *malignant reason* as it were, a thoroughly evil will . . . and thus the subject would be made a *devilish* being'. Kant adds quickly that this kind of case 'is never applicable to man' (*RL*, p. 30). No doubt, when faced with the menace of absolute wrong, there is no longer any point in arguing, one chooses one's side: if this inconceivable case ever came to be presented, human reason would no longer make Law and the humanity of man would end. It is therefore important to contain that menace in the unpresentable – and in this genre of ruse we recognize a master exorcist – by substituting for its unsustainable presentation the vicarious figuration of an analogous case, one that can be absorbed into the system of reason without causing any damage. Wary lest this inhuman evil be directly presented, pure reason re-presents it to itself symbolically in the appropriate – that is, assimilable – form of its substitute: an evil that would have retained its human face, that would have remained properly human. The advantage of this lesser evil, which preserves us from the greater, is that 'it must be possible to *overcome* it, since it is found in man. . . . We are not, then, to call the depravity [*Bösartigkeit*] of man *wickedness* [*Bösheit*] taking this word in its strict sense as a disposition . . . or to adopt evil *as evil* into our maxim as our incentive (for that is diabolical); we should rather term it the *perversity* of the heart . . . [which] may coexist with a will which is in general good' (*RL*, p. 32). The case of this figure for radical evil, this *Bösartigkeit* which encounters itself everywhere in experience, would have its sole burden in countering the unfigurable menace of *Bösheit*, absolute or diabolic evil that must remain forbidden to presentation. This is to say that, in the end, if there is a 'radical' evil in us, it is only proof that we are not so bad, and Kant will only have thought about our wrong to keep us from being absolutely wrong.

If this operation is to have some chance of success, the devil must deign to be exorcized, the unpresentable must not return to be presented in substitute representations – the fetishes of pure reason – which were supposed to supplant him. For there is always a case in which one finds oneself confronted by that which, properly, should not present itself at all. We can reread in this perspective the long and wild note to the *Doctrine of Right* in which Kant tries to explain, to strange effect, the 'horror' evoked in us by the French Revolution and more particularly by that monstrous crime of regicide.[20] What seems to unveil this 'historical sign' would be the abject reverse of the political, its Medusa face – the Terror as the figure of absolute wrong, as that abyss of thought that it is necessary at all costs to evade. Thus Kant does his best to demonstrate that the king's death sentence does not originate in an absolutely evil intention, in a rebellious will 'diametrically opposed' to the Law, but is the result of a limited transgression, committed as if accidentally by a people in panic 'so that their killing him would not be an enactment of punitive justice but merely a dictate of self-preservation'. The French would have behaved like a savage people, but their cruelty would have remained properly human. If, that is, the king had been secretly assassinated in a tower of the Temple, or lynched by the sans-culottes in the course of a revolutionary *journée*. Then the crime would have remained a simple infraction, the private act of a handful of rebels. Evil would not have pretended to raise itself to a universal principle, it would not have dared to defy the Law to the point of simulating it, usurping its place and its dignity. But this was not what happened, and the most atrocious forfeit of which a people will have been guilty is precisely the execution of its sovereign through legal forms: 'while his *murder* is regarded as only an *exception* to the rule that the people makes its maxim, his *execution* must be regarded as a complete *overturning* of the principles of the relation between a sovereign and his people. . . . Like a chasm that irretrievably swallows everything, the execution of a monarch seems to be a crime from which the people cannot be absolved, for it is as if the state commits suicide.' We are rightly horrified: and, because the most extreme evil can occur only in politics, the French are accordingly a people of demons. But this must remain impossible, forbidden to presentation, even though the case has just presented itself. Unless the French didn't really judge and condemn Louis XIV, unless they gave a simple murder, committed in the heat of passion, the appearance of a legal execution and 'these formalities were undertaken only to give that deed the appearance of punishment, and so of a *rightful procedure*'. We thought we had found ourselves in the presence of absolute wrong, but it was only a simple parody. That it will be necessary to think the impossible, to discover reason in meaninglessness: this is the courage of thought. And Kant will not have failed, he who at times comes closest to the border of the chasm, even if he never stops avoiding and recanting it, at grips with the troubling singularity of the event that he is trying desperately to occlude with an ambiguous gesture of discovery and denial that seems at one with the very movement of his thought. In this movement, Kant exposed himself to the aporia and condemned himself to keep unthought the enigma of evil. But Heidegger has taught us that the unthought is not a lack, it is rather the highest gift that thought can make.

Translated by Debra Keates

Notes

1. The title initiates an untranslatable semantic chain: literally the phrase would be rendered 'It gives us wrong', *ça nous donne tort*, and this giving will play itself out in a series of derivative words – *don, donne, donné*. Where there is no English equivalent, the French will be included.
2. Immanuel Kant, *Religion within the Limits of Reason Alone* (*RL*), trans. Theodore M. Greene and Hoyt H. Hudson (New York: Harper and Row 1960), p. 15.

3. Let us be precise: analogous themes can be found early in Kant's work, from the *Essay on the Concept of Negative Quantities* (1763). See O. Reboul, *Kant et le problème du mal* (Montréal: Presses de l'Université de Montréal 1971), pp. 43–59, which poses the question of their occultation during the period of the three critiques and their sudden reappearance during the French Revolution. See also E. Weil, *Problèmes kantiens* (Paris: Vrin 1936).

4. It would be necessary to confront the Kantian doctrine of radical evil with the theses of Hannah Arendt on the 'banality of evil'. See my essay, 'Hell on Earth: Hannah Arendt in the Face of Hitler', *Philosophy Today*, Fall 1993. [See also, in this volume, Juliet Flower MacCannell's 'Fascism and the Voice of Conscience'.]

5. *RL*, p. 92. On this motif of 'curvature', see the clarifying commentary of A. Philonenko in *Théorie et Praxis* (Paris: Vrin 1968), pp. 28–30. Philonenko points out other appearances of this theme in Luther and St Augustine.

6. There is another linguistic linkage here that the English translation cannot capture; the French sentence sets up an associative chain which revolves around the word I translate as 'wrong': *tort*. The sentence in the original speaks of framing 'cette *torsion* qui exède tout cadrage', and of making disappear that 'pliure *retorse* d'un *tort* primordial'. The reader should hear in every wrong the hint of a twist .

7. Immanuel Kant, *Critique of Pure Reason* (*CPR*), trans. Norman Kemp Smith (New York: St Martin's Press 1965), pp. 469–75.

8. On the notion of *duratio noumenon* evoked by Kant in the *End of All Things* (1794), and on the set of problems concerning practical temporality, we should return to the classic studies of Brunschvig, Havet and Ricoeur, as well as to the discussion of J. L. Bruch in *Philosophie religieuse de Kant* (Paris: Aubier 1968), pp. 79–94.

9. Immanuel Kant, *Critique of Practical Reason* (*CRp*), trans. Lewis White Beck (Indianapolis, Ind.: Bobbs-Merrill 1956), p. 98.

10. Immanuel Kant, *Foundations for the Metaphysics of Morals* (*FM*), trans. Lewis White Beck (Indianapolis, Ind.: Bobbs-Merrill 1959), p. 23.

11. On this 'second Copernican revolution', implied by the 'paradox of method' in the second critique, see my essay, 'Le paradoxe de l'éthique', *Césure*, no. 6, 1993.

12. See J. -L. Nancy, *L'impératif catégorique* (Paris: Flammarion 1983), p. 16.

13. G. Krüger, *Critique et moral chez Kant* (Paris: Beauchesne 1961), p. 246.

14. Immanuel Kant, *The Metaphysics of Morals* (*MM*), trans. Mary Gregor (Cambridge: Cambridge University Press 1991), pp. 225–6.

15. Immanuel Kant, *Sur un prétendu droit de mentir par humanité* (1797). Published in a French edition by Vrin.

16. Jean-François Lyotard, *The Postmodern Condition*, trans. G. Bennington and B. Massumi (Minneapolis, Minn.: University of Minnesota Press 1979), p. 10.

17. On the *Verstimmung* of the two voices, see J. Derrida, 'D'un ton apocalyptique adopté naguère en philosophie', in *Les fins de l'homme* (Paris: Galilée 1981), pp. 448–55. A version of this text is translated by Peter Fenves in *Raising the Tone of Philosophy* (Baltimore, Md.: Johns Hopkins University Press 1993).

18. Immanuel Kant, *Critique of Judgement*, trans. J.H. Bernard (London: Hafner Press/Collier Macmillan 1951).

19. *FM*, p. 55.

20. *MM*, pp. 131–2. On the conception of politics and sovereignty implied by the *Doctrine of Right*, see my essay, 'Un crime inexpiable: Kant et le régicide', *Rue Descartes*, no. 4, 1992.

3 FASCISM AND THE VOICE OF CONSCIENCE

JULIET FLOWER MACCANNELL

The less you eat, drink, and buy books, the less you go to the theatre, the dance hall, the public house; the less you think, love, theorize, sing, paint, fence, etc., the more you *save* – the greater becomes your treasure which neither moths nor dust will devour – your *capital.*

Karl Marx[1]

Democracy is under serious assault these days. Global capitalism in tandem with the displacement of community by 'networking' have asserted themselves as major anti-democratic forces (although apologists of both would disagree, believing that the equation of 'democracy' with the 'free market' was established long ago). Along with the minority election of congressional representatives and the self-destruct mode of legislative bodies, a stylistic fascism has begun to creep back into fashion in every sense (for example, 1930s Italy has inspired recent clothing). In the new, improved stylized fascism, overt racial hatred is disavowed under the banner of 'love' (under the united colors of . . .).[2] The 'colourful' is championed as exotic, yet local; all sorts are welcome. While it is also clear that such excesses as 'ethnic cleansings' are also occurring, they are depicted in the media as marginal, unrelated to mainstream political forms and legal structures. One speaks of 'fundamentalisms' with a religious basis or 'deep-seated historic conflicts'. Critical analyses of racism, even some of the psychoanalytically inflected ones, underplay racism's genocidal telos; but more damagingly, they have failed to implicate fascist structural arrangements in contemporary ethnic hatreds and their implicit end.[3] Why are current instances of fascism, which have taken on a 'down home' air, especially in the media, exempted from reminders of their historical connection to genocide? Why are we skittish about political generalizing from what Hannah Arendt called the unprecedented and horrendous event known as the Holocaust? Why does democracy itself seem to have a bad conscience on this topic, even to the point of ignoring the issue as long as lip service is given by crypto-, proto- or openly neofascists to the 'unthinkability' of genocide? One answer, on the conservative side, is the lure of a nostalgia for fascism's 'patriarchal' aura (let us remind ourselves that this aura is false – our nostalgia feeds off the forms fascism destroys).[4] There is also, on the left, an understandable desire to preserve the Holocaust as absolutely unique. This would be fine if such an event were truly never to recur. Unfortunately, the uniqueness of the Holocaust is being challenged by the horrifying outcomes of countless contemporary ethnic clashes, clashes whose stated goal of clean-sweeping, of 'cleansing', force us to recall the precedent and doubt its status as hapax.

In this light it is important to review fascism's historic opposition to democracy. For fascism is still the only real and persistent opponent, politically and economically, of democracy (no one fears a return to monarchy, and communism is 'dead'). Founded on this opposition, fascism defines itself against democratic principles for structuring not only relations between owners and producers, but also those between different races and between the sexes.[5]

As a preliminary to recalling the link between fascism and genocide, we should also remind ourselves that 'fascism' is a technical term, not simply an epithet hurled by 1960s radicals at oppressive authority figures. Fascism is first of all an industrial economic mode of production of a special type, detailed below.[6] Cultural critics are not doing enough to increase our understanding of the basic *economic* differences between fascism and democracy (industrialization, self-taxation, entrepreneurship, and so on); nor have they adequately drawn the appropriate legal and ethical distinctions between them. But it is most critical, in my view, to detail the differences at the *psychic* level, the level of the heart,[7] since it is at this level that fascism's appeal to the individual persists. My focus here, then, will be on the mechanism of its appeal to the reserves of antidemocratic impulses in any individual subject, intensified under an existing fascist regime. That appeal is not, as enunciated by the inaugural terms of democracy, to our dreams and our desires – the 'right to pursue happiness' – but to our enjoyment and its loss. If democracy opened with the assertion of our right to *pursue* happiness (which is nothing more than the freedom to desire), it soon devolved in some places, as Lacan pointed out, into 'the freedom to starve'. Wherever this happened, the promise to provide the 'missing' happiness developed into a political and an economic project that could only be delivered phantasmically in a set of appeals to a full enjoyment and to an undivided subject.

Fantasy in Democracy and Fascism

Such freedom to desire as is proclaimed in democracy is by no means necessarily a happy experience from the point of view of a subject. Desire divides the subject, as the mise-en-scène of desire, fantasy (or fiction) clearly shows. The split is as simple as that exhibited by the daydreamer, who for Freud was both author and hero of his dream. In Lacan, the subject arrays its fantasy around the enjoyment of an object (its cause) which it secretly knows to be a lost cause, since the very nature of fantasy is only to fulfil a wish. The subject who 'enjoys' the object in the fantasy is also the subject who bears witness to the nonrealization of its own *jouissance* of this object. What has happened in modern life, however, according to Lacan, is that we have experienced a 'cultural loss of the object'.[8]

In his essay on the 'Subversion of the Subject', Lacan envisaged the *Che vuoi?* – the question of the Other – as liberating us from alienating identifications. By recognizing that the Other 'wants' and is as devoid of enjoyment as we are ourselves, we are able to face our own desire. Alienation begins with an original 'eclipse' of the subject in the unary signifier (characterized earlier by Lacan as 'traumatic non-meaning');[9] it is increased in identifications with an ideal I in the imaginary, and is crowned with an utterly nonsensical signifier – the proper name – in the symbolic. 'Liberation', if it comes at all, arrives via the fantasy, and then only 'by linking it essentially . . . to the condition of an object',[10] rather than another subject or another signifier. It must be an object, that is the crucial point. In fantasy, desire confronts the fact that the cause of enjoyment (an enjoyment that is imagined to have been alienated from the subject or expropriated by the Other) only appears after it apprehends its original 'alienation' in and by the signifier (or, one's access to the symbolic) as a 'castration'. In the fantasy the signifier is displaced by an object *a*. Where does this object *a* come from? Lacan's answer is that it is produced in one field by means of a renunciation of *jouissance*; this is the field of castration, where this object *a* seems to embody the enjoyment the subject has renounced. In the opposing field (that of *jouissance*), the object *a* appears through an avowal of castration. In contrast to the renunciation of enjoyment demanded by castration, its appearance here (hallucinatory, fantasmic) is produced by an intensified form of desire called drive. *Jouissance* is the satisfaction of drive. Drive 'postdates' desire; it is the response to castration at the point where it produces the fantasy, wherein the desire of the object is staged – a ($ \text{\$} \diamond \text{a} $).

The presence of the object *a* in this second field thus indicates not renunciation, but the possibility of another sort of *jouissance*. Unlike the signifier, which generates an endless number of other signifiers, the object *a* is 'without alterity'.[11] By its nondialectical quality, the object *a*, to which the fantasy pays homage, can finally evoke the concomitant idea of a *subject* 'without alterity', that is, a unique, independent subject, 'liberated' from its alienation in the signifier. The process by which this utopian horizon is attained is, needless to say, complex and difficult.

Fascism and Fantasy

Fascism has to do with the way the subject relates to fantasy by short-circuiting it. Fascism therefore remains within the field of the very threat it promises to disable: castration. Structurally, fascism always demands excessive sacrifices from its adherents. Thus it is primarily empowered through its short-circuiting of the constitution of the subject of enjoyment by robbing the fantasy of its object *a*. As Slavoj Žižek has recently described it:

> Fascist ideology is based upon a purely formal imperative; Obey, because you must! In other words, renounce enjoyment, sacrifice yourself and do not ask about the meaning of it – the value of the sacrifice lies in its very meaninglessness; true sacrifice is for its own end; you must find positive fulfilment in the sacrifice itself, not in its instrumental value; it is this renunciation, this giving up of enjoyment itself, which produces a certain surplus-enjoyment. This surplus produced through renunciation is the Lacanian *objet petit a*, the embodiment of surplus-enjoyment.[12]

For Lacan, the region 'beyond' desire and fantasy is a horizon of *jouissance* where a 'unified subject' *might* emerge.[13] This is also where fascism pretends to aim; but, as it pre-empts the subject's freedom to fantasize, to desire, to reach the level of a disruptive drive, fascism implicitly or explicitly declares that *jouissance* is already achieved, or, if not, then that it is readily available. Rather than being, as for psychoanalysis, a utopic horizon, the unified subject is, for fascism, already at hand. *Jouissance* is right here, provided one gets 'beyond' desire and mere dreaming. What emerges when the subject gives way on his desire is, however, harrowing: reality *as* a fantasy, but one that is fixed or static, ready-to-wear.[14] The horror lies in that, by virtue of this short circuit, fascism's real field is that of *castration*, where a split is made permanent between the subject of enjoyment and the subject of lack.

Voice as Object *a* in Fascism

We can now evaluate why in the fantasy, that sole mode of desire where its object can be recognized, the role of the object becomes critical. For where sacrifice (or, in other words, the foreclosure of desire) is called for, hearts and minds are moved to renunciation by something. The question is, by what? The answer offered by Lacan is: by the voice as object *a*, apprehended as beyond the laws of desire. The voice is the most omnipresent of the objects *a* for Lacan: in contrast to the way the other sense organs are libidinally attached to desire, the ear cannot be closed. The voice requires no recognizable fantasy frame to be experienced as irrupting within the subject from without – extimately, but as an Other, not as an object.

As such, a *vocal imperative* (as distinct from *written law*) is capital in securing the renunciation that allows fascism its grip on the subject. And in the case of genocide, the role of the voice is decisive. Voice takes shape, for Lacan, as one of the objects *a* around which the 'partial drives' turn: the drives find their specific embodiment in fantasy objects. In other words, the partialness of Freudian drives is translated in Lacan by the partialness of objects: gaze, voice, breast, faeces. While the drives themselves are defined as death seeking (Lacan, *Seminar XI*, p. 205) their objects are all representatives of a life force or libido. For the subject of the unconscious they represent various forms of *jouissance* which life in society forbids, though they are, in fact, less forbidden than unbearable and unavowable.[15] Classically, symbolically, these 'partial drives' and their objects are subordinated to a larger ideological construction of identification for the subject, however much that identification may invert the real relations of production. In recent times, when the drives have become the only site left for an enjoyment denied in workaday reality, more perverse twists are at work. Through sacrifice, surplus enjoyment becomes fantasmatically located wholly in the Other. In a second move, the 'subject', fantasizing prematurely its over-coming of alienating identifications, has now merely become the instrument of that 'Other's' enjoyment, by unconsciously *identifying* with the object *a*, rather than taking it on as an object of desire.

In a perversion of the classical structure, 'the *objet a* . . . is never found in the position of being the aim of desire. . . . It is either pre-subjective, or the founda-tion of an identification of the subject, or the foundation of an identification disavowed by the subject.'[16] Who, after all, would admit to being identified with a piece of shit?[17] More to the point here, Lacan introduced, with the object *a* in the fantasy (and its disavowal), the material form of a second-order alienation of the subject's desire. That this alienation takes place in the perversion known as fascism not through just any object, but specifically through the *voice* has been noted by several analysts. Mladen Dolar, for example, writes:

Fascism feeds on the voice, unto death. This is the case of Peter Gemeinder, who died of exhaustion, in August, 1931, after a speech of two hours, preceded by 2000 other speeches. . . . But what does this exalting voice say exactly? We don't get to know by reading the fascist reports of fascist speeches. We find a flood of words on the impressions of the reporter . . . on the atmosphere of the public, dead silences, ovations, etc. In the long poetization by Goebbels on his first encounter with the Führer we find only three specific words that the Führer speaks . . . 'honor, work, flag.'[18]

Dolar concludes that, 'merely by emitting a voice the master becomes master, and merely by virtue of being the receiver of this voice ("his master's voice") a crowd becomes a crowd'.[19] In short, fascism submits itself to what Lacan called 'the invocatory drive' and its object.

In what follows I will try to show how the *voice* implicated in fascism's appeal is connected to the superego and the disavowal of castration. But I must reaffirm my intent to retain genocide as central to the issue of fascism's difference from, or opposition to, democracy. I will analyse the role the voice played in enabling the 'banality of evil', the way it normalized the acts that resulted in the Holocaust. My case is that of Eichmann, as detailed in Hannah Arendt's penetrating study, *Eichmann in Jerusalem*.[20] I use a firmly Lacanian, rather than Derridean, approach because Derrida's critique of *voice* (which relates to Lacan's voice as object *a*) was obscured, in the Anglo-American translation of his work, under the blanket term 'speech'. For Lacan, and for the earliest Derrida, speech is not voice but *parole*, which has an entirely different ethical inflection. Speech, in classic Lacan, is the signifier, the symbolic pact, the social contract that divides us from each other as mutual aggressors: 'Speech is always a pact, an agreement, people get on with one another, they agree – this is yours, this is mine, this is this, that is that.'[21] For Lacan, the signifier in speech determines the unconscious relation of the subject to enjoyment (*jouissance*).[22] 'Voice' is different. Voice is already a phantom locus of enjoyment: object *a*. It is, for the unconscious, the embodiment or bearer of a principle behind the law of speech,[23] of speech as social pact: the 'will of . . . ' – the people, the Other.

I also want to distinguish my approach from Foucault's in so far as voice, as unconscious fantasy object, exists on a different plane from *discourse*. The discursive is that broader set of practices (for example, Lacan's four discourses) that results from positions taken up in relation to speech.[24] In my analysis, however, I will treat discursively (in Lacan's sense) the problematic relation of discourse to voice in two parallel, competing, but strangely complementary ethics – Kant's and Sade's, both contrived at the dawn of modern democracy. These distinctions are necessary if we are to understand how fascism – and its strong arm, genocide – was unwittingly allowed to enter the world stage when modern democracy also made its debut.

The Law

There is a technical and crucial reason why genocide, although it is abhorred, has not been legislated against in our modern democratic states.[25] But before we can understand this reason, we must first go back to the transformation of the notion of law that was the very condition of modern democracy. We must go back to Kant, and to the notion of *will*, or *goodwill*, which subtends a notion of Law as an imperative rather than as a repression of a desire.

In Kant, the Law becomes a formal, empty universality through an evacuation of all content.[26] This emptiness is what permits the universality of the Law, which is both liberatory for the subject and an obvious prerequisite to any democratic order. But Kant did not leave things with this negative moment of merely formal emptiness; he insisted instead on the need to pass to the act. While empty, the law is not entirely mute, but appears as 'a voice', a maxim, a universal 'ought' or pure positive command to duty ('You must!').[27] In contrast to an understanding of law as that which inhibits an action ('You must not!'), Kant's practical reason demands, in the form of duty, 'that a man do more than obey the law': he must 'go beyond the mere call of obedience and identify his own will with the principle behind the law – the source from which the law sprang'.[28]

Let me be blunt about my thesis: it is that the origin of the possibility of what Arendt names the 'new crime' of bureaucratic genocide arises *only* with the opening of modern democracy (the attribution of will to the individual and hence, as in Rousseau, to the 'people');[29] that this crime is democracy's chief and most constant danger, made possible wherever the 'will' is appropriated by fascism under very particular but not uncommon conditions; and that the reason why this crime continually threatens democratic civilization is that there is no *written* commandment, no written law against genocide. A written law – independent of the voice of conscience – against genocide, which would prohibit the annihilation of one people by another as the moral equivalent of murder for the individual, is unthinkable for us. Why? Because the people, not the individual, would be the subject of such a law. Under such a hypothetical law, many issues would be subjoined. For example, capital punishment, abortion and state-run sterilization programmes, the destruction of viable lands, euthanasia, suicide doctors, hate crimes, and so on, would all be argued as matters transcending issues of individual rights and choices, and would become subject to other kinds of questions: the racial make-up of death row inmates,[30] the statistical distribution of the availability of prenatal care, sterilization, abortion by race, and so on.

Under traditional circumstances, one would imagine that what is known as common law would – as the normal, customary and ordinary way we relate to each other – take care of the matter, by precluding the tacit or overt legitimation of genocidal practices. But these are not traditional and customary times: the case can be made, as Arendt argues, that such customary forms of conscience are precisely what was openly overcome by fascism. Unfortunately, then, it may be necessary to consider the need for a positive law on genocide. Perhaps, after so much freedom to prescribe our own laws, we need a reminder, by means of an alien or dead letter, that all law must ultimately seem to come to us as if from an Other.[31] When that Other becomes too close to us, appearing as our own from within, we risk the worst.

Self-legislation, whether Kantian (or superegoic), is the necessary risk of democracy. But some of its riskiest aspects might be diminished by a less naive version of the goodwill than Kant was able to articulate.[32] This version would question our reliance on our 'inner voice', which is insufficiently alien to mark its own limits.

The Economic Basis

Fascism as an economic structure was modelled on, but not materially connected to, patriarchal (especially feudal) forms. Though firmly hierarchical, it is supposed to incorporate all members of a productive unit in one structure. From the lowest floor sweeper to the CEO and the owner, all are part of a single corporate body.[33] Produced goods are owned by *patrons* who are supposed to care for their workers. The structure superficially resembles the lord/peasant relation, though in the feudal arrangement the lord needed his producers to live (if only barely) to produce and harvest the food they all required to subsist, while in a modernized world of global networks, the products are not necessities of life, but luxuries, consumer goods. Workers are expendable to the degree that they are replaceable. (The 'consumer' part of the 'consumer goods' they produce is an interesting transformation of the agricultural model.) Work is increasingly disconnected from access to these products, as salaries do not begin to cover the 'cost of living'. The worker-producer is in constant jeopardy. As a pseudopatriarchy industrial fascism calls up and calls upon a repertoire of fixed stereotypes for purposes of nostalgia (most often for the very things it had been instrumental in destroying). Historical fascism, Mussolini's party, was politically nationalistic, less from a concern for nationhood than from an antipathy to the internationalism of unions, which cut across national boundaries to secure rights and resist abuses of the producing classes. Today, fascism can be internationalist in proportion to the waning of the union movement.

Ethics

That a ferocious will-to-*jouissance*, expressed through unconscious fantasies, currently inhabits the discourse of rights is not to be doubted. But how did this situation evolve? Is it enough to say that this will-to-*jouissance* is itself fascist when early capitalism similarly exhibited such a will through its dream of unlimited profit? The critical figure for thinking through this question is undoubtedly Sade, with his depiction of endless orgasms. This aristocrat turned sans-culotte understood 'right' in the new Republic as the right to unlimited enjoyment. Sade provided Lacan with a foil for Kant and his notion of moral law; while for Horkheimer and Adorno he represented a precursor of fascism. Which was he? We can begin to answer this question by noting that Sade figures an unlimited 'will-to-*jouissance*'[34] that applies, *theoretically*, more to democratic equality than to hierarchical fascism. Sade's maxim, 'I have the right to enjoy your body, and you have the right to enjoy mine', sums this up. One should not, then, too casually connect the sadism of Sade with fascism, but neither should one presume that his version of democratic equality as reciprocity is not abusive and deluded. It is. Lacan's four fundamental discourses (which all relate the subject of desire to the object *a*) had to be stretched to account for Sade, just as postdemocratic political philosophy has to stretch to account for its evil clone, fascism. Sadism is a response, according to Lacan, to the *jouissance* of the Other as *voice*, rather than to the desire of (lack in) the Other as *speech*. But this is not yet a fascist response.

Lacan's reading of Sade's *La philosophie dans le boudoir* as companion piece to Kant's *Critique of Pure Reason* forces us to recognize the parallels that exist between the two imperatives: 'Enjoy' and 'Obey!' By stripping the Law of any mythic-rhetorical pretence of being 'motivated' by the Good, Kant placed the Law in the territory of the drive. That is, though he successfully eliminated every pathological object as source of the moral law, Kant, like Sade, allowed the law a source in another kind of object – the object *a*.[35] The cost, then, of Kant's foundation of ethics on a nonpathological basis was an unwitting empowerment of the Thing (*das Ding*).[36] While Kant seemed to believe that distance, or the sacrificial eradication of the object of desire, would provide a guarantee for the autonomy of the will, this has turned out not to be the case. For the distance that was supposed to intervene between us and the Thing has turned instead into a kind of Sadean apathy that draws us closer to the object in the drive.

Kant/Eichmann

Kant's moral philosophy, which displaced Aristotelian ethics once and for all, is ultimately linked to man's faculty of judgement, which rules out blind obedience, and condemns the instrumentalization of the other.[37] As such, the sadistic-perverse fantasy relation, in which the other becomes the object/instrument or agent of the Other's enjoyment, should be precluded. In Nazi Germany, however, the faculty of judgement failed in this regard, thus inserting a permanent warp into Kantian ethics, our ethics. This warp was almost simultaneously detected by Lacan, who published 'Kant avec Sade' in 1963, and Hannah Arendt, who published *Eichmann in Jerusalem* in *The New Yorker* that same year.[38] Thinkers from quite different fields, they each found themselves disturbed at precisely the same moment by the excess or perversion which Kant's moral philosophy, if it did not exactly lend itself to, did not preclude.[39] Lacan analysed the scandalous closeness between Kant's maxims and Sade's. Arendt, writing about a different kind of perversion, documented and analysed the proclamations of Adolf Eichmann, who administered the Final Solution, that in faithfully carrying out his 'duty' he was enacting a 'version of Kant "for the household use of the little man"'.[40] Eichmann's invocation of Kant at his trial was for him no hypocritical cover-up; Arendt concurs that by *all* accounts, not only his own, Eichmann was motivated by only one thing: his sense of duty. 'He did his *duty*, as he told the police and the court over and over again; he not only obeyed *orders*, he also obeyed the *law*.'[41] Dimly struggling, nonetheless, to make clear that he was not just a 'soldier carrying out orders that were clearly criminal in nature and intent' (p. 135), he 'declared with great emphasis that he had lived his whole life according to Kant's moral precepts, and especially according to a Kantian definition of duty' (pp. 135–6).

Arendt, aghast, at first adamantly objects to Eichmann's self-declared Kantian ethics. 'This was outrageous on the face of it, and also incomprehensible, since Kant's moral philosophy is so closely bound up with man's faculty of judgment, which rules out blind obedience,' she contests, and then goes on to argue:

> In this household use, all that is left of Kant's spirit is the demand that a man do more than obey the law, that he go beyond the mere call of obedience and *identify his own will with the principle behind the law – the source from which the law sprang.* In Kant's philosophy that source was practical reason; in Eichmann's household use of him, it was the will of the Führer. (p. 136; italics mine)

Yet, although he clearly distorted it, Eichmann actually had specifically singled out *The Critique of Practical Reason* as his personal moral guide, and spontaneously spouted an 'approximately correct definition of the categorical imperative' (p. 136) to the astonishment of Judge Raveh and the audience at his trial in Jerusalem: 'I meant by my remark about Kant that the principle of my will must always be such that it can become the principle of general laws (which is not the case with theft or murder, for instance, because the thief or the murderer cannot conceivably wish to live under a legal system that would give others the right to rob or murder him).' Eichmann then adds that he had

> read Kant's *Critique of Practical Reason*. He then proceeded to explain that from the moment he was charged with carrying out the Final Solution he had ceased to live according to Kantian principles, that he had known it, and that he had consoled himself with the thought that he no longer 'was master of his own deeds', that he was unable 'to change anything'. (p. 136)

Eichmann thus ultimately did confess to having abandoned Kant and to betraying the Law rooted in the Kantian principle, claiming as his excuse that he had been 'mastered' or overpowered by a force or will beyond his own. But though this admission ought to have vindicated Arendt's severe objections to his claim to having been guided by Kant, she shows some hesitancy. She worries the question of whether Eichmann had really 'forgotten' Kant as he set to work accomplishing the Final Solution, finding 'the Kantian formula . . . no longer applicable', or whether he had employed it in a twisted way. She is inclined to believe that rather than abandoning it altogether,

> he had distorted it to read: Act as if the principle of your actions were the same as that of the legislator or of the law of the land – or, in Hans Frank's formulation of 'the categorical imperative in the Third Reich' which Eichmann might have known: 'act in such a way that the Führer, if he knew your action, might approve it'. (p. 136)

The scandal here is less that Kant's principles did not hold against a will to transgress them, than that something in Kant's very principle seemed to an Eichmann (and a Hans Frank) to lend itself to this particular distortion. At best, nothing in the structure of the law conceived on Kantian lines worked to disable this particular perversion – in the end the law failed to resist the will-to-*jouissance*. Not Eichmann's will, but that of the Führer. Here we have stumbled upon the paradox of democracy's peculiar susceptibility to totalitarianism: people who rule themselves with absolute freedom find themselves perpetually threatened with rule by dictatorship.[42]

Thus, while Arendt details the philosophical *errors* that permitted such a deadly misreading of the upright German idealist she does not totally exonerate him or his theory from the consequences of this misreading. She thereby suggests that the empty moral law is inherently vulnerable to the fascist perversion. 'To be sure,' she argues, 'Kant had never intended . . . anything of the sort; on the contrary, to him every man was a legislator the moment he started to act: by using his "practical reason" man found the principles that could and should be the principles of law. But it is true that Eichmann's unconscious distortion agrees with what he himself called the version of Kant "for the household use of the little man"' (p. 136).

The Voice, Moral Conscience and the Law

Let us observe that the herald of the maxim does not need to be anything more than a point of emission. It can be a voice on the radio. . . . Such vocal phenomena, notably those of psychosis, indeed have this aspect of the object. And psychoanalysis was not far in its dawn from referring the voice of conscience to them. (Lacan, *Kant with Sade*)

At this point we need to focus more directly on the remainder for which Kant left us unprepared, that is, the object left behind by his clean sweep of pathological objects of desire: the *object-cause-of-desire*. Analytically, this means we must address the question of castration, and the way it installs the modern superego, the voice of conscience and successor to the 'father' of Oedipal patriarchy.[43] For if fascism hooks the hearts and minds of a people by *determining its will* rather than democratically permitting it *to ask what it wants*,[44] it does so through the implied threat, even in the popular mind, of castration. Anecdotally, Lyndon Baines Johnson was reputed to have provided the (truncated) name for the US community development programme for South Vietnam – 'Hearts and Minds' – with his pithy: 'When you've got them by the balls, their hearts and minds will follow.' Not castration but its disavowal *articulates* the appeal of fascism.

Before Kant, to act ethically meant to conform one's desires to the moral law, which described the set of behaviours conducive to the achievement of the goal of happiness. After Kant, the subject of *desire* could no longer conform to, but rather came into fateful conflict with, 'moral law'. In Lacan's rereading, Kantian moral law is nothing but 'desire in its pure state',[45] which means that the subject must not give in to but *resist* the voice-commands of the superego. For it is precisely by ceding to its commands that we surrender our desire. While the 'original' moral voice – the Jewish God – proffered the Ten Commandments as an alien, the moral voice evoked in the texts of Rousseau, Kant and Freud proceeds from an Other *within the self*. This pseudo-other, or superego, increasingly obscene, is felt 'within like a stranger':

[A]s it [the I] progresses in its experience, it asks itself [this] question and asks it precisely in the place where strange, paradoxical, and cruel commands are suggested to it by its morbid experience.
Will it or will it not submit itself to the duty that it feels within like a stranger, beyond, at another level? Should it or should it not submit itself to the half-unconscious,

paradoxical, and morbid command of the superego, whose jurisdiction is moreover revealed increasingly as the analytical exploration goes forward and the patient sees that he is committed to its path.

If I may put it thus, isn't its true duty to oppose that command?[46]

Arendt likewise backs away from granting the inner voice of conscience the function of moral law: '[J]ust as the law in civilized countries assumes that the voice of conscience tells everybody "Thou shalt not kill," even though man's natural desires and inclinations may at times be murderous, so the law of Hitler's land demanded that the voice of conscience tell everybody: "Thou shalt kill"' (p. 150). Genocide by administration fully depended on that inner voice, unassimilable to any of its previous iterations. Speaking of the simplistic and overly traditional way in which the new crime, administrative massacre, was treated by the prosecutors in Jerusalem, Arendt complains: 'To fall back on an unequivocal voice of conscience – or, in the even vaguer language of the jurists, on a "general sentiment of humanity" (Oppenheim-Lauterprach in *International Law*, 1952) – not only begs the question, it signifies a deliberate refusal to take notice of the central moral, legal, and political phenomena of our century' (p. 148).

Lacan, arguing that the *perverted* position with respect to the voice as object was taken up by Sade, the aristocrat turned republican, provides a certain instructive model for analysing Adolf Eichmann, chief administrator of the Final Solution under Hitler. The perverse position, which disavows castration, works, as I claimed earlier, through a perverse identification of the self with the object *a* in its role as agent of the *jouissance de l'Autre*.[47] With this in mind, I would like to re-examine Arendt's analysis of the relation between Eichmann and Kant. Before beginning, it is important to note that whereas under monarchy the subject could, structurally, remain a subject no matter how much he laboured for the king's pleasure, the same does not hold when the leader, like the self, is also sacrificing.

In Eichmann's Case: Voice as Object *a* and the Normalization of Excess

In her chilling, difficult and heartbreaking report on the banality of evil, Hannah Arendt portrays Adolf Eichmann as a kind of neutral functionary, neither hero nor victim of his criminal acts. His actions cannot be viewed, in her opinion, in the perspective of a traditional morality play. In this she goes against the grain, accepting analytically Eichmann's self-professed normality. But she sees this 'normality' less as an index of his mental health than of the fact of the existence, on the world scene, of a state whose norm was 'thou shalt' rather than 'thou shalt not' kill.

Watching without sentimentality Eichmann's long-drawn-out trial – tellingly, *not* on charges of genocide, but on 'crimes against the Jewish people' and 'crimes against Humanity' – unfold in Jerusalem,[48] Arendt waits in vain for the customary theatre of justice to open its dramatization of good and evil in his case. The dramatization does not catch fire. Arendt grows alarmed when the traditional scene of judgement does not materialize either: the stage which places the evil doer between a judge who represents the community and the community for whom the judge speaks. Instead, it is Eichmann who commands centre stage.

A man of 'rather modest mental gifts' (p. 135), Eichmann is the man in the glass booth, whose transparency and shielding is both a metaphor for the trial itself and what places him in the typical posture of the female subject, weak and on display. For Arendt sees his physical position – placed *below* tier upon tier of judges, translators and officials, and *between* the prosecutors and the courtroom – as precluding the traditional work of justice. Those who watch Eichmann ('medium-sized, slender, middle-aged, with receding hair, ill-fitting teeth, and nearsighted eyes' [p. 5]) over the shoulders of the prosecutors form no 'community' whose standards he could be said to have violated. Why are the charges of 'crimes against the Jewish people' and 'crimes against Humanity' *separate* charges? The charges themselves err by over- or underspecificity. The result is that the 'Jewish people/Humanity' – the 'victims' – are not as concrete and defined as 'the man in the glass booth'. In fact, both 'the Jewish people' and 'Humanity' have a reduced, remote role, relegated to being an 'audience' of literally *no one* – which means, really, that they are an audience composed of everyone in the world (former victims and bystanders both). Cast as mere onlookers, peering *over the shoulders* of the prosecutors at the man who ordered and arranged for the deaths of a whole people, they can and will have their opinions shaped mainly by the physical appearance of the man, not by the standards of their 'community'. Under these conditions, Arendt makes clear, Eichmann is the one who looks like a victim, not an instigator, capable at best of having been an instrument but not an originator of evil, whose source will be as inexplicable, nebulous and undefined as the 'humanity' he sinned against.

There is an evil, though its shape is still obscure. Arendt proposes that something 'altogether unprecedented' *was* at work in the very acts of the man who is on trial, a 'new crime', for which the 'prevailing legal system and current juridical concepts' (p. 294) are entirely inadequate. What cannot be dealt with – justly – under the older forms of separation of individual guilt and group responsibility is 'administrative massacre organized by state apparatus' (p. 294). And yet Arendt wants to be able to refer it to Eichmann, to his personal 'judgement'. She terms her work a 'report on his conscience'. Thus, though she is a political philosopher, Arendt, like the psychoanalyst, insists Eichmann is an individualized *case*. She seeks not to determine a generic model, but to ascertain the point at which Eichmann's will, his relation to his desire (and to the Law), was a factor in his political acts. Though her aim differs, and she will not facilitate his 'cure' but only a judgement on the man, she will have reframed the question of the Law to which his drive and his desire respond (as no limit). But Eichmann himself will never be able to 're-order' the elements of his discourse, his own narration of his life, in other than ready-made formulaic terms.

Why is the 'new crime' of 'administrative massacre', which is simply the term for modern as opposed to traditional genocide, not yet able to be brought to the bar of justice? Why do those crimes committed 'above' the 'individual' level not yet have to face the *decision*, a judgement (between good and evil)? Perhaps this should be put another way: can we not mark Eichmann's original 'ethical' decision (to do his 'duty') as Lacan marked Kant's and Sade's, that is, with a *vel*? The alienating *vel* is a logical connective which denies one of its terms. It is a choice made in such a way as to avoid a decision by absolutely eliminating one of the options. It means no choice at all: as 'Your money or your life', wherein the 'choice' of the latter destroys the option of enjoying the former. We can mark Eichmann's 'choice' thus, if we make the link Lacan does, between this *vel* and the *v* of the *volonté de jouir* (the will-to-*jouissance*). A simulacrum of judgement, the *vel*'s act of absolute cutting away pre-empts and precludes the need for any further judgement or decision: it is a form of final solution.[49]

Hannah Arendt makes a double argument. She argues first that the escape from the area of ascertainable facts and personal responsibility that became pandemic in Germany during the Nazi years, and of which Eichmann is an example, is the only thing that justice can deal with and call to account; the failure to be able to *decide* between good and evil is the only moral failing. Hence her criticism of the widespread response to and accusation of the trial of Eichmann ('Who are you to sit in judgment? You might have done the same in his place', and so on). All generalities ('it's humanity itself on trial') are in her eyes incorrect from any standpoint that takes justice as its goal: justice is a judgement to be rendered on deeds and misdeeds, the decisions of a person, an individual.

Second, Arendt argues that there is, beyond the individual level, a *political* responsibility which 'exists quite apart from what the individual member of a group has done, and therefore can neither be judged in moral terms nor brought before a criminal court' (p. 298). It is this political responsibility that she feels must be separated from the question of the individual's guilt or innocence, which are the only things, she tells us, 'at stake in a criminal court'. Whence her profound repugnance for putting a whole people, or humanity itself on trial, in the showcase way that she believes Ben-Gurion attempted to do. One can take on the guilt of his group's evil only in a metaphorical way, and no one can be held responsible for the acts of a whole society. Conversely, an entire society cannot be judged guilty, since there will always be individual members who dissented and disagreed (as in Arendt's example of the acts of the simple soldier, Anton Schmidt). What is at issue in the case of Eichmann, however, is that he felt no need to engage in the *individual* decision as to good or evil; he was 'beyond' them by virtue of his being a mere executor of the will of the group, which had its own grounds for the decision at which it had arrived.

Thus the central structural problem – self-legislation – remains. It is even emblematized in Eichmann's case by the locale of the trial itself: Eichmann is tried not in a supreme court, but in a parliamentary building: Beth Ha'am, the House of the People, is where this Beth Hamispath, or House of Justice, has been installed. Arendt, of course, concludes her book as she must, by reaffirming that 'the question of individual guilt and innocence are the only things at stake in a criminal court' (p. 298). That she nonetheless felt compelled to raise the question of the guilt or innocence of 'political responsibility' is telling. 'It is quite conceivable that certain political responsibilities among nations might some day be adjudicated in an international court' (p. 298), which she immediately qualifies as necessarily not a criminal court ('[w]hat is inconceivable is that such a court would be a criminal tribunal which pronounces on the guilt or innocence of individuals'). She has also shown how far Eichmann's 'Kantianism' protected him from bearing responsibility for any criminality or evil to be attached to an openly expressed 'political will'. The question remains, then, how can the crime of genocide be adjudged a crime as such? On whose head would the guilt lie?

Despite her tremendous reluctance to consider 'political responsibility' as falling within the realm of criminal justice, Arendt has, I think, actually opened a path. Her inquiry turns into one concerning the relation of genocide to written and unwritten law – the same one I proposed at the outset. That it was a woman, and as such classically 'suspicious of the signifier',[50] who was able to define this problematic first and to call tentatively for a response of the signifier is, in my view, highly significant.

The Otherness of Laws and the Reason for Writing Them

For Arendt, the simple decision to keep its Laws unwritten – free of content, of pathological objects – granted tacit permission for National Socialism's plan of genocide. Any law explicitly directing genocide would have already been the result of a *vel*, and the expression of a specific *will-to*.[51] Single individuals were not so much loath to engage in such expressions as structurally impeded from doing so: their will was not their own, as Eichmann recounted. One had to be attuned to the 'principle behind the law',[52] which should be, for Kant, the individual will or, for Rousseau, the *volonté générale* – the will of the people as a whole taking itself for an object – both of which are problematic and difficult to access. But functionaries like Eichmann had no difficulty in locating this will, because they identified it with the actual, if only indirectly heard, voice of the Führer.

For very practical reasons, of course, Hitler's genocidal programme had to remain unwritten because of its criminal nature: international public opinion would have mobilized more quickly against it were it to have been written down. The only language ('Officialese') to which the Nazi regime condescended to transmit its orders constituted a new kind of 'discourse' framed by a 'language rule' (the new *Amtssprache*; the *Sprachregelung*). This rule was to remake what once, under common civil agreements, had been called 'the lie' into the form of a specially honoured 'secret': 'Those who were told explicitly of the Führer's order were no longer mere "bearers of orders", but were advanced to "bearers of secrets", and a special oath was administered to them' (pp. 84–5). The 'secret' therefore was, in formal communication terms, also technically 'content free'.

All speech 'calls for a reply'.[53] The error – in politics as in the analytic session – lies in mistaking an *appel* for an *appeal*. This mistake is made by placing primary emphasis on the 'feelings' of the hearer:

> If the psychoanalyst [but could we not also say political subject?] is not aware that this is how the function of speech operates ['to call for a reply'], he will simply experience its appeal all the more strongly, and if the first thing to make itself heard is the void, it is within himself that he will experience it, and it is beyond speech that he will seek a reality to fill this void.[54]

Self-absolved from any need to *reply* (if only with silence), the unaware listener will 'echo his own nothingness' in the other, and it is this echo which is the source of the appeal of 'empty' speech: an 'appeal' to the 'very principle of truth', which Lacan tells us is first and foremost 'the appeal of the void, in the ambiguous gap of an attempted seduction of the other by the means of which the subject has come compliantly to rely and to which he will commit the monumental construct of his narcissism'.[55] What this 'mere formalism' or *evacuation* of pathetic content does is to deliver us over to the all-or-nothing game of a 'full' meaning, yielded entirely to an Other who is thus empowered to reward us with the nugatory remainder, an empty 'senselessness' for our being – but a senselessness experienced as a sensory impression, a certain *jouissance*. One 'responds' (not answers) to an insistent excess of *jouissance* in the Other, whose final mastery over all meaning is sufficient sign of its ownership of the signified-of-all-signifiers – the *jouissance* excised by speech.[56]

Listening to Eichmann from the 'pre-Kantian', sympathetic or pathological posture (that is, trying to 'think from the standpoint of somebody else'), the Jerusalem judges imagined that Eichmann's perpetual recourse to 'empty talk' showed that the 'accused wished to cover up other thoughts which, though hideous, were not empty' (p. 49). But Arendt finds otherwise. The presumption of especially savage passions is perfectly refuted by Eichmann's verbal demeanour. His clichés are purely formal. Arendt asks, parenthetically, 'Was it these clichés that the psychiatrists thought so "normal" and "desirable"?' (pp. 48–9).

Eichmann showed 'great susceptibility to catch words and stock phrases, combined with his incapacity for ordinary speech' (p. 86). According to Arendt's analysis of Eichmann's speech, the 'inner voice' of conscience in Eichmann was perhaps less silent than voiced over. 'Genuinely incapable of uttering a single sentence that was not a cliché', Eichmann claimed that 'Officialese [*Amtssprache*] is my only language' (p. 48). At times, of course, Eichmann showed 'uplift'. He thrilled whenever he was able to re-voice or utilize a cliché that made him feel part of the perpetual 'movement of the Universe' (p. 27). Eichmann reports being 'elated' when he was able to link his 'mood' with its 'catch phrase' (p. 62), labelling such phrases with the German term for touchstone quotations, *Geflügelte Worte* (winged words, p. 48). With them, he was 'in movement' (p. 43), he 'lived for his idea' (p. 42).[57] That attunement with the idea had no room for 'pathological' emotions:

> When he said in the police examination that he would have sent his own father to his death if that had been required, he did not mean merely to stress the extent to which he was under orders, and ready to obey them; he also meant to show what an 'idealist' he had always been. The perfect 'idealist,' like everybody else, had of course his personal feelings and emotions, but he would never permit them to interfere with his actions if they came into conflict with his 'idea.' (p. 42)

Indeed, Eichmann's whole posture parallels that of the sadist in Lacan's analysis, who is not a man filled with irresistibly savage urges, but the executioner of the will-to-*jouissance* of the Other.[58]

For Eichmann, a 'death whirl' circulated around the Führer's voice. Arendt writes that the Führer's words had the 'force of law' for Eichmann (*Führerworte haben Gesetzkraft*): which meant, 'among other things, that if the order came directly from Hitler it did not have to be in writing. He tried to explain that this was why he had never asked for a written order from Hitler . . . but had demanded to see a written order from Himmler' (p. 148). A barely perceptible thread, then, leads from the evacuation, opened by Kantian philosophy, of specific, affective content in the Law, to the absolute emptiness at the centre of Eichmann's thought, the absolute void to which Arendt points in her report on Eichmann's conscience. Eichmann's salient 'inability to speak' was, according to Arendt, 'closely connected with an inability to *think*, namely, to think from the standpoint of somebody else' (p. 49).

Precisely because no written Law specifically prohibited (or permitted) genocide, the command to genocide appeared as a pure function of the will of the Other, completely unrelated to Eichmann's own wishes and desires. As such, it became Eichmann's duty, but not only his. It had an astonishingly immediate appeal to the state's chief functionaries, few of whom owed their careers to the Nazis, and might not have been thought reliable or responsive to Hitler.[59] Wannsee, where the Final Solution was laid out as the government's programme in 1942, was a 'cozy little social gathering' (p. 113). Eichmann was secretary to this conference of the undersecretaries of state that resolved all his doubts. Arendt quotes Eichmann's deposition:

> 'Here now, during this conference, the most prominent people had spoken, the Popes of the Third Reich.' Now he could see with his own eyes and hear with his own ears that not only Hitler . . . but the good old Civil Service were vying and fighting with each other for the honor of taking the lead in these 'bloody' matters. 'At that moment . . . I felt free of all guilt.' *Who was he to judge?* (p. 114)

Arendt comments, 'Well, he was neither the first nor the last to be ruined by modesty' (p. 114); but when such modesty was a function of what Eichmann himself termed a 'death whirl' (p. 115), his failure to 'judge' becomes obscene. His modesty instead marks Eichmann as the one who renounces his personal judgement, desires and emotions to serve the will-to-*jouissance* of Hitler.

Just what 'satisfying Hitler' meant – the sacrifice or 'ethical renunciation' he demanded of the German people of the 1930s and 1940s – is described movingly by Arendt. What the average German had to sacrifice was precisely his or her hard-won place in the symbolic order, in 'civilization' – he or she had to give up the symbolic modes of fending off the call of the will-to-*jouissance*:

> Evil in the Third Reich had lost the quality by which most people recognized it – the quality of temptation. Many Germans and many Nazis, probably an overwhelming majority of them, must have been tempted *not* to murder, *not* to rob, *not* to let their neighbors go off to their doom. . . . But, God knows, they had learned how to resist temptation. (p. 150)

The 'voice of conscience' called on the people to ignore their desire. After the administration and execution of Hitler's genocidal plan, justice can no longer presume a certain content or character to the 'voice of conscience'. In order for there to be justice based on 'conscience', Arendt writes, unlawfulness must 'fly like a black flag above . . . as a warning reading "Prohibited!"' (p. 148). By contrast,

> in Hitler's criminal regime this 'black flag' with its 'warning sign' flies as 'manifestly' above what normally is a lawful order – for instance, not to kill innocent people just because they happen to be Jews – as it flies above a criminal order under normal circumstances. To fall back on an unequivocal voice of conscience – or, in the even vaguer language of the jurists, on a 'general sentiment of humanity' (Oppenheim-Lauterprach in *International Law*, 1952) – not only begs the question, it signifies a deliberate refusal to take notice of the central moral, legal, and political phenomena of our century. (p. 148)

More broadly interpreted, the status of the law is up for grabs: laws can no longer easily claim symbolic status if they are not simply isomorphic with the signifier (ultimately the phallus). Castration within the symbolic is nowhere near as radical as what fascism required: a sacrifice to the *jouissance* embodied in the 'principle behind the law'.

Psychoanalytically, the 'principle behind the law' in Eichmann's case is obscene: a popular will that masks a 'maternal' will-to-*jouissance* beyond the regulation of the signifier. I would concur with Arendt that genocide and its peculiar 'call to conscience' are the 'central moral, legal, and political phenomenon of our century'. Lacan's analysis of the pivotal role played by the object *a* – in this instance, the 'maternal' *voice* – contributes, then, to developing an ethics that would acknowledge the force of drive and fantasy over desire in the postdemocratic era in which a fascist perversion of democratic principles continues to threaten us.[60]

Arendt's account does not identify the voice as organ of the obscenely enjoying Other, or 'principle behind the law' with the superego. She does, however, demonstrate the (potentially) fatal weakness in modern self-governance. Modern forms of state, as she demonstrates here and as confirmed in our subsequent experience, relentlessly and remorselessly lend themselves to the recurrence of genocide. If Arendt proposes no solution; if her imperturbable analysis of evil allows of no remedy but the supranational written law, this is because, absent of psychoanalytic insights, it is unable to account for the workings of fascism on the level of the subject. This task can only be shouldered by a politically informed psychoanalysis.

Sacrifice

I will end my discussion where I began, by recalling the link of fascism with its sacrificial imperative to genocide. Lacan has remarked on the 'resurgence' of this 'imperative':

> I would hold that no meaning given to history, based on Hegelian-Marxist premises, is capable of accounting for this resurgence – which only goes to show that the offering to obscure gods of an object of sacrifice is something to which few subjects can resist succumbing, as if under some monstrous spell . . . for whoever is capable of turning a courageous gaze towards this phenomenon – and once again, there are certainly few who do not succumb to the fascination for the sacrifice in itself – the sacrifice signifies that, in the object of our desires, we try to find evidence for the presence of the desire of this Other that I call here, the dark God. (Lacan, *Seminar XI*, p. 275)

While, from a historical standpoint, the uniqueness of the Holocaust must never be denied (something 'unprecedented' was Arendt's term for it, and Hilberg concurs that there was more than 'ordinary' anti-Semitism at work in it), we should not shrink – as Lacan does not – from recognizing the signs of a resurgence of the genocidal imperative. Ethnic cleansing, the demand for racial purification, the Khmer Rouge, the Bosnian war: these indicate not imitative repetitions, but that a new evil has entered the world, which wears the face or mask of a certain detachment. 'Administrative massacre' Arendt called it, enabled by a transcendental subjectification on the one hand, and by an unconscious identification with the object *a* on the other. While mass killings on a large scale have occurred before in world history, the calculating decision to cleanse, to expunge, to obliterate is altogether new. Mass murder was committed during the Holocaust with an industrial efficiency and an appropriate distance (executioners who appeared to enjoy killing in the camps were immediately relieved of their duties). Today's systematic mass rapes in Bosnia are accomplished, it seems, coolly, without lust. What I am suggesting is not passion and empathy as alternatives, but an analysis of the basis of this pseudodistance. Not *critical* as Kant would have had it, this distance is instead *apathetic*, in the sense of Sade. Such apathetic engagements by the political subject mark a resistance to temptation – the temptation, as Arendt puts it, '*not* to murder, *not* to rob . . . *not* to let their neighbors go off to their doom'. In short, this apathy marks the sacrifice of one's own symbolic mandate. This stubborn and persistent resistance to one's own desire, encountered again and again in the executioners of genocides, indexes the preservation of a *jouissance* the subject disowns. It marks the advent of a new and radical evil.[61]

In the passage above, one of his most enigmatic pronouncements, Lacan concluded his eleventh seminar by linking Nazism with 'a sacrifice', an 'offering to obscure gods'. Dismissing 'Hegelian-Marxist premises' as unable to account for 'the drama of Nazism', he intimates that his psychoanalysis has access to a more compelling explication than that provided elsewhere. This access issues from the notion of *sacrifice*. The question we must ask ourselves is how and why millions of human beings became objects of sacrifice. Behind these words of Lacan, which have haunted me from the first time I read them, I have asked you to hear Arendt's chilling report on the 'sacrifice' demanded from the German people by Hitler, the 'dark god' whose will-to-*jouissance* seemed insatiable. Lacan brackets his remarks on sacrifice with allusions, on the one side, to mass media and the voice as object,[62] and on the other side, to Kant, who *should* counterbalance them. One of the questions I have tried to pose, if not definitively answer, in this essay is: why *doesn't* he? Without questioning the invaluable contribution Kant made to the notion of a 'democratic' law, we cannot mistake the dark overtones this law takes on in Lacan's text. Whose hair has not been raised by the verbal coloration at the point in *Seminar XI* where Lacan describes the relation of moral law to the object? '[T]his moral law . . . looked at more closely, culminates in the sacrifice, strictly speaking, of everything that is the object of love in one's human tenderness. I would say, not only in the rejection of the pathological object, but also in its sacrifice and murder. That is why I wrote "Kant avec Sade"' (pp. 275–6). Only a few paragraphs separate this 'sacrifice and murder' of the object of love from the sacrificial aspect of the Holocaust. With these words, Lacan forges an alliance between what he called the 'malevolent superego' and the moral law: each lives only on the fantasy of the sacrifice of desire.

For many, Kant's 'moral law', the law of 'pure desire', seems to guide the aim of analysis: to bring the subject to ask itself what it wants. A propos of Freud's famous 'Wo Es war soll Ich werden' Lacan writes: 'That "I" which is supposed to come to be where "it" was, and which analysis has taught us to evaluate, is nothing more than that whose root we already found in the "I" which asks itself what it wants.'[63] Lacan's denunciation of normative ideals (genital primacy, adulthood, happiness) as goals of psychoanalysis likewise repeats Kant's fundamental ethical gestures, by clearing the ground of sentimental cant. Nevertheless, on the matter of the 'purity' of desire, Lacan seems to *distinguish* his position from Kant's by insisting that the analyst's desire 'is not pure' (p. 275). That the attraction to and distancing from an equation of Kantian and psychoanalytic ethics comes in the context of unsettling remarks on the Holocaust must give us pause. If nothing else, these remarks set an agenda for analysing and overcoming the fascist temptation that inhabits all forms of self-governance: superegoic, democratic.

It has not been my purpose here to trace 'blame' for the Holocaust to

Kantian philosophy (though others have tried to do so),[64] nor conversely to exonerate Kant (as Derrida has, by honouring him as the 'Jew' unassimilable to the fascist tendencies of Hegelian grand dialectics). My purpose has been less philosophical, less embroiled in contemporary academic politics. It has been rather to delineate a structure, available through a study of certain obscurities in Kant's thought, in which the vulnerability of the symbolic order to the particular, new and ferocious excess of our postdemocratic time – genocide, ethnic cleansing – might come to be better understood.

The fantasmatic character of human enjoyment must be accounted for in any ethic today, it must take primacy. Unconscious fantasy formations grow ever more central in our lives; they are the support of our 'reality'.[65]

The law counters unconscious fantasy with desire: but it has no purchase unless it accounts for where the subject *enjoys*. The obverse also holds: only where the subject knows how its desire and the law respond to its *jouissance* can it encounter its own enjoyment. In centring on the object that Kant too naively swept away, Lacanian analysis shows the relation of desire, and its alienation, to the general will. To write the law against genocide would provide a way for the increasingly stateless 'citizens' of the postmodern, global community to once again be asked, as individuals, *to decide, to judge*: and this means facing, not disavowing, a relation to *jouissance*. Paired sets of alternatives (good or evil, to kill or to love) share the same object: separating this object out as that which joins them is the goal of the psychoanalysis of the alienated subject. It should now be clear that it needs also to be related to the alienation of the political subject. Only this kind of decision, as separation – which is the reversal of the *vel* – permits the individual to resist 'the will of the people' when it has become a malignant will-to-*jouissance*.

Notes

1. Karl Marx, *Economic and Philosophical Manuscripts* (New York: International Press 1964), p. 150.
2. A rare mention in recent news report of the openly neofascist soccer clubs in Italy notes that membership is reputed to require 'killing a nigger'; *San Francisco Chronicle*, 16 December 1994.
3. One of the few is Renata Salecl. See her article, 'Society Doesn't Exist', *American Journal of Semiotics*, vol. VII, nos 1–2, 1990, pp. 45–52; and her recent book on Eastern Europe, *The Spoils of Freedom* (London and New York: Routledge 1994).
4. In my book, *The Regime of the Brother: After the Patriarchy* (London and New York: Routledge 1991), I argued that fascism is *not* patriarchal or related to the father, but has to do with a phantasmic fraternalism.
5. In the party Mussolini started to construct before and after World War I (1909–19), he introduced 'no systematic exposition of its ideology or purpose other than a negative reaction against socialist and democratic egalitarianism'. *New Columbia Encyclopedia* 1975, p. 925.

6. Fascism's potential translation into new and unknown forms of production (especially in the media and technology) remains to be seen.
7. Lacan says that the place of the partial drives is the domain of the heart for Freud. Jacques Lacan, *Seminar XI: The Four Fundamental Concepts of Psychoanalysis*, trans. Alan Sheridan (New York and London: W. W. Norton & Co. [1973] 1978), p. 139.
8. Jacques Lacan, *Seminar VII: The Ethics of Psychoanalysis*, trans. Dennis Porter (New York: Norton 1993), p. 99.
9. Lacan, *Seminar XI*, p. 251.
10. Jacques Lacan, *Ecrits: A Selection*, trans. Alan Sheridan (New York: W.W. Norton and Co. 1977), p. 313.
11. Lacan, *Ecrits*, p. 315.
12. Slavoj Žižek writes: 'Fascism is obscene in so far as it perceives directly the ideological form as its own end, as an end in itself – remember Mussolini's famous answer to the question "How do the Fascists justify their claim to rule Italy? What is their programme?"; "Our programme is very simple: we want to rule Italy!" The ideological power of Fascism lies precisely in the feature which was perceived by liberal or leftist critics as its greatest weakness; in the utterly void, formal character of its appeal, in the fact that it demands obedience and sacrifice for their own sake. For Fascist ideology, the point is not the instrumental value of the sacrifice, it is the very form of the sacrifice itself, "the spirit of sacrifice", which is the cure against the liberal-decadent disease. It is also clear why Fascism was so terrified by psychoanalysis: psychoanalysis enables us to locate an obscene enjoyment at work in this act of formal sacrifice.' *The Sublime Object of Ideology* (London: Verso, 1989, pp. 82–3).
13. Lacan always keeps alive a sense of the subject's alienation in and by the signifier, its "fading" or eclipse . . . that is closely bound up with the *Spaltung* or splitting that it suffers from its subordination to the signifier' (*Ecrits*, p. 313). To visualize the terms of my analysis here, I ask the reader to consult the 'Completed Graph' of desire on p. 315 of the *Ecrits*.
14. Or a 'statics of the fantasy,' Jacques Lacan, 'Kant with Sade', trans. James Swenson, *October 51* (Winter 1989), p. 63.
15. Mental life springs from desire, according to Freud, in the form of hallucinated enjoyments: 'Whatever was thought of (desired) was simply imagined in an hallucinatory form.' 'Formulations Regarding the Two Principles of Mental Functioning' in *General Psychological Theory: Papers on Metapsychology* (New York: Collier Books 1963), p. 22.
16. Lacan, *Seminar XI*, p. 186.
17. Julia Kristeva's *Powers of Horror* (New York: Columbia University Press 1982) tried to link fascism and anti-Semitism in Céline to this abject identification. But her analysis lacks the clarity and rigour which Lacan's provides via his notion of the object *a*.
18. Mladen Dolar, 'Prolégomènes à une théorie du discours fasciste', in *Perspectives psychanalytiques sur la politique* (Paris: Navarin Éditeur 1984), p. 42; my translation. See, additionally, Jacques Derrida, *The Ear of the Other*, trans. Peggy Kamuf and Avital Ronell (New York: Schocken Books 1985). See also Avital Ronell, *The Telephone Book* (Lincoln, Nebr.: University of Nebraska Press 1990). Mladen Dolar's essay provides greater specificity. From Cracauer on, critics have sensed that without radio or film, Hitler could not have come to power. By using Lacan, we can narrow this to the field of operation of the object *a*.
19. Dolar, 'Prolégomènes à une théorie', pp. 42–3.
20. Hannah Arendt, *Eichmann in Jerusalem: A Report on the Banality of Evil* (Harmondsworth: Penguin Books [1963] 1964).
21. Jacques Lacan, *Seminar III: The Psychoses, 1955–56*, trans. Russell Grigg (New York: Norton 1993), p. 39.
22. The object *a* is the bearer of that bit of *jouissance* excised by accession to the symbolic, and yet produced, retrospectively, by that accession. The object *a* is a remainder, unaccommodated by and unaccountable to the symbolic.
23. 'Principle' is intertwined with 'drive' throughout Freud. See my exposition in an

earlier version of this paper, 'Facing Fascism: A Feminine Politics of Jouissance', in *Topoi* 12, September 1993, pp. 137–51; reprinted in R. Feldstein and W. Apollon, *Lacan and Politics*, State University of New York Press, forthcoming.

24. It would he useful to free democratic and poetic versions of *voice* from the onus of a misapplied Derridean critique. For it is the monology and monotony of the fascist voice, not the plurivocality fundamental to both democracy and poetry which is, or should be, the target of critique. See my essay, 'On Woman's Speech', *American Journal of Psychoanalysis*, vol. 58, no. 2, June 1994, pp. 143–58.

25. I was shocked to learn that the United States has consistently refused to ratify the antigenocide treaty devised by the United Nations. Apparently, if, after Rousseau, the Law is deemed the repression of a desire than a positive form of the will – *la volonté générale*, or the formal force of the democratic polity – it seems the 'popular will' in democracy must imagine itself to be good, presumed innocent, in all senses of the term. Law that would express an evil will could not afford to recognize its desire.

26. 'The law as empty form in the *Critique of Practical Reason* corresponds to time as pure form in the *Critique of Pure Reason*. The law does not tell us *what* we must do, it merely tells us "you must", leaving us to deduce from it the good, the object of this pure imperative.' Gilles Deleuze, *Kant's Critical Philosophy*, trans. Hugh Tomlinson and Barbara Habberjam (Minneapolis, Minn.: University of Minnesota Press 1984), p. x.

27. Žižek in *For They Know Not What They Do: Enjoyment as a Political Factor* (London and New York: Verso 1991), suggests that such exhortation denotes an absolute prohibition at work – it is the other side of 'you must not!' The point is that the absolute freedom to enjoy beyond the limit of the Law brings with it countless prohibitions. 'Partial' enjoyments – witness, for example, the vegetarianism of Hitler, and bans on smoking, drinking, meat, loud music, free speech, noise – are sacrificed. Such bans on one's own enjoyment produce the excess hatred of perceived *jouissance* of the other, what Lacan called *Lebensneid* (*Seminar VII*, p. 237). See Jacques Alain Miller, 'Extimité', in Mark Bracher et al., eds, *Lacanian Theory of Discourse: Subject, Structure and Society* (New York and London: New York University Press 1994), pp. 74–87.

28. See Arendt, *Eichmann*, p. 136. See also P.T. Geach, 'Good and Evil', in *Theories of Ethics*, ed. Philippa Foot (London: Oxford University Press 1967), pp. 64–73: 'Since Kant's time peoples have supposed that there is another sort of relevant reply – an appeal not to inclination but to the Sense of Duty. Now indeed a man may be got by training into a state of mind in which "You *must* not" is a sufficient answer to "Why shouldn't I?"; in which, giving this answer to himself, or hearing it given by others, strikes him with a quite peculiar awe; in which, perhaps, he even thinks he "must not" ask why he "must not". . . . Moral philosophers of the Objectivist school, like Sir David Ross, would call this "apprehension of one's obligations"; it does not worry them that, but for God's grace, this sort of training can make a man "apprehend" practically anything as his "obligations". (Indeed they admire a man who does what he thinks he *must* do regardless of what he actually does; is he not acting from a Sense of Duty which is the highest motive?' (pp. 70–71).

29. Rousseau was by no means unaware of such dangers when he developed his concept of *la volonté générale* in the *Social Contract*, especially in the chapter on 'La religion civile'. 'There is often a great deal of difference between the will of all and the general will. The latter considers only the general interest, whereas the fomer considers private interest and is merely the sum of private wills. But remove from these same wills the pluses and minuses that cancel each other out, and what remains is the general will.' *The Social Contract*, trans. Donald A Cress (Indianapolis: Hackett Publishing Company 1983) pp. 31–2. Rousseau, needless to say, identifies 'civil society' as intrinsically antagonistic, founded in and by inequity and injustice, to which his *volonté générale* is conceived simply as an antiweight. The general will is their common loss, the lack they all hold in common. It is obvious, however, that as in the

case of Kant, such a definition was susceptible of being misconstrued once it became a received idea.

30. The media dramatization of the execution of Robert Alton Harris, who is white, overtly mobilized public sentiment against capital punishment, but a major side effect of this sentiment was a suppression of awareness that such punishment is disproportionately meted out to men of colour.

31. On this point, Lacan, in *Seminar VII*, and Rousseau, in *The Social Contract*, might be said to agree; as Rousseau insists, in his chapter on 'The Legislator', the law giver must present himself as either a foreigner or a divinity, for no one would agree willingly to submit to a law made by one's equal and peer.

32. See Lacan's lightly ironic treatment, in *Seminar VII*, pp. 108–9, of Kant's overly rational sense of the psychology involved with sex: Kant fails to recognize, in his famous example of the gibbet awaiting the man who would sleep with his lady love and who thus 'naturally' chooses against it, either the compulsions of the over-estimated object (love) or the impulses of the sadist (the pleasure of possibly cutting up her body).

33. See Žižek, *The Sublime Object of Ideology*, pp. 83–4.

34. 'The right to *jouissance*, were it recognized, would relegate the domination of the pleasure principle to a forevermore outdated era. In enunciating it, Sade causes the ancient axis of ethics to slip . . . for everyone: this axis is no other than the egoism of happiness. It cannot be said that all reference to it is extinguished in Kant' (Lacan, 'Kant avec Sade', p. 71).

35. See Slavoj Žižek, 'Why is Sade the Truth of Kant?' in *For They Know Not What They Do*, pp. 229–33.

36. Sent 'off to the unthinkability of the Thing-in-itself' (Lacan, 'Kant avec Sade', p. 60). But it has a remainder, the object-*cause*. Here the reader is asked to recall the creation of surplus enjoyment by virtue of sacrifice outlined by Žižek (*The Sublime Object of Ideology*, pp. 82–3, cited above).

37. Although his views on marriage as the even exchange of sexual parts could give us, as it has others, pause.

38. See my earlier paper, 'Facing Fascism'. As the documentation and testimony piled up at the trial of Eichmann, it became quite clear to Hannah Arendt, who reported on it, that he had killed not out of blood lust, nor any of the traditional passions. He did not participate emotionally in the *Endlösung*; he could not even bear the few glimpses he had of the actual deaths and killings he routinely ordered. Eichmann was, as Arendt showed, a murderer only 'by administration'. He 'felt' desire very little if at all (at most he wanted to rise and succeed in the government's hierarchy). He always acted in accordance with the rules, and, far from simply following orders, he reported he felt compelled to 'go beyond' the written law and attributed this to his Kantian ethics. In the end this compulsion led to his being 'mastered' by a will not his own.

39. Lacan called Kant an obsessional, keeping him this side of psychosis and perversion. But he also saw how Sade would find his perverse position in a way quite parallel to Kant. Lacan also said that 'the realization of full speech' began with the opposite of 'obsessional intrasubjectivity': 'hysterical intersubjectivity' (*Ecrits*, p. 46).

40. Arendt, *Eichmann*, p. 136.

41. Ibid. p. 134.

42. See Lacan, *Seminar VII*, p. 73, on the link between the superego and *das Ding*. Kant ruled out *the Gut, das Ding* as determining reason. But at the 'level of the unconscious', Lacan tells us, '*Das Ding* presents itself . . . as that which *already makes the law*. . . . It is a capricious and arbitrary law, the law of the oracle, the law of signs . . . the law to which [the subject] has no *Sicherung*, to use another Kantian term. That is also at bottom the bad object that Kleinian theory is concerned with. . . . *The subject makes no approach at all to the bad object, since he is already maintaining his distance in relation to the good object*. He cannot stand the extreme good that *das Ding* may bring him, which is all

the more reason why he cannot locate himself in relation to the bad. . . . At the level of the unconscious, the subject lies [about evil],' my emphasis.

43. In his *Seminar VII*, pp. 307–10, Lacan interprets all of Freud's versions of the father as adumbrations of the 'malevolent superego' that, in Freud's later work, replaces the Oedipus complex with the castration complex.

44. Endless opinion polls, of course, address only prepackaged, prepared goods: they rarely tap people's desire.

45. Lacan, *Seminar XI*, p. 275.

46. Lacan, *Seminar VII*, p. 7.

47. Recall that this '*jouissance de l'Autre*', with respect to Freud's discussion of *drive* and 'the two principles of mental functioning' (the pleasure and reality principles), is always a *retrospective illusion*.

48. Arendt follows Raoul Hilberg in utterly rejecting the long European tradition of *anti-Semitism* as the principal cause of the Holocaust, an opinion for which she has borne much criticism by her fellow Jews.

49. Lacan maps three sorts of *vel* in *Seminar XI*, p. 241: the indifferent 'either/or' (where the choice does not matter); the absolute 'either/or' (where choice eliminates one side); and 'neither/nor'. In any case, each side or set of possible outcomes holds its object in common with the opposed set. If an absolute choice is made and one set over the other is elected, the object once shared by the sets, and which is needed to complete them, is retained by only one, and the other side ceases to exist at all. Conversely, the object itself loses a portion of its own existence, its resonance in the other set.

50. Willy Apollon, 'Four Seasons in Femininity', *Topoi* 12, September 1993, p.3.

51. Recent examples of 'unwritten laws' and their connection to modern mass slaughter include the more or less complete abandonment, since World War II, of formal declarations of war whenever hostilities are undertaken; and the burial alive of 'thousands of Iraqi soldiers' by the United States Armed Forces in the Persian Gulf War, because, as Pentagon officials explained, there was no written law against it. The Pentagon said there was a 'gap' in the law. 'The Pentagon said yesterday that a "gap" in laws governing warfare made it legally permissible during the gulf war for U.S. tanks to bury thousands of Iraqi troops in their trenches and for the U.S. warplanes to bomb the enemy retreating along the so called Highway of Death. . . . *Newsday* disclosed in September that many Iraqi troops were buried alive when the First Mechanized Infantry Division attacked an 8,000 man division defending Saddam Hussein's front line.' Patrick Sloyan, 'US Defends Burying Alive Iraqi Troops: Pentagon Cites a "Gap" in International Law', *San Francisco Chronicle*, 11 April 1992, p. A10.

   The Pentagon later claimed that the 'heat of the battle' obscured Iraqi efforts to surrender; but no *a priori* constraint on the right to such mass solutions is conceded by US officials. The law of war, they state, 'permits the attack of enemy combatants at any time, whether advancing, retreating or standing still'.

52. Or 'above the written law', as in the famous statement by Oliver North's secretary, Fawn Hall, by which she sought to justify her illegal destruction of government records in the Iran-Contra Affair. '[A] few minutes later, she retracted her statement. "I don't feel that", she said.' Cited in *The California Aggie*, 10 June 1987, p. 6.

53. Lacan, *Ecrits*, p. 40.

54. Ibid.

55. Ibid.

56. Granted that the drive to 'senselessness' in the discourse of fascism is utterly without the concomitant and flexible comprehension of 'form' found in Kant and in post-Kantian critical aesthetics.

57. Eichmann's fantasy at first is that he will save the Jews by his actions. He calls himself a Zionist: 'He hardly thought of anything but a "political solution" . . . and how to "get some firm ground under the feet of the Jews"' (Arendt, *Eichmann*, p. 41). That

'expulsion' under the guise of salvation inevitably turned to extermination is, however, predicted by Eichmann's relation to *jouissance*. Since he only felt 'elated' when he was swept up as a part of the 'Movement of History', Eichmann's desire to pin the Jews to the 'ground' 'spares' them this 'elevation', and 'movement', which he himself terms a 'death whirl'. The Jews would thus go 'below' and remain in 'the past', reaching the endpoint of the death drive without having to suffer its *jouissance*.

58. The true sadist, as Slavoj Žižek says, is the one who works not for his own desire, but on behalf of the Other's *jouissance*, as its agent or executioner. See 'The Limits of the Semiotic Approach to Psychoanalysis', *Psychoanalysis and* . . . , Richard Feldstein and Henry Sussman, eds (New York and London: Routledge 1990), pp. 89–110, as well as Žižek, *For They Know Not What They Do*, p. 234.

59. Arendt reports (*Eichmann*, pp. 112–13) that Heydrich was pleasantly surprised at how few difficulties he had enlisting the active help of all the ministries and the whole civil service needed for the Final Solution. There was 'more than happy agreement on the part of the participants'; the Final Solution was greeted with '"extraordinary enthusiasm" by all present'.

60. See Jacques Lacan, *Television: A Challenge to the Psychoanalytic Establishment*, ed. Joan Copjec, trans. Denis Hollier, Rosalind Krauss and Annette Michelson (New York and London, W. W. Norton and Co. 1990), pp. 32–3, for remarks on the growth of racism.

61. 'What is Alexander's proclamation when he arrived in Persepolis or Hitler's when he arrived in Paris? . . . "Carry on working. Work must go on." Which of course means, "Let it be clear to everyone that this is on no account the moment to express the least surge of desire." The morality of power, of the service of goods, is as follows: "As far as desires are concerned, come back later. Make them wait"' (Lacan, *Seminar VII*, p. 315). Joan Copjec's recent book, *Read My Desire: Lacan against the Historicists* (Cambridge, Mass.: MIT Press 1994), is recommended for its concrete expansion on desire.

62. Like others from Adorno to Ronell, Lacan implicates the mass media; but in contrast to the thinkers of technology, Lacan underscores the problematic of subject and object as essential to an anatomy of fascism.

63. Lacan, *Seminar VII*, p. 7.

64. Notably Horkheimer and Adorno in *The Dialectic of Enlightenment*, trans. John Cumming (New York: Continuum 1982).

65. Note that EuroDisney in France is restricted to only one of the 'lands' Disney's company devised for the Anaheim Disneyland: 'Fantasyland'.

4 THE BAD SEED
'Auschwitz' and the Physiology of Evil

ANDREW HEWITT

In *The Differend*, Jean-François Lyotard characterizes the
impossible demand for proof made by historical revisionists
on the survivors of a camp aimed at total destruction, in the
following terms:

> Either the situation did not exist as such. Or else it did exist, in
> which case your informant's testimony is false, either because he or
> she should remain silent, or else because, if he or she does speak, he
> or she can bear witness only to the particular experience he had,
> it remaining to be established whether this experience was a
> component of the situation in question.[1]

Lyotard rehearses in this passage the rhetoric of a
revisionism he seeks to refute, and yet he takes seriously
the dilemma that revisionism exploits. The very ability to
bear witness to the camps does violence to what the
camps 'name' in history. At stake is the very possibility of
characterizing the 'Auschwitz' experience as an experience.
On the one hand this is a general problem, as Lyotard notes:

> It follows that reality does not result from an experience. This does
> not at all prevent it from being described from the standpoint of an
> experience. The rules to respect in undertaking this description are
> those of speculative logic . . . and also those of novelistic poetics. . . .
> This description, though, has no philosophical value because it
> does not question its presuppositions (the I or the self, the rules of
> speculative logic). (§73)

But 'with Auschwitz, something new has happened in
history (which can only be a sign and not a fact), which is
that the facts, the testimonies which bore the traces of *here*'s

and *now's*, the documents which indicated the sense or senses of the facts, and the names . . . all this has been destroyed as much as possible' (§93: 57). The general problem of speculative logic and novelistic poetics – their clinging to the notion of an I or a Self – acquires a specific historical importance through 'Auschwitz', in which the maintenance of the I or the Self was a physical rather than a merely speculative imperative.[2] Speculative logic cannot deal with a discourse that does not problematize the I or the Self: and survivors of the camps are unlikely to question such constructs when the experience of the camp was itself that of attempting to *survive* as I or Self.

Though Lyotard's rhetorical analysis serves as one of the most powerful refutations of a vulgar and pernicious revisionism, he too is led to reframe 'Auschwitz' as something other than an 'experience'. 'It could not therefore be said to be an experience', he writes 'since it would have no result. Its not having a speculative name, however, does not preclude the need to talk about it' (§153: 89).[3] How are we, then, to deal with the 'experiences' of those survivors whose texts play out 'the need to talk about it' while negating the very category of experience itself as it has traditionally been understood? What I seek here – through a return to the notion of radical evil developed in Kant's late essay *Religion within the Limits of Reason Alone* – is to supplement Lyotard's approach to 'Auschwitz' by suggesting that the problems of unrepresentability and inconceivability turn on a traditional philosophical coupling of representation and conception.[4] If, as Lyotard argues, 'Auschwitz' obliges us to rethink a model of verifiable history predicated on the production of a *Resultat* ('Auschwitz' would not be an experience because 'it would have no result'), it necessarily challenges the concept of history. If the dilemma – as Lyotard paraphrases it – is the impossibility of bearing witness to one's *death* in the camps, might we instead seek out witnesses to *life* in the camps?

In *Negative Dialectics*, Adorno refuses to privilege the survivors' insistence on the 'I or the Self',[5] arguing that an insistence on personal narrative presupposes a kind of subject that the very possibility of the camp liquidated. To perpetuate personal narrative is, potentially, to act as though the camps never happened. He remains suspicious of an 'experience' of the end of 'experience'; of any narrative that purports to be the narrative of a subject subjected to 'Auschwitz', where subjects were destroyed and where the destruction of subjectivity necessarily led to an ideological renaissance of the subject in extremis. Hannah Arendt, meanwhile, in *The Origins of Totalitarianism*, privileges the perspective not of the survivors, but of what she calls the 'fearful imagination', for:

> If it is true that the concentration camps are the most consequential institution of totalitarian rule, 'dwelling on horrors' would seem to be indispensable for the understanding of totalitarianism. But recollection can no more do this than can the

uncommunicative eyewitness report. In both these genres there is an inherent
tendency to run away from the experience.... Only the fearful imagination of those
who have been aroused by such reports but have not actually been smitten in their
own flesh, of those who are consequently free from the bestial, desperate terror which,
when confronted by real, present horror, inexorably paralyzes everything that is not
mere reaction, can afford to think about horrors.[6]

Of course, Arendt and Adorno rework a similar question in very different ways.
Arendt's insistence on those fearful imaginations that 'have not actually been
smitten in their own flesh' and can therefore move beyond 'mere reaction' is an
appeal to a reflective, mediating and meditative subject. The 'fearful imagination', in a conventional philosophical gesture, must distance itself from the
immediacy of bodily pain. 'Fear' is the modality of an embodied subjectivity: I fear
therefore I am. If fear is the fear of my demise as a speculative *and bodily* subject,
it reasserts my subjectivity in negative form. For Adorno, however, the first
reaction of the subject under bodily threat is to resort to precisely those fictions
of subjectivity on which Arendt relies. In his rendering, Arendt's meditative and
mediating subjectivity is itself the result of 'mere reaction', of the immediacy of
fear. Precisely when she de-privileges the (bodily) 'experiences' of the survivors,
Arendt in fact re-privileges the category of experience per se by invoking a notion
of the subject without which experience would be unthinkable.

For Adorno, the body is no longer that which distracts the spirit from the task
of self-sublating reflection, but rather that which insistently recalls the fatuous
and ideological nature of such a task. Confronted with his or her corporeality in
the camps, the individual survives, according to Adorno, through the fiction of
subjectivity. Consequently, in *Negative Dialectics*, Adorno will insist that 'a new
categorical imperative has been imposed by Hitler upon unfree mankind' and
that 'the course of history forces materialism upon metaphysics' (p. 365). Where
Arendt retains a mind-body dichotomy, Adorno at least proposes a move beyond
it. What he will insist on, however, is that 'the somatic, unmeaningful stratum of
life is the stage of suffering, of the suffering which in the camps, without any
consolation, burned every soothing feature out of the mind, and out of culture,
the mind's objectification' (p. 365).

While advocating a retreat from metaphysics, Adorno never satisfactorily
elaborates any discourse of the body that might counter what he takes to be an
ultimately murderous metaphysical project. His bodies suffer. Adorno clearly
ranges himself against a Kantian metaphysical tradition with his recognition
that:

a new categorical imperative has been imposed by Hitler upon unfree mankind: to
arrange their thoughts and actions so that Auschwitz will not repeat itself, so that

nothing similar will happen. When we want to find reasons for it, this imperative is as refractory as the given one of Kant was once upon a time. Dealing with it discursively would be an outrage, for the new imperative gives us a bodily sensation of the moral addendum – bodily, because it is now the practical abhorrence of the unbearable physical agony to which individuals are exposed even with individuality about to vanish as a form of mental reflection. (p. 365)

But his retention of Kantian terminology indicates the extent to which he still relies on an ethics drawn from early Kant. Countering a sublation of the body in spirit, Adorno sees this sublation taking place ironically in a collapse of spirit into matter. He values the body only as the trace of suffering – as the agony, the death throes of the ideal subject. To this extent, he imagines not the embodiment of a new economy – with its own flows and circuits – but the trace of a rupture in another economy, that of metaphysics. The body is always already a corpse, or a corpse in abeyance, or the 'remains' – that which 'remains' of the idealist project, resisting it, yet decimated by it.

Perhaps Adorno is right to insist, in the face of 'Auschwitz', on the physicality of the body as a resistance to 'absolute identity' or 'pure identity as death', but he does not examine the body in terms of the economy it inaugurates. I shall examine this economy as the physiology that underpins even Kant's most apparently rigoristic moral writing. I would argue that philosophy's attempts to come to terms with the *death* camps in fact attend to the body only in its negative sense: as lack, as suffering and as resistance to another (totalizing) discourse. This conception of the body, which is ultimately privative, further corresponds to a privative notion of evil central to precisely those Kantian moral categories Adorno would challenge. Though he rejects 'an ontologically pure being named Death', in the name of 'that which the stench of cadavers expresses' (p. 366), Adorno nevertheless figures the body always as cadaver. Might it be possible, instead, to examine *life* in the camps in such a way as to attend to the flows and functions of the body without resorting to either a vitalist discourse or a eugenics? How would we 'read' this life; and would such a reading permit of a moral rigour that would not always be a rigor mortis?

So long as philosophy has tried to conceive of 'Auschwitz' – or where it has allowed itself to be thought through 'Auschwitz' – it has necessarily resorted to death: Adorno's insistence upon the return of the body to metaphysics has led to the cadaver. But does not the cadaver, the body deprived of its animating spirit, annul the very problem to which it attests: namely, the division of body and spirit? Is the corpse not the production of an inverted sublation, in which spirit becomes body, *absolute matter*, rather than the reverse? And if the body in this sublation represents (if representation be still possible) the contingent and relative, does it not become *absolutely* relative, even without any ontological notion of death? Adorno's privileging of the body leads, instead, to a merely suffering conception of the somatic. If, as Adorno argues, the cadaver embodies the murderous end of 'the philosophy of pure identity as death', what are we to say of birth and conception, those tropes central, as we shall see, to Kant's reflection on evil? If death, and the stench of cadavers, comments immanently on the metaphysical project, what status is to be accorded to a mechanism of birth and conception upon which that tradition has consistently drawn to figure its own movement?

Lyotard's study of the possibility of 'phrasing "Auschwitz"' also raises the question of genre in a more traditional and limited sense. For 'the idea of an experience presupposes', he writes, 'an I which forms itself [*Bildung*] by gathering in the properties of things that come up [events] and which constitutes reality by effectuating their temporal synthesis' (p. 45). The collapse of experience, at least in Lyotard's rendering, is linked to the question of *Bildung*, and the recounting of those experiences, therefore, to the status of the *Bildungsroman*. In this paper, I will conclude with some writings of Primo Levi that – in so far as they can, with some violence, be recuperated within the parameters of the *Bildungsroman* genre – trace the specificity of the camp experience back to a physical, biological economy. Looking back with amused condescension at his life as a resistance fighter before being captured, Levi comments that it was 'a world inhabited by civilized Cartesian phantoms, by sincere male and bloodless female friendships'.[7] By taking seriously this negative linkage of body and spirit, a Cartesianism that is 'bloodless', I seek to examine the way in which accounts of 'Auschwitz' as an instantiation of radical evil necessarily suggest not only a physical metaphysics in Adorno's sense, but also a metaphysics of the physical – a moral physiology – that turns upon a conception of *life* rather than *death*.

One of the few studies of camp narratives to take at face value the observations of internees regarding the day-to-day physical degradations of *life* in the camps poses the challenge of a 'physical reading' in the following (rather simplistic) terms:

> The basic structure of Western civilization or perhaps of any civilization, insofar as the processes of culture and sublimation are one, is the division between body and spirit, between concrete existence and symbolic modes of being. In extremity, however, divisions like these collapse. The principle of compartmentalization no longer holds, and organic being becomes the immediate locus of selfhood. When this happens, body and spirit become the ground of each other.[8]

Building on this erasure of the body-spirit differential in the camp, the author further notes:

When civilization breaks down, as it did in the concentration camps, the 'symbolic stain' becomes a condition of literal defilement, and evil becomes that which causes real 'loss of the personal core of one's being.' In extremity man is stripped of his expanded spiritual identity. Only concrete forms of existence remain, actual life and actual death, actual pain and actual defilement: and these now constitute the medium of moral and spiritual being. Spirit does not simply vanish when sublimation fails. At the cost of much of its freedom, it falls back to the ground and origin of meaning – back, that is, to the physical experience of the body. Which is another way of saying that, in extremity, symbols tend to actualize.

We might say, then, that in extremity symbolism *as symbolism* loses its autonomy. Or, what amounts to the same thing, that in this special case everything is felt to be inherently symbolic, intrinsically significant. Either way, meaning no longer exists above and beyond the world; it reenters concrete experience, becomes immanent and invests each act and moment with urgent depth. And hence the oddly 'literary' character of experience in extremity. (p. 69)

By returning to Kant's *Religion within the Limits of Reason Alone*, I seek to examine the status of the 'symbolic stain' we read of here. If 'Auschwitz' marks the collapse of evil as a symbolic structure – through its *bodily* inscription of evil – it may very well confront us not simply with a reformulation of the conception of evil in literal and physical instead of 'symbolic' terms, but rather with the fact that the displacement of moral judgement from the symbolic to the physical realm is *itself* constitutive of evil. In other words, the possibility of thinking morality in physiological terms, in so far as it compromises the distinction between nature and morality, *is* evil, as such. Could this not lie at the core of the unrepresentability of 'Auschwitz', namely the fact that 'symbolism *as symbolism* loses its autonomy'? Could Arendt be completely wrong in arguing for a distancing from bodily sensations? And further, what does it mean to conflate, as the author of the passage just quoted does, 'the literal' and 'the literary'? Does the collapse of the symbolic lead at the same time to a new 'intrinsic' or 'inherent' symbolic order? For precisely when the possibility of a 'symbolic' literary representation of 'experience' seems impossible, 'experience' itself apparently takes on an immanently literary quality. The 'symbolic stain' would need to be read, then, not simply as a symbol of inherited evil, but as the stain of evil that is inscribed on the body. What this would mean, in effect, is that the stain marks the end of 'symbolism *as symbolism*'; it no longer 'symbolizes', in fact, evil or even the end of evil, but *is* evil and *is* evil's end as a symbolic structure. The stain is evil because it is *not* a symbol.

Retracing the genealogy of this 'symbolic stain' returns us directly to Kant's late essay on radical evil, for it is in this essay that Kant likewise posits evil as a 'foul taint in our race' (p. 34). The need to posit such a taint as a physical and racial category is itself a measure of the taint itself, which is (or should be) a purely moral rather than physical fact. What does it mean when, as in Kant's essay and in the camps, such 'symbols tend to actualize'? Is the victim of the camp in fact the victim of a supposed 'foul taint in [his] race'? The taint is tainted by its physical instantiation. But this question of the stain throws us back also onto the question of the break that Kant's essay made with his writings on morality up to that point.

Religion within the Limits of Reason Alone, the late text in which Kant proposes and explores the notion of radical evil, has traditionally posed problems to Kant scholars as well as to those seeking to derive from his work a philosophy of history in the Enlightenment tradition. For in this work Kant moves startlingly close at times to traditional Christian notions of original sin, repudiating positions he had elaborated only a decade before in the *Lectures on Philosophical Theology*, for example. The late essay moves so far beyond the purely privative notion of evil inherent in the Enlightenment's faith in human perfectibility that Goethe, for one, would claim in a letter to Herder that Kant 'had criminally smeared his philosopher's cloak with the shameful stain of radical evil, after it had taken him a long human life to cleanse it from many a dirty prejudice, so that Christians too might yet be enticed to kiss its hem'.[9] The stain, then, has been read as a stain on Kant's ethical project. Even among those who instinctively rejected Kant's position, the 'stain' enters the discourse on evil.

Other critics, meanwhile, have argued that *Religion within the Limits of Reason Alone* serves as a necessary corrective to the moral dilemmas posed by some of Kant's earlier writings; a dilemma of responsibility that Jean-Luc Nancy identifies with Kant's earlier arguments 'that authentic freedom was the freedom of the good, whereas evil was the fact of nonfreedom letting itself be dragged along by the mechanics of the sensible'.[10] What the *Religion* essay offers instead is a positive, substantive and active model of evil.[11] My aim here is not to reconcile this late work with the corpus of Kant's earlier moral writings, but to suggest a way in which the essay perhaps provides an ethical framework within which 'Auschwitz' can, again, be thought. More specifically, I wish to examine National Socialism and the experience of the concentration camp as an instantiation of radical evil and to indicate the limits that the Kantian formulation necessarily places upon any such attempt. In its Nazi form, fascism would be the historical instantiation of what Nancy terms a '*fascination with evil*' (p. 123) that cannot, however, be thought as a countertradition to Enlightenment optimism because, as Nancy again points out, it is 'absolutely relative'. What is evil about this fascination is its reduction of the *good* to a condition of relativity and contingency; its introduction of what Kant calls the *adiaphoron morale* into rigorous moral critique. The relativity of evil is absolute precisely in so far as it is (in its very relativity) the *negation*, rather than the opposite, of the absolute. In what follows, I examine the pertinence of Kant's essay to a consideration of Nazism in two respects: first, I will show how it prefigures the aporia in moral and juridical discourses – let us say, the discourses of judgement – that 'Auschwitz' seemed to inaugurate (I hope to show that the responses of Nazi war criminals to their accusers would prove exemplary in this sense); second, and more importantly, I will use it as a framework for understanding the narratives of those who experienced the camps.

Returning to the *Religion* essay, we might begin by situating it (as Kant himself does) within an eighteenth-century debate on the possibility of evil; for the problems Kant poses in this essay derive from his repudiation of a variety of positions prevalent at the time. This essay poses several enigmas to those who would derive from it any definitive position. It is an essay that turns delicately on the niceties of a distinction between man's 'original predisposition to good' and his 'natural propensity to evil', and between conceptions of radical evil as both 'innate' and forced upon us by our freedom. Likewise, radical evil is '*inextirpable* by human powers' (p. 32), and yet man is obliged to free himself from it, even if divine aid is necessary to accomplish this (p. 40).

Kant begins the essay by outlining two broad models of history: one assuming gradual decline and the other gradual progress. The former is exemplified by Christian notions of the Fall (but also by the worship of Rudra, the God of Destruction in Indian religion); the latter, 'more modern, though far less prevalent' (p. 15), is identified with 'the moralists, from Seneca to Rousseau' (p. 16) and with the Enlightenment. Stated schematically, this 'Enlightenment' tradition would argue, as Kant himself had in the *Lectures on Philosophical Theology*, that evil was of the order of a 'lack' rather than a positive entity or concept in itself. Evil would result, then, from a 'lack' of Enlightenment, an underdevelopment of the free use of individual understanding, an ignorance. Kant's own Enlightenment instincts clearly predispose him in presenting the dilemmas toward what we might call the 'optimistic' model, after all: 'We may note that since we take for granted that man is by nature sound of body (as at birth he usually is), no reason appears why, by nature, his soul should not be deemed similarly healthy and free from evil. Is not nature herself, then, inclined to lend her aid to developing in us this moral predisposition to goodness?' (p. 16). I stress here not the tentative position Kant hypothesizes only to reject subsequently, 'optimistic' rather than 'pessimistic' in the schematized form he has set forth, but rather the terms in which he presents the case. Despite the fact that Kant's moral argument rests on a strict distinction between (amoral) physical phenomena and moral or spiritual phenomena, this essay will be peppered with rhetorical invocations of nature and the body, of natural flows and economies that Kant must ultimately reject as soon as they are evoked. Moral health will again and again depend upon an image of physical health, even where the slippage from moral to physical is itself presented as the very modality of evil. It is from this rhetorical strategy, rather than from the essay's ostensible moral argument, that the disturbing possibility of a *physiological* morality opens up in Kant's essay. Is it this physiology that realizes itself in 'Auschwitz'?

In fact, the radical evil proposed in *Religion within the Limits of Reason Alone* confounds both the optimistic and the pessimistic position by insisting upon evil's dependence upon *Wille.* Those who see this essay as a response to the aporias of earlier Kantian strictures on morality present their case in the following terms: if, as Kant argues in *Foundations for the Metaphysics of Morals,*[12] the will acts virtuously only when it is truly acting freely – for to act on the impetus of an external determinant is to adulterate the moral judgement with an extraneous or pragmatic consideration (thereby undermining the function of the moral maxim as the subjective principle of volition) – the will fails morally by subjugating itself to a heteronomous determinant. Where I act morally, I act freely, for conformity to moral law frees me; and where I act immorally, I act unfreely, for any abnegation of moral freedom is by definition an immoral act. In other words, freedom and morality are potentially conflated to the extent that it becomes impossible to conceive of an immoral act that is the free choice of an individual will.[13] If the abnegation of personal freedom is immoral, the reverse seems also to be true: immorality is the abnegation of freedom.

To be immoral is to be unfree, but can we hold an unfree nonsubject responsible for his or her acts? If evil results from my surrender of *Wille* to the heteronomous determination of pragmatic or objective concerns, 'I' am never, in a sense, responsible for my evil acts, which derive not from 'me' but from the *absence* of me, and my maxims, as the subjective principle of volition. By associating evil with ignorance, we characterize it as 'lack', this time, the 'lack' of the subject in the determination of his own actions. Evil is privative in this sense, precluding a subject rather than proceeding from one. The very immorality of an act paradoxically attenuates the subject's responsibility, for in the committal of that act one is no longer a subject in the moral sense. The *Religion* essay responds to this problem of responsibility deriving from a privative conception of evil (evil as lack) by thinking a *positive* evil that is the result of will, rather than of will's self-abnegation. I would argue that it is precisely the historical experience of Nazism that obliges us to move beyond the moral framework of works such as the *Lectures on Philosophical Theology* and to countenance the possibility of a radical and positive evil as developed in the *Religion* essay. To contend that the Nazis 'knew' that what they were doing was evil not only raises questions of moral responsibility, but also reformulates the very nature of evil itself, as something substantive rather than privative.[14]

Kant's essay is especially relevant to the examination of fascism in regard to the question of responsibility; for the paradox of Kantian moral responsibility is nowhere more dramatically exemplified than in the protestations of war criminals such as Eichmann and Höss that they were merely following orders and cannot therefore be held responsible for the acts they committed in the name of another. The juridical unfreedom they claim to mitigate their acts mimics the unfreedom Kant generally posits at the root of all immorality. Indeed, the problem is complicated, as Hannah Arendt has pointed out, by the fact that the 'other' who commands the actions of Eichmann and Höss in fact personifies the law in whose name morality would otherwise become possible. In *Eichmann in Jerusalem*, Arendt describes how Eichmann 'declared with great emphasis that he had lived his whole life according to Kant's moral precepts, and especially according to a Kantian definition of duty'.[15] She is further astonished at the conciseness of Eichmann's quotation of Kant. In such criminals, the law itself has become an external determinant: for not only do they deny their own supra-sensual identity with the law, they reduce the law itself (in the very absolutism of their *submission* to it) to a contingent and accidental force. If we can see in this gesture a mimicry of the potential aporia opened up by Kant, the *Religion* essay nevertheless frames a 'way out' of the dilemmas of responsibility for 'Auschwitz'. For Eichmann and Höss, in Arendt's presentation, obedience to the law *negates* personal responsibility by effectively effacing the subject of the crime ('*I* have no axe to grind with the Jews. Indeed, I have – as Eichmann would claim – "special reasons" to be favorably disposed to them. I was simply following orders'). The arguments of these men become doubly reprehensible to the extent that they reduce the law to a finite and external determinant: not only do they abjure all personal responsibility, they negate the transcendent and inherent quality of the law by invoking it as an external and objective determinant of their actions. Obedience no longer legitimates law: I know the law is absurd, but I obey.

This, in a sense, is precisely what radical evil would be: the law, the principle of moral action in accordance with which moral maxims can be developed by the subject, has itself become the merely *external* determinant that in fact renders all actions fundamentally immoral. When Eichmann cites his 'special reasons' for liking Jews, he buries beneath the contingency of the specific the categorical imperative and thereby reduces the law itself to the level of a contingency. He considers his acts morally accountable only in so far as they *negate* rather than actualize his subjective volition. Citing his biographical 'special reasons' for liking Jews, Eichmann elucidates negatively the analysis of moral behaviour in the *Religion* essay, in which Kant writes:

Thus, for example, in order to know whether I should (or indeed can) be truthful in my testimony before a court, or whether I should be faithful in accounting for another man's property entrusted to me, it is not at all necessary for me to search for an end which I might propose to achieve with my declaration since it matters not at all what sort of end this is; indeed, the man who finds it needful, when his avowal is lawfully demanded, to look about him for some kind of [ulterior] end, is, by this very fact, already contemptible. (p. 4)

Ostensibly, Kant argues that a moral decision that needs to cite some practical or ulterior motive to prove its own conformity to the law ('Of course I will observe the law in this instance, because it is even in my interests to do so. Common sense and practical reason tells you that I will observe the law') thereby proves its nonconformity. In such a case, the law, rather than functioning as an internal and self-sufficient rationale for action by a subject, functions as a purely *external* determinant. Whereas the Kantian formula aims at the reconciliation of the subject and objective morality through the notion of a suprasensual and moral self, Eichmann actually assumes their radical antinomy. Obedience that knows itself as such is necessarily immoral, for it renders the law a merely contingent and finite determinant rather than an indwelling principle. This is the sense in which evil would be 'absolutely relative'. That which is to liberate man, the moral law, has itself truly become corrupted as a source of evil. 'This evil is *radical*', Kant insists, 'because it corrupts the ground of all maxims; it is, moreover, as a natural propensity, *inextirpable* by human powers, since extirpation could occur only through good maxims, and cannot take place when the ultimate subjective ground of all maxims is postulated as corrupt' (p. 32). In other words, radical evil is an evil in which the means of overcoming evil are themselves contaminated by the evil that is to be overcome.

While Eichmann's self-exculpations caricature a certain Kantian conception of evil, questioning his status as the subject of his own acts, the responses of Nazi camp doctors to the charges laid against them go one step further in confounding – as, I will argue, Kant himself cannot help confounding – the otherwise mutually negating (rather than opposing) discourses of physiology and morality. In a study of these trials, for example, Mitscherlich notes the response of a certain 'Edwin Katzenellenbogen, erstwhile member of the Faculty of Harvard Medical School. He asked the court for the death sentence in the following words: "You have placed the mark of Cain on my forehead. Any physician who committed the crimes I am charged with deserves to be killed. Therefore I ask for only one grace. Apply to me the highest therapy that is in your hands."'[16] This is a curious admission of guilt indeed. At no point does the doctor posit himself as the subject of his crimes, hypothesizing instead a 'physician who committed the crimes I am charged with'.[17] He further experiences his guilt only as a physical mark, the mark of Cain that has been placed on his forehead by others, rather than as the consequence of his own actions. His guilt, like the guilt of the Jews, is inscribed on his body, which functions in this rhetoric as the empty vessel of a subjectivity. The 'admission' of guilt not only replicates Eichmann's self-distantiation from moral agency, but also replicates the crime by once again confounding the physiological and the moral. One might say that the subject's awareness of his guilt results from an unawareness, a loss of consciousness and a falling into materiality. He is aware of his guilt only in so far as he experiences himself merely as a body. Most shocking, however, is the way in which this 'admission' replays precisely the ideological horrors that led to the crime in the first place. Because of a physical mark, the doctor feels he does not deserve to live. Death becomes a therapy: respect for life, the therapeutic process, necessitates death. It is this, I think, that we must recall in approaching the questions of *life* in the camps, and of the camps themselves as a regimen of life; death is no longer simply the termination of and opposition to life, but a therapy.

Perhaps most interesting, however, is Karl Brandt, the leading defendant at the doctors' trial and the most defiant. Brandt, Mitscherlich informs us, 'offered to cheat the gallows by offering his living body for medical experiments like those he had conducted' (p. 147). Dr Brandt was apparently surprised at the American judges' refusal of the offer: how are we to understand this strange gesture? Whereas Katzenellenbogen and others could not conceive of themselves as sane ethical subjects (a circular logic, of course, since the inability to conceive of one's subjectivity itself strikes at the very root of that subjectivity) and saw death, the mortification of the body, as a 'therapy' that might somehow restore them as subjects, Brandt more thoroughly conflates the conditions of physicality and moral agency. One might read his gesture as a kind of retroactive invocation of the categorical imperative: Brandt consents retrospectively to the generalization of his acts, so that what he did to others might be done to him. His gesture is a reparation rather than a retribution; the experiments will function not as punishment but as the reconstruction of his acts as the acts of a subject. And where Katzenellenbogen imagines the possibility of a future 'therapy', death, that might reconstitute the subject, Brandt seeks a measure that will reconstitute him as a subject of his past acts and therefore render them moral (as the acts of a subject). The conditions of physiological and moral subjectivity are no longer mutually indifferent, then, but mutually interdependent. The doctor will have become the subject of his acts through the immolation of the body. But is this not also the logic of genocide: paradoxically seeking to render the victims the subjects of the crimes they cannot be responsible for as vermin? Genocide not only destroys, but also, in this sense, produces subjects.

Similar questions of subjectivity arise for the victims: if the victim is not (or is not viewed as) a subject, then murder cannot necessarily be viewed as murder. The problem of defining 'life' is directly linked to the problem of defining moral culpability. Thus, for example, after the war the World Medical Association responded to the crimes of Nazi doctors by administering a new Hippocratic Oath obliging all physicians to 'maintain the utmost respect for human life from the time of its conception' (quoted in Mitscherlich and Mielke, *Doctors of Infamy*, p. xxviii). Clearly the aim is to acknowledge the embodiment of the ethical subject, that is, to conflate the physical and the intellectual origins of life, which Kant seeks to keep apart. But are we being enjoined by this oath to respect a life as soon as it has been conceived (a physiology), or to respect a mere conception of life (a morality)? What is the status of this conception? Moral, physiological or both?

The radical evil of which Kant writes contaminates the very possibility of escape, and it is therefore fitting that he should conceive of both escape from and entry into evil through the same trope: as a conception and (re)birth. The inability of thought to escape radical evil is linked to its inability to conceive of conception outside the framework of a physiology, that is, as a birth. Kant figures the possibility of a 'revolution' in man's disposition, for example, as 'a kind of rebirth, as it were, a new creation' (p. 43), at the same time as the act of conception (and, I would argue, the action of the concept) has itself become the mode of transmission of evil. What I am proposing is that Kant's essay begins by presupposing a division between morally indifferent nature and the morality of human nature only to see nature re-emerge with a moral urgency at the level of the physical. While invoking parallels from natural history to support a moral argument, Kant must reject with equal consistency the relevance of those parallels.

Clearly, 'nature' is a highly problematic term in the *Religion* essay. To clarify this term, which he acknowledges as problematic, Kant will explain: 'Lest difficulty at once be encountered in the expression *nature*, which, if it meant (as it usually does) the opposite of *freedom* as a basis of action, would flatly contradict the predicates *morally* good or evil, let it be noted that by "nature of man" we here intend only the subjective ground of the exercise (under objective moral laws) of man's freedom in general' (p. 16). *Religion within the Limits of Reason Alone* will struggle incessantly with this problematic redefinition of 'nature'. Since the very idea of a 'human nature' suggests a moral indifference contrary to Kant's project, human nature will have to become something thoroughly 'unnatural'. In and of itself, this troublesome redefinition of nature need not startle us: the idea that man's natural instinct is to rise above nature is a recurrent Enlightenment theme. More troubling, however, is Kant's inability to discard the natural historical and physiological framing tropes that help develop his argument. The body keeps reasserting itself, and this insistence of the body, I would argue, *is* radical evil, for it marks the recurrence of a physiological moral indifference (*adiaphoron morale*) at the very heart of Kant's rigoristic moral project. It is as nature that evil is absolutely relative.

Characterizing the shift in concepts of evil from the *Lectures on Philosophical Theology* to *Religion within the Limits of Reason Alone*, one critic comments:

> [A]t the time of the *Religion*, moral evil is for Kant definitely not a 'lack' or a privation, but a positive reality: it *becomes* a reality, moving from not being to being real, in the course of maxim-making. This fundamental point, which runs through the first two books of the *Religion*, marks a significant departure from the view that Kant espoused a decade earlier in his university lectures on philosophical theology, where he suggested that radical evil can be viewed as the 'incompleteness in the development of the seed toward good.' Evil itself 'has no special seed,' Kant said in that earlier context, for 'it is only a negation, and consists only in a limitation of what is good.'[18]

The shift, then, is from a privative to a substantive notion of evil, from evil as lack to evil as substance. Moreover, the propensity to evil tends now to arise from an excess in an opposing predisposition to good: there is no strict opposition, then, between good and evil. According to Kant's essay, these predispositions to good are threefold:

1. The predisposition to *animality* in man, taken as a *living* being;
2. The predisposition to *humanity* in man, taken as a living and at the same time a *rational* being;
3. The predisposition to *personality* in man, taken as a rational and at the same time *accountable* being. (p. 21)

What is striking, of course, is the possibility of good and evil raised here even at the level of *animality* – at the level, that is, preceding the emergence of an ethical subject. Explicitly, Kant raises at least the possibility of a physiological ethic, dividing this most basic predisposition (which, as a natural phenomenon, one might expect to be a- or pre-moral) into three subgroups: the predispositions to self-preservation, to the preservation of the species and to community with other men. The reproductive preservation of the species, then, is being accorded as direct a moral value as the preservation of the community. It is important to note, however, the process whereby these animal predispositions to good are converted, or, as Kant will insist, perverted, into evil. The first two predispositions (to self-preservation and to the preservation of the species) become vice by virtue of an excess, or at least a plenitude. Self-preservation becomes gluttony or licentiousness (the term *Völlerei* suggests the logic of plenitude that brings this

about); while the preservation of the species leads in its excesses to lascivious-
ness. In both cases, then, we can see a move beyond a *privative* to an explicitly
excessive conception of evil. Only the third animal predisposition, toward
community with other men, becomes a vice through lack or absence. The vice of
'law-*less*-ness' (emphasis mine) resulting from this predisposition suggests
instead an *absence* of the grounding virtue rather than a vicious excess of it.
Why should it be that Kant does not envisage excess in this regard, and what
would 'community with other men', the system of social intercourse, become in
a state of excess? Kant does not countenance the possibility of an excess of men's
'communion', I would argue, for it is an exchange that does not permit of a
conception.

Evil is *radical* not when it is absolute, but when it allows for moral indifference
in man. Thus, for example, the question of whether 'radical' evil would be an evil
'innate' in man provokes from Kant the following elaboration of the concept of
the 'innate': 'it follows that good or evil in man (as the ultimate subjective
ground of the adoption of this or that maxim with reference to the moral law) is
termed innate only in *this* sense, that it is posited as the ground antecedent
to every use of freedom in experience (in earliest youth as far back as birth)
and is thus conceived of as present in man at birth – though birth need not
be the cause of it' (p. 17). We should dwell a while on this notion of the 'innate'
and the rhetoric of natality and conception it inaugurates. We have here two
conceptions: (1) the physical act of conception that is, indeed, 'the cause of'
man's birth; and (2) the concept that conceives of this conception as a 'ground
antecedent to every use of freedom'. The innate, Kant wishes to assert, inheres
only in the latter: it is a purely conceptual origin. That which is innate is so
only in the concept; what man has from his physical birth is not fundamental to
the *concept* of man and therefore not innate in the sense elaborated here. The
tropological philosophical concept, we are asked to believe, is more originary
(more 'radical') than natural birth. In other words, the invocation of a natural
tropology serves to denature by rendering the natural ground a merely
secondary, rhetorical and therefore nonoriginary origin.

Though Kant wishes to insist that 'birth need not be the cause of' what
is innate, he fails to convince even himself of this. He intends to present
physiological conception as a mere trope of the act of moral and intellectual
conception, but again and again the physicality of the act returns to render
impure this immaculate conception. The operation of radical evil within the
essay would be precisely that failure of 'symbolism *as symbolism*' that renders the
trope, itself drawn from indifferent nature, literal. This 'failure of symbolism *as
symbolism*' should be thought, then, not as a failure of meaning, but as the
failure to restrain meaning within the symbolic structures that generate it: the

failure to prevent 'meaning' from *actualizing* itself and coming to life in conceptions. Thus, commenting on the question of moral indifference in his *Experience of Freedom*, Jean-Luc Nancy arrives at the following formulation:

> But evil is, if we can say it thus, 'absolutely relative' to good in that it is the ruin of the good as such, not its privation, but its crushing in a night where nothing any longer gives one the slightest right to say that it would still be the gloomy evening preceding a dawn. . . . Evil does not impair the good (it could not be impaired), nor does it disregard it (for evil knows and wills itself as evil and is therefore knowledge of the good), but it refuses its coming to life. Wickedness causes evil by withdrawing from the good its possibility *in statu nascendi.* (p. 126)

The question of evil turns upon the question of the concept and the question of conception in both the moral and physiological senses. Is evil contraceptive in nature, the ruination of good *in statu nascendi?* Or is this evil transmitted in (re)birth, in the act of concept(ion)? And would the concept in the rigorous sense itself function as the reconception of a birth that Kant dare not think physiologically?

Kant returns to the conception of conception considerably later in the essay, in a lengthy footnote reflecting on his own tropological unsettling of the spirit's moral primacy. Considering the function of the virgin birth as a Christian response to radical evil, Kant observes that 'to conceive the possibility of a person free from innate propensity to evil by having him born of a virgin mother is an idea of reason accommodating itself to an instinct which is hard to explain, yet which cannot be disowned, and is moral, too' (p. 74). Since the virgin birth does not involve sensual pleasure, argues Kant, it figures the possibility of a generation in which no admixture of finite or sensual determinants operates. To this extent, a natural birth *would* be the 'cause' of evil, in so far as it renders undecidable the determining role of sensual pleasure (that is, of a mundane experience that withstands the totalizing urge of the suprasensual) in the (literal and figural) conception of man. Though Kant seems somewhat embarrassed by the theological quibbles that the 'symbol' of a virgin birth entails – arguing only that 'it suffices for practical purposes to place before us as a pattern this idea taken as a symbol of mankind raising itself above temptation to evil' (p. 75) – he nevertheless enters the game, aware that what is at stake is not so much a point of doctrinal exegesis as the very concept of the concept. The body functions 'as a symbol of mankind' and yet the *physical* processes of conception seem, in fact, to determine the moral law.

Leaving aside the theological and doctrinal assumptions of Kant's arguments, let us point out merely that he assumes the Virgin herself to have been of natural birth and potentially capable, therefore – if birth were the mode of transmission of Original Sin, the foreclosure of the good *in statu nascendi* – of passing on her own sinful nature to her child. Before giving up on the whole debate as a merely 'symbolic' enterprise, Kant provides the following explanation: 'To avoid this conclusion, we should have to adopt the theory that the seed [of evil] *pre-existed* in the parents but that it did not develop on the part of the *female* (for otherwise that conclusion is not avoided) but only on the part of the *male* (not in the *ova* but in the *spermatozoa*), for the male has no share in supernatural pregnancy' (p. 75). In an essay that takes as its premise the moral indifference of the natural world, Kant has moved in a rather bold direction here. Evil will be transmitted only through the spermatozoa, the bad seed. From the assertion in the earlier work that evil 'has no special seed' we have by now arrived at a spermatozoal evil: evil not only *has* a seed, it *is* the seed.

This notion of the bad seed is far from peripheral to Kant's central argument in this essay. If we asserted earlier that the essay marks a break in Kant's conceptualization of evil, the spermatozoon is central to this reconception. The footnoted spermatozoon is of central conceptual and methodological importance in Kant's redefinition of evil in this essay. It is a shift Kant will explain in the following algebraic terms:

> If the good = a, then its diametric opposite is the not-good. This latter is the result either of a mere absence of a basis of goodness, = 0, or of a positive ground of the opposite of good, = –a. In the second case the not-good may also be called positive evil. . . . Now if the moral law in us were not a motivating force of will, the morally good (the agreement of the will with the law) would = a, and the not-good would = 0; the latter, as merely the result of the absence of a moral motivating force, would = a × O. In us, however, the law is a motivating force, = a; hence the absence of agreement of the will with this law (= 0) is possible only as a consequence of a real and contrary determination of the will, *i.e.*, of an *opposition* to the law, = –a, *i.e.*, of an evil will. (p. 18)

In other words, if we are to accept that man is a being determined by the moral law, we must accept evil not as mere absence (since the moral law cannot be absent in man qua man) but as a positive force. Thus evil is no longer good multiplied by zero, but rather a substantial opposition (–a) that in turn creates a moral void, the mere appearance of an *adiaphoron morale.*[19]

The insistence upon the positive (im)moral force of evil leads also to a re-emergence of the body in Kant's philosophy: the function of the will in this newly substantive notion of radical evil goes hand in hand with an equally insistent discourse of the body. The physiology of the bad seed (this embodied evil, or evil as embodiment) will be of further importance to Kant as a model of reading. For example, in the passage where he discusses the function of Christ as redeemer (the passage to which the question of the virgin birth is appended as a footnote), Kant proposes two possible readings of the career of Christ:

[T]he event can be viewed either in its legal or in its physical aspect. When we regard it as a physical event (which strikes the senses) the good principle is the worsted party; having endured many sorrows in this combat, he must give up his life because he stirred up a rebellion against a (powerful) foreign suzerainty. Since, however, the realm in which *principles* (be they good or evil) have might is a realm not of nature but of freedom . . . this death (the last extremity of human suffering) was therefore a manifestation of the good principle, that is, of humanity in its moral perfection, and an example for everyone to follow. (pp. 76–7)

The disposition of 'physical' and 'legal' readings is somewhat complicated here; for the 'physical' defeat is the result only of the legal privilege of 'a (powerful) foreign suzerainty', while the moral victory results from the fact of physical death. Nevertheless, Kant's aversion to what we might call 'physical reading' is palpable. This embroilment of legal and physical modes of reading is typical of the problems Kant faces in establishing an ethic in the face of radical evil. Not only is the physical a- or pre-moral in Kant's ethics, it now becomes *positively* evil. To read Christ's struggle physically is to read it as a defeat. Only legally or juridically can the act of reading restore moral order. Yet because good 'made its appearance in an actual human being', the question of morality can and must be thought through the medium of the body.

Ostensibly, then, Kant argues that the act of being born is not itself the *source* or *cause* of good or evil, but merely the medium of its transmission. But the very physicality of birth renders Kant incapable of separating morality from the realm of the physical, of escaping, in other words, the materiality of his tropological system. He seems to fear that his recourse to physiological imagery will serve to de-moralize human actions by presenting them as merely physical and pre-conscious rather than as the effects of a conscious human will. At the same time, however, an equal and opposite danger persists: namely, that the tropological link of body and spirit will serve not to de-moralize the spirit, but rather to subject the body (physiology) to the dictates of morality, and morality, in turn, to the cycles of the body. Narratives of spiritual de-moralization suggest at the same time a moral discourse surrounding and emanating from the body, a discourse which Nazi eugenics perversely realizes (fusing a philosophical trope with a tradition of nineteenth-century Social Darwinism). This logic of the 'bad seed' can help us reformulate a discourse of evil in the face of the camps.

I am suggesting, then, that there is a strain of eugenicism issuing not only from nineteenth-century bastardizations of Darwinian theory, but from the very ethical categories of the idealist project. If the *Religion* essay exemplifies this idealist strain, however, it also suggests a way of continuing to think 'Auschwitz' – and a project of physical annihilation – 'this side of good and evil'. It offers both a moral and an experiential framework for the understanding of camp life and the accounts that life fosters. We cannot simply regress beyond 'Auschwitz' to a speculative discourse that would resist the de-generation of idealist thought. In arguing for the unrepresentability of 'Auschwitz', theory has failed to move beyond Kant's earlier privative notions of evil. The following reframing, taken from Michalson, whose exposition of Kant is otherwise so useful, is paradigmatic in this regard:

> In its starkest forms, moral evil is a kind of void in our experience, an absence of meaning that leaves us unable to configure our contact with the external world in narrative form. The revelation of Nazi death camps at first produced numbness more than an articulate outrage, and a sustained Jewish response to the camps did not really take shape until well into the 1960s. Evidently, the experience of evil in such a degree points us not only in the direction of religious skepticism, but toward something utterly inexplicable in ourselves. It is not by accident that the word 'monster' is often used following the capture of a true evil-doer, such as a former concentration camp guard. Our inability to explain finally signals the inscrutability of human behavior itself and, especially, of our deepest motivations; moral evil radicalizes the difficulty already latent in the question, 'Why does anybody do anything?' (pp. 14–15)[20]

If it is often observed that 'Auschwitz' demands a break from 'Enlightenment' notions of morality, it is nevertheless true that post-'Auschwitz' philosophy has had great difficulty making that break. Rarely is the *Religion* essay – in which Kant posits radical evil as a positive force – invoked to frame the reconsideration of evil, which remains a void in these presentations. The privative notion of evil in turn creates a void of meaning, a representational 'numbness'; the lack of a representation is felt as the lack of any bodily sensation of 'Auschwitz'. That this absence should take the form of a bodily sensation – numbness, or sensation of the lack of sensation – is not insignificant: for the rhetoric of the body reasserts itself precisely where it is denied. The absence of the body is figured paradoxically as an absence (of sensation) *in* the body: the body marks its own absence. Upon this numbness (philosophical and physiological) turns the question of a radical and positive evil: is numbness a sensation or a lack of sensation – or the sensation of sensation's lack?

What we must seek to understand here is the status of good and evil in a radical situation where *specific* physical sensations, and bodily fluids, dry up. To reconfigure the philosophical question in the physiology of the camps: what happens to a positive spermatozoal evil in the neutering conditions of the concentration camp? When humans are robbed at the physiological level of the ability to conceive, when an 'inconceivable' crime is itself embodied in the physiology of the victim, what moral ground remains? The foreclosure of a conceptual and reproductive economy – exterminating the physiological seed – seems to take at a 'literal' level (and we shall deal with this term later) the idea of a 'bad seed'. From Kant to the camps, we encounter 'the failure of symbolism *as symbolism*'. What happens when the precarious rhetorical structure of Kant's essay – in which the natural will represents the moral, yet through the very act of representation risks undermining the purity of moral categories – collapses; when the merely rhetorical identification of body and soul has been realized? What social and moral economy remains where women cease to menstruate, while men, robbed of sexual desire, might nevertheless seek homosexual release as a 'hygienic' measure? What hygiene, or eugenics, is implied in this deployment of the (bad) seed?

In his accounts of camp life in *The Drowned and the Saved*, Primo Levi is quite explicit and insistent concerning the physiological impact of the camps. For example, he draws a distinction between the concentration camp inmates and the regular prisoners of war that lived alongside them:

> The mental mechanisms of the *Häftlinge* were different from ours; curiously, and in parallel, different also were their physiology and pathology. In the Lager colds and influenza were unknown, but one died, at times, suddenly, from illnesses that the doctors never had an opportunity to study. Gastric ulcers and mental illnesses were healed (or became asymptomatic), but everyone suffered from an unceasing discomfort that polluted sleep and was nameless.[21]

Levi, like Arendt, understands the camps not only as the *means* utilized within a eugenic and genocidal physiology, but as themselves the realization of that project as a biosocial experiment: for him 'the Lager was pre-eminently a gigantic biological and social experiment' (p. 87). Nazism succeeds not simply by eradicating a life it finds intolerable, but by reducing that life to the concept it already entertains of it: in other words, by reducing the Jews to a certain regime of *living*. 'For us,' Levi writes, 'the Lager is not a punishment; for us, no end is foreseen and the Lager is nothing but a manner of living assigned to us, without limits of time, in the bosom of the Germanic social organism' (pp. 82–3). The camps reduce their victims to the level of the parasite they were always supposed to have been within the 'Germanic social organism'. To this extent, the reduction of the inmate to the level of vermin paradoxically renders them the mimetic subjects of their putative crimes: 'Auschwitz' produces subjects as it eradicates them. It is notable, also, that Levi contrasts this physiologically parasitic existence with the absence of a 'punishment', or of any *legal* discourse in which the experience would be thinkable as punishment. We are reduced – as the inmate was reduced – to that level of physical reading outlined and resisted by Kant.

But if we are considering here the reduction of life to a concept and the emergence of a physiological morality, how are we to treat the process of reproduction and conception that is at the root of that concept of life? The trope – or is it a trope? – of conception through which eugenics conflates moral and material discourses obliges us, as Levi points out, to examine the question of life and its reproduction in the camps, rather than subordinate that life to the consideration of death. If, as Adorno insists in *Negative Dialectics*, we are to return in an antimetaphysical gesture to the level of the body, we cannot think that body (as Adorno himself tends to) simply as cadaver. For the body as cadaver is already the body whose suffering has been conceptualized at the cost of the body itself: it is doubly dead.

Though Levi writes very little on the specific question of birth, reproduction and sexuality, perhaps the most important physiological change in the camps has elsewhere been reported as follows:

> One of the striking things about the concentration-camp experience – and there is enormous evidence on this point – is that under conditions of privation and horror the need for sex disappears. It simply is not there, neither in feeling, nor in fantasy, neither the desire nor the drive. As one survivor says, 'Many of us young men ceased to have any sexual feelings whatever; Karel and I, during all the time we were in Treblinka and for a long time afterwards, were men in name only'. Or, as another puts it, 'After two or three weeks of the regime at Maidanek, sex problems disappeared. Women lost their periods; men lost their urge'. In Buchenwald, according to the report of a doctor imprisoned there, 'one hundred percent of the female prisoners ceased to menstruate at the very beginning of their term of captivity; the function did not reappear until months after the liberation'.[22]

What is being described is the fulfilment, *avant la lettre*, of the Nazi project of genocide: the superimposition of death on life in the condition of sterility. To this extent, the camps do not only put life to death, but also bring death to life. If, as Lyotard insists, 'Auschwitz' marks the end of 'beautiful death', it seems to mark also the impossibility of any (re)birth. In Kant's terms, 'this evil is *radical* because it corrupts the ground of all maxims'.

This, it would appear, is the function of the concept in thinking 'Auschwitz' – if life is put to death, death itself is brought to life as that which allows us to 'conceive'. Whereas Nancy wrote of a contraceptive evil, foreclosing any conception of the good *in statu nascendi*, here we have an evil that gives birth to a death. But can there be a system of sexuality that escapes this eugenic surveillance, a system that is not organized around the function of (racial) reproduction and thus facilitates exchanges that do not bring death to life in this way? We find an answer in another account that considers specifically the treatment of homosexuals in the camps in the light of the drying up of spermatozoa. 'Even the stronger prisoners came to loathe their emaciated bodies, infected with parasites and covered with dirt. For the majority of prisoners homosexual activity was, at best, tolerated as "locational sex", a hygienic relief measure – if it did not put others at a disadvantage.'[23] While both accounts of camp life just cited attest to the widespread physiological degradation, there is also a tension between them. One talks of a complete suppression of the sexual instinct, while the other speaks of the persistence of that instinct among the men.[24] It is this new 'hygienic' discourse, itself unsettlingly reminiscent of the eugenic hygiene in whose name the camps were originally founded, that I would like to foreground. Though ostensibly detailing the difficulties of homosexual prisoners in the camps, the second writer nevertheless attests to what I might term the 'insistence of the seed' as a principle of economy. In other words, even though urge and desire have ceased to operate within the subject, the physiological economy continues: semen still flows. This flow, in the absence of female menstruation, is, however, no longer a generative (conceptual) one, but rather an economy of excess, in which the men's semen is 'hygienically' disposed of in homosexual relations. Homosexuality in the camp serves to recirculate the 'bad seed' as the 'hygienic' avoidance of a conception.

From the heteroconceptual economy of Kant we seem to have arrived at a homoeconomy in which physiological depletion nevertheless yields to hygiene, to economy, in the production and redistribution of the bad seed. If the virgin birth served as a moral parable of generation and conception without the spermatozoa of (physical) evil, 'Auschwitz' reverses the Christian paradigm 'symbolically' explicated by Kant. Now there is only seed – and no economy of conception that might take it up. But what does it mean to speak of homosexuality in the camps as hygiene? Is this recirculation of seed the moment of excess in which man's predisposition to community and intercourse with other men becomes 'immoral', is it to be thought as a resistance to the possibility of spermatozoal evil, as an economy of conception?[25] I suggest that this persistence of the seed must be read as a *physiological* rejection of the conceptualizations of the body effected in idealist tradition: as the persistence of the physical, material *signifier*.

For, as recounted by Primo Levi in *The Drowned and the Saved*, the very defining experience of the concentration camp seems to have been less an absence or void of significance than a proliferation. His accounts of the camp experience attest not only to a search for meaning in an apparently meaningless and horrifyingly illogical existence, but also to the persistence of such a meaning in what he will (perhaps not altogether accurately) call a 'symbolic' form: 'We had an incorrigible tendency', he writes, 'to see a symbol and a sign in every event' (p. 77). That which makes possible the retention of a moral judgement 'this side of good and evil' is a tendency – 'incorrigible', no doubt – to seek and find significance.[26] Levi consistently argues that 'no human experience is without meaning or unworthy of analysis, and that fundamental values, even if they are not positive, can be deduced from this particular world which we are describing' (p. 87).

It would be easy to read Levi's assertion as simple humanism; and such a reading would not be entirely wrongheaded, since Levi's point of departure is, indeed, an insistence on the meaning-constitutive nature of all human experience. We can, however, only understand this incorrigible persistence of meaning by examining a second metaphoric strain with which it is consistently linked in his discourse. For this 'incorrigible tendency' mediates the relation of the body and its flows and secretions to the possibility of communication in the camps. It emanates, as I hope to show, from the body rather than from a spirit of humanism. But what sense does it make to offer definitions of humanity in a situation where even the physiological make-up of man will be changed? Despite insisting on the physiological nature of the political experiment of the camps, Levi (not unlike Kant) consistently reverts to physiological definitions of human essence, in which the possibility of language is always already encoded. For example, in *The Drowned and The Saved* he insists:

> Except for cases of pathological incapacity, one can and must communicate, and thereby contribute in a useful and easy way to the peace of others and oneself, because silence, the absence of signals, is itself a signal, but an ambiguous one, and ambiguity generates anxiety and suspicion. To say that it is impossible to communicate is false; one always can. To refuse to communicate is a failing; we are biologically and socially predisposed to communication, and in particular to its highly evolved and noble form, which is language. (p. 93)

Levi's analysis operates within the same paradoxical structure that characterized Kant's essay. A refusal to communicate is immoral or, at the very least, a failing. In other words, Levi redisposes freedom and nature in the same way Kant does – desirous, on the one hand, of retaining their opposition, but insisting, ultimately, on their affinity. The moral is no longer a willed and conscious triumph over nature, but rather an attendance *to* nature, to the physio-logical aspect of human existence. Levi's apparent 'humanism' retreats to the level of the body, where communication – let us call it intercourse – becomes inevitable. The body speaks its own language.

What others have described as the stemming of reproductive flows – that is, the flows of semen and menstrual blood – Levi has described as the drying up of language in *The Drowned and the Saved*: 'If you are fortunate enough to have next to you someone with whom you have a language in common, good for you, you'll be able to exchange your impressions, seek counsel, let off steam, confide in him; if you don't find anyone, your tongue dries up in a few days, and your thought with it' (p. 93). The 'drying up' of thought is related directly to a drying up of language figured in physiological terms. This stemming of flows and of language is overcome, however, at vital points in Levi's descriptions of camp life, and I wish to consider these instances now as events that go beyond moral, linguistic and bodily 'hygiene'.

The displacement from sperm to saliva in the moral consideration of language leads Levi to a final, minimal parable of the inextirpability of the linguistic impulse as a physio-logical given: 'To this day', Levi writes, 'I remember how one pronounced in Polish not my registration number but that of the prisoner who preceded me on the roster of a certain hut. . . . In fact, that "stergishi steri" functioned like the bell that conditioned Pavlov's dogs: it stimulated an immediate secretion of saliva' (*DS*, p. 94). What are we to make of Levi's secretions? What this passage seems to enact is precisely that collapse, posited earlier, of 'symbolism *as symbolism*' through the de-differentiation of body and language, language and identity. Particularly interesting in this passage, however, is the way in which the concept – or, minimally, the name – of the self-identical subject has become uncoupled from the physio-logy of that subject.[27] Levi does not recall his own name or number, nor does his own name activate those vital gastric juices that mark the body's simple 'will' to exist. It is the name of the 'other', the name of another *man*, that calls forth these secretions. The physiological experimentation of the camps, then, seems to effect a shift in the nature of the subject. It is no longer a matter of the autonomous subject, but a subject whose dependence on the body (and language's effects on the body) simultaneously activates a visceral desire for and at the name of *another* (man). From the outset, Levi has linked the collapse of the autonomous subject – the theme of the parable of 'stergishi steri' – to the question of 'a world inhabited by civilized Cartesian phantoms, by sincere male and bloodless female friendships' (*DS*, p. 13). If, however, the collapse of these 'Cartesian phantoms' leads also to a break with such sterile, nonphysical relationships, it will *not* lead to a renewed flow of blood enabling conception between man and woman, but to a newly physicalized relation between *men* through the medium of language, through the name of the other. That this issue becomes, ultimately, a question of repro-duction for Levi should be apparent from the conclusion to his reflection on the flow of language. Nazism, ultimately, will have been an attempt (impossible, of course) to silence the body; and Levi implicitly rejoins the school of 'totalitarianism theorists' when he expands his reflection into a political judgement: '[I]n countries and epochs in which communication is impeded, soon all other liberties wither; discussion dies by inanation, ignorance of the opinion of others becomes rampant, imposed opinions triumph. The well-known example of this is the crazy genetics preached in the USSR by Lysenko, which in the absence of discussion (his opponents were exiled to Siberia) compromised the harvests for twenty years' (*DS*, p. 103). The broader political framework of totalitarianism is encapsulated in a political 'genetics'. What Nazism threatens, and what Levi seeks to reinstate, is the possibility of a reproduction, of a *conception*. What it cannot extinguish is a language of ejaculation. Lysenko's experiments are an experiment with the *seed*, and are evil and pernicious in the way that all such privileging of the seed must be post-Kant. Even if Levi can smile at the bloodless Cartesianism of his youth, he necessarily rejoins a philosophy of consciousness in so far as that philosophy depends on a conception of conception. Heterosexual relations are what the camps threaten (as the locus of a physical and cultural reproduction such relations must, of course, form the target of a genocidal project) and what Levi seeks to reinstate. Homosexuality, meanwhile, constitutes a physical urge that does not attain the level of conceptuality/conception and cannot, therefore, be contra-ceived.

Notable in Levi's formulations is the Kantian dissociation of a language of rights, a legal reading, and a language of the body, a physical reading. But what forms, what *secretive* forms, will this language take? Because they do not ground a conception, it is the homoseminal impulses that remain 'incorrigible'. Even where communicative language breaks down, Levi posits the persistence of an ejaculatory language. Reflecting further on the essentiality of language to man, Levi recalls 'imprecations, curses, or small everyday often repeated sentences' that were 'the fruit of a useless and unconscious effort to carve a meaning or sense out of the senseless. They were also the mental equivalent of our bodily need for nourishment' (*DS*, pp. 94–5). Such linguistic ejaculations seem, on the surface, to insist upon the inevitability of linguistic interaction; they reinstate a *bodily* language rather than a philosophy of consciousness. This rather unhygienic ejaculation is all that remains of Levi's faith in language.[28]

The question remains, then, whether this ejaculatory language permits of a discourse, or (re)produces any narrative of truth about the camps: whether, in other words, it admits of a conception. This minimal language, coeval with the insistence of the seed, seems necessarily to resist an economy of meaning-production, to the extent that any attempt to reflect on 'Auschwitz' seems inappropriate. Consequently, the experience of evil in the camps has produced no new concept of evil. Arendt, for example – perhaps the most influential

philosopher to reflect on the fate of philosophy post-'Auschwitz' – offers little
in the way of an advance on existing (let us call them early Kantian) notions of
evil. She writes in *The Origins of Totalitarianism*:

> It is the appearance of some radical evil, previously unknown to us, that puts an end to
> the notion of developments and transformations of qualities. Here, there are neither
> political nor historical nor simply moral standards but, at most, the realization that
> something seems to be involved in modern politics that actually should never be
> involved in politics as we used to understand it, namely, all or nothing – all, and that is
> an undetermined infinity of forms of human living-together, or nothing, for a victory of
> the concentration-camp system would mean the same inexorable doom for human
> beings as the use of the hydrogen bomb would mean the doom of the human race.
> (p. 443)

In this passage, Arendt identifies radical evil with a certain mutation in the
appearance of history; the end of historical 'developments and transformation'.
Just what sort of history is it, then, that meets its end in totalitarianism? With the
historical shift comes a shift in the terms of the political, which now becomes a
language game of 'all or nothing'. Politics seems to lose its provisionality and to
essentialize itself through Nazism. Thus, radical evil would consist in the belief
that politics is itself a radical discourse, capable of treating root problems.
Radical evil in this political context would be (1) the very *possibility* of an
appearance of evil; and (2) its appearance within the contingency of a political
discourse, as something 'absolutely relative'. With regard to the first point, the
privative notion of evil we have derived from Kant's earlier texts – and that
Eichmann cites so succinctly – would foreclose the possibility of evil's *appearance*,
for evil would have been that which prevents the appearance of good. Once evil
no longer prevents appearance, but instead appears, the possibility of the moral
indifference of appearance as a criterion and characteristic of truth itself
is raised. With regard to fascism, then, we are faced with a methodological
dilemma. If fascism itself functions as the 'appearance' of evil, and if the modus
operandi of this evil is to hypostatize the possibility of evil's appearing, we risk
replicating a fascistic discourse; fascism cannot be accorded the status of the
'appearance of evil' because such a notion is itself intrinsically fascistic when
proposed within a political discourse (for example, the Jews as the 'appearance'
of evil). Radical politics seems inevitably to lead to a politics of eradication,
whether that eradication takes the form of a physical destruction or a discursive
deconstruction.

This would mean that while *Religion within the Limits of Reason Alone* provides a
model for the thinking of 'Auschwitz', it does not permit of a conception. If,
as Adorno and others point out, it is incumbent on philosophy to rethink itself

so that 'Auschwitz' may not reoccur, it is nevertheless necessary to acknowledge that 'Auschwitz' did, in fact, happen, and that we still inhabit the episteme it inaugurated. We cannot refer to what I have termed the early Kantian moral framework for an assessment of 'Auschwitz'. Thus, for example, the passage just cited from Arendt is significant for its differentiation (and paralleling) of the camps and the bomb. The bomb threatens the 'human race', while the camps threaten 'human beings'. But what status can be accorded the distinction between 'race' and 'being' Arendt wants to maintain, given the genocidal project that has sought to eradicate it? Surely 'Auschwitz' must be the place where race and being can no longer be distinguished, however discomforting this may be. If it is imperative that we reject any such Nazi ethical construction, it is no less imperative that we recognize what that construction itself demonstrated about the possibility of evil. If we are to reject Nazism, it cannot be from the position of an ethics that the very *appearance* of Nazism has vitiated. We can understand and condemn it only from the perspective of a radical rather than a privative notion of evil, even if, and this is the risk, it was Nazism itself that enacted historically that ethical shift.

Where, then, are we to place the death camps between two traditions of thinking about evil: between a tradition in which the seed is the spermatozoa of evil, and one in which conception is the model of the production of the good? Is evil contraceptive or reproductive, privative or substantive? A traditional language of conception seems to have entered easily into the vocabulary of those, such as Arendt, who have sought to understand Nazism. She refers specifically in works such as *The Human Condition* to natality – a physical embeddedness in the world – as the essence of the human condition, thereby acknowledging (in accordance with Adorno's injunction) the insistence of the body in the face of any totalitarian sublation. Whereas for Kant it was the physicality and sensuality of birth that potentially rendered contingent the purity of the virgin birth, for Arendt the opposite is now true. Only natality guarantees the ontico-logical embeddedness of man in the world. It is no longer worldliness, but transcendence that is to be resisted.[29] Arendt will explicate her reversal of Kant's model in terms that make clear, however, that the reversal is in no sense an inversion in the sexual sense – it is grounded in a heterosexual economy of (re)production.[30] 'Natality', and the act of generative conception it implies, she writes, 'is intrinsic to the human condition', as a 'condition of action' that is 'implicit even in Genesis ("Male and female created He *them*") if we understand that this story of man's creation is distinguished in principle from the one according to which God originally created Man (*Adam*). "Him" and not "them," so that the multitude of human beings becomes the result of multiplication. . . . Moreover, since action is the political activity par excellence, natality, and not mortality, may be the central category of political, as distinguished from meta-physical thought.'[31] To take this natality as the definitive 'human condition' is to accept, of course, a (hetero)sexual economy, a physio-logy of flows of blood and semen. Birth marks man's embeddedness in a nature that no moral discourse can eradicate: and again, natality is tied to conception in a broader sense – as Genesis and origin. The very discourse of the political seems to depend, for Arendt, on the coupling of a heterosexual 'them'. Like Adorno, Arendt suggests the necessity of an ethical shift – post-'Auschwitz' – in the direction of the body, but a living body rather than Adorno's putrefying cadavers. In the light of that nonconceptual, inconceivable ejaculatory language that speaks to us from the camps, however, we must go a step further, freeing the physical not only from the closure of death, but also from the truth-producing economy of a 'conceptual' logic.[32] Thus, 'Auschwitz' would remain for us a seminal experience in a radical, physiological sense, obliging us to acknowledge the body not in any *conception* of the camps, but in those ejaculations of language that no terror could eradicate. What 'remains' is to trace the physio-logy of the 'bad seed'.

Notes

1. Jean-François Lyotard, *The Differend: Phrases in Dispute*, trans. Georges Van den Abbeele (Minneapolis, Minn.: University of Minnesota Press 1988)§ 1.

2. I use the term 'Auschwitz' throughout this paper in the sense elaborated in Lyotard's *Differend*. I do not, however, enter into the terms of Lyotard's debate with Adorno's usage of 'After Auschwitz' in *Negative Dialectics*, as I have dealt with this question elsewhere (see 'Coitus Interruptus: Moravia and the Deaths of History', in *Postmodern Apocalypse*, ed. R. Dellamora (Philadelphia: University of Pennsylvania Press 1995). The question framing both this paper and the sense of unrepresentability it seeks to unsettle is posed by Lyotard as follows: 'How can "Auschwitz," something thought from the outside, a referent placed only "near itself" *[an sich] [auprès de soi]* "for us" *[für uns]*, be interiorized, suppressed as an unmediated position, and show itself to itself, know itself, in the identity (be it ephemeral) of a for-itself *[für sich] [pour soi]*?' (§153: p. 89). In a sense, I am seeking – by looking at the camps as a regimen of life, rather than as an instrumentalization of death – to address Lyotard's further question, if it is 'possible that some kind of phrase, in accordance with some other logic, takes place "after" the antonym "Auschwitz" and which would not be its speculative result' (§153; p. 89). I place what I will call 'conceptual logic' in the position of Lyotard's 'speculative' in order to question the implication of a discursive production of 'results' in a certain sexual economy of reproduction and truth. For Adorno's position, see *Negative Dialectics*, trans. E.B. Ashton (New York: Continuum 1987).

3. Lyotard works with a Hegelian conception of experience as the '"dialectical process which consciousness executes on itself". In the sphere that belongs to it, experience supposes the speculative element, the "life of the mind" as a life which "endures death and in death maintains its being"' (§153).

4. Immanuel Kant, *Religion within the Limits of Reason Alone*, trans. Theodore M. Greene and Hoyt H. Hudson (Chicago: Opencourt 1934).

5. Citing a survivor who argued 'that if Beckett had been in Auschwitz he would be writing differently, more positively, with the front-line creed of the escapee', Adorno

concedes that 'the escapee is right in a fashion other than he thinks. Beckett, and whoever else remained in control of himself, would have been broken in Auschwitz and probably forced to confess that front-line creed which the escapee clothed in the words 'Trying to give men courage' (Adorno, *Negative Dialectics*, p. 367).

6. Hannah Arendt, *The Origins of Totalitarianism* (George Allen and Unwin: London 1963), p. 441.
7. Primo Levi, *Survival in Auschwitz: The Nazi Assault on Humanity*, trans. Stuart Woolf (New York: Collier 1993), p. 13.
8. Terrence Des Pres, *The Survivor: An Anatomy of Life in the Death Camps* (New York: Oxford University Press 1976), p. 65.
9. Quoted in Karl Barth, *Protestant Thought from Rousseau to Ritschl*, trans. Brian Cozens (New York: Simon and Schuster 1969), p. 178.
10. Jean-Luc Nancy, *The Experience of Freedom*, trans. Bridget Macdonald (Stanford, Calif.: Stanford University Press 1993), p. 125.
11. Obviously the work on Kant's conception of evil is voluminous. But for a detailed consideration of the shifts I trace only in outline here, see Olivier Reboul, *Kant et le problème du mal* (Montréal: Presses de l'Université de Montréal 1971); Ann Loades, *Kant and Job's Comforters* (Newcastle upon Tyne: Avero Publications 1985); Emil Fackenheim, 'Kant and Radical Evil', *University of Toronto Quarterly*, vol. 23, 1954, pp. 339–53; James Collins, *The Emergence of Philosophy of Religion* (New Haven, Conn. and London: Yale University Press 1967). Particularly helpful, however, is Gordon E. Michalson, Jr. *Fallen Freedom: Kant on Radical Evil and Moral Regeneration* (Cambridge: Cambridge University Press 1990).
12. Immanuel Kant, *Foundations for the Metaphysics of Morals*, trans. Lewis White Beck (New York: Bobbs-Merrill 1959). See, for example, the notes to pages 17 and 38.
13. In *Act and Idea in the Nazi Genocide* (Chicago: University of Chicago Press 1990), Berel Lang has traced this notion of evil, which renders 'Auschwitz' unimaginable, back to Plato, schematizing 'the concise premise of the ethical theory as a whole – that it is impossible to do evil when the knowledge is fully present that the contemplated act *is* evil' (p. 33).
14. Lang makes this point: 'it should also be possible to show that the principle from which this conclusion of exculpation is drawn, whether in its general, Platonic conception, or more specifically in relation to the Nazi genocide, may be mistaken; that is, that evil *can* be done knowingly, and, more specifically, that the Nazis were aware of the nature of the wrongs they were doing' (pp. 35–6). His concern seems to be more the reconstruction of a subject of evil: a calculating, evil Nazi subject. This is less my concern here: I am more interested in tracing the impact of a substantive notion of evil on the object of study – evil itself.
15. Hannah Arendt, *Eichmann in Jerusalem: A Report on the Banality of Evil* (New York: Viking 1963), p. 136.
16. Alexander Mitscherlich and Fred Mielke, eds, *Doctors of Infamy: The Story of the Nazi Medical Crimes*, trans. Heinz Norden (New York: Henry Schuman [1948] 1978), pp. 146–7.
17. Likewise, another defendant, Dr Hans Eiser, 'is reported to have said that if he was found guilty the court "should not confine me to prison, but rather to an insane asylum"' (Mitscherlich and Mielke, *Doctors of Infamy*, p. 147). In other words, like Eichmann, Eiser cannot present himself as the subject of his own evil, for evil would be the foreclosure of his subjectivity.
18. Michalson, *Fallen Freedom*, p. 35. Michalson quotes from Kant's *Lectures on Philosophical Theology*, trans. Allen W. Wood and Gertrude M. Clark (Ithaca, N.Y. and London: Cornell University Press 1978), p. 117.
19. Clearly Kant's tone in treating the 'symbolic' construct of the virgin birth is somewhat embarrassed. However, he does acknowledge the motivation for such symbolic constructs in 'an instinct which is hard to explain, yet which cannot be disowned, and is moral too' (p. 74). Kant's reasoning here involves him in a conceptual circularity,

however, regarding the function of 'instinct'. For in a footnote on terminology – in which he differentiates between 'propensity', 'inclination', 'instinct' and 'passion' – Kant writes of the '*instinct*, which is a felt want to do or enjoy something of which one as yet has no conception (such as the constructive impulse in animals, or the sexual impulse)' (n. 24). If sexual desire is paradigmatic for the instinct 'which is hard to explain, yet which cannot be disowned, and is moral, too' (p. 74), and to which the parable of the virgin birth responds, then the possibility raises itself that the sexual urge, as instinct, provides a model for and impetus toward the construction of this symbolic moral parable of the virgin birth.

20. Michalson, *Fallen Freedom*, pp. 14–15.
21. Primo Levi, *The Drowned and the Saved* (*DS*), trans. Raymond Rosenthal (New York: Summit 1988), p. 84.
22. Des Pres, *The Survivor*, p. 185.
23. Richard Plant, *The Pink Triangle: The Nazi War against Homosexuals* (New York: Henry Holt 1986), p. 171.
24. I am aware, of course, of the masculine coding of this persistence of the seed in hygienic homosexuality. The persistence of feminine flows and their grounding of economies other than that of reproduction would necessarily also give rise to a rethinking of camp life that I do not even begin to undertake here. Perhaps a model for such thought is indicated in the materially grounded analysis to be found in Gayatri Chakravorty Spivak, *In Other Worlds: Essays in Cultural Politics* (New York: Methuen 1987).
25. One might begin to evaluate the flow of the seed from the perspective of Levi's analysis of the camp black market, another illicit economy. In *Survival in Auschwitz*, Levi observes that 'every exchange . . . is explicitly forbidden' (p. 78). The intercourse of hygienic emissions – like 'every exchange' – proves for Levi the necessary inter-relatedness of men, rather than the need to fulfil a vestigially idiotic desire.
26. Herded onto the train, the Italian Jews of *Survival in Auschwitz* learn of their destination 'with relief. Auschwitz: a name without significance for us at that time, but it at least implied some place on this earth' (p. 17). The qualifier 'at that time' perhaps suggests the commencement of a *Bildungsroman*, a process of learning as a consequence of which Auschwitz will – at some other time in the future – acquire a significance for the protagonist. In fact, this is not the trajectory of the narrative.
27. It is important to stress that the physiology of the camps does not consist in a simple shrinkage of the experience of identity to the minimal immanence of the body. As we have seen in Levi's salivation, there is a crucial rupture effected between the desire for self-preservation and the sense of identity. It is the name of the *other* that activates the desire for self-preservation. In fact, Levi gives an even clearer example of this dissociation in the story of Ziegler, who – observing that 'a double ration will be given to those selected' for extermination the next day – 'holds out his bowl, collects his normal ration and then waits there expectantly'. The point is, Ziegler was *not* among those selected; he is to survive, and is therefore not 'entitled' to extra rations. But 'Ziegler returns and humbly persists. He was on the left [among the condemned], everybody saw it, let the *Blockältester* check the cards; he has the right to a double ration' (*Survival in Auschwitz*, p. 29). The very act that is driven by the body's desire to exist – the demand for food – brings about the death of that which it was to preserve. By seeking to save himself, Ziegler must condemn himself, place himself in the ranks of those who are to die. The calculus of survival is robbed of its ultimate ground – survival itself. The act that seeks to ensure survival jeopardizes it, the impulses of the body in fact betray the subject rather than present it. Identity and body are not identified, but dis-identified. To *identify* the body with identity is, in fact, to subjugate the body *to* identity. This is not what happens in any of those examples Levi offers. This too, I would argue, is the failing of a post-'Auschwitz' theory that attends to the body only in its suffering and lack; a theory that might paradoxically identify the body with the nonidentical.

28. John Kekes likewise links Kant with a sophisticated strain of what he calls 'choice morality', behind whose assumptions lie 'the metaphor that morality is like language. All normal human beings are supposed to acquire it and become variously adept at following its rules, so immorality must be interpreted, the metaphor suggests, as deficiency in learning or using a skill'. John Kekes, *Facing Evil* (Princeton, N.J.: Princeton University Press 1990), p. 124.

29. Rainer Schürman has traced in broad terms the transformation of the notion of evil in 'Conditions of Evil', trans. Ian Janssen, in *Deconstruction and the Possibility of Justice*, Drucilla Cornell, Michel Rosenfeld and David Gray Carlson, eds (New York: Routledge 1992), pp. 387–403.

30. Richard Dellamora has elaborated in some detail on the heterosexual 'conceptual' structure of a philosophic tradition that is 'framed within binary oppositions of male and female, heterosexual and homosexual, which lend it the authority of the compulsory heterosexuality that it also enforces'; *Apocalyptic Overtures: Sexual Politics and the Sense of an Ending* (New Brunswick, N.J.: Rutgers University Press 1994), pp. 17–18. He also elucidates what I mean here in utilizing two different regimes of 'inversion': 'Apocalyptic "inversion" as it usually occurs within philosophy is an aspect of logocentrism. Although it has referents both in love-hate between male rivals and in the erotic scenes of instruction in which philosophy originates and in which it continues to be instilled, this particular kind of inversion exists within the terms of hegemonic sexuality. As such, it is by no means the same inversion as that which is subjected to scrutiny by late nineteenth-century sexologists. Rather, the "truths" that this inversion establishes are opposed to what sexologists refer to as "sexual inversion" which they define as the negation of the normal rules of sex and gender' (p. 20). I am proposing that 'Auschwitz' likewise presses upon us an inversion that cannot – unlike that proposed by Arendt – reinstate either a normative heterosexual economy of discursive truth-production, nor the sexual dyad of male and female that produces it. I propose that we take seriously in our philosophizing the bodily secretions at the name of the other and the ejaculatory language that escapes from the terror of the camps.

31. Hannah Arendt, *The Human Condition* (Chicago: University of Chicago Press 1958), pp. 8–9.

32. The logic I have in mind with this formulation is that identified by Lyotard in *The Differend* as the logic of the result (*resultat*). See Lyotard, *The Differend*, pp. 86–106.

5 KANT WITH DON JUAN AND SADE

ALENKA ZUPANČIČ

Speaking about Zeno's famous paradox of Achilles and the tortoise, Lacan remarked: 'To the extent that a number has a limit, it is infinite. Clearly, Achilles can only overtake the tortoise, he cannot catch up with her. He rejoins her only in infinity.'[1] This remark enables us to discern 'two faces of Achilles', the 'Sadian' and the 'Don Juanian' face. One could say that these two faces articulate the diapason of the sexual (non)relationship, its fundamental either/or: either it is always still too soon or always already too late; either we fail to come close enough to the object of our desire or we go beyond it.

The Sadian motion implies that we approach the whole of the object of desire ad infinitum. With each step we come closer to it, yet we never really cover the whole distance. Therefore, as Sade puts it in his famous statement, we (always) have to make one more effort. This is why the Sadian paradigm strikes us as ultimately boring: the story progresses exceedingly slowly, 'little by little', it is overloaded with all kinds of 'technical details' and digressions. It appears that the heroes of these stories have 'all the time in the world' and that they are postponing the pleasure that gives them the greatest pleasure. This paradigm also governs what we call the *erotic*. On the other hand, there is the Don Juanian motion, which is best described as hasty. Here, each time we approach the object of desire, we start off too quickly and overtake it with the first step. So we have to start again and again. If the Sadian paradigm is monotonous (yet attracts us with its suspense), the Don Juanian is repetitive (yet full of adventure). The difference between the two approaches can also be formulated in terms of 'part by part' versus 'one by one'. In the first case, we enjoy the body of the other part by part, but when we want to 'put the pieces together', they never make a *whole*, a One. In the second case, we start with One and enjoy them 'one by one', yet we can never say that we have enjoyed them *all.* 'She', each *one* of them, is essentially *One-less-than.* According to Lacan: 'This is why, in every relation between man and woman – and it is woman who is at stake here – she has to be viewed from the angle of One-less-than (*Une-en-moins*). I have already pointed this out to you in connection with Don Juan.'[2] It is probably no coincidence that both attempts (trying to rejoin the Other 'part by part' or 'one by one'), when undertaken seriously, enter the territory of radical evil.

The Stone Feast of the 'Eternal Feminine'

What makes Don Juan – we will focus essentially on one of the most sophisticated versions of the myth, Molière's play – a figure of radical evil is not his debauched life, his sinning. Don Juan's position is not governed by the logic of transgression and negation (opposition, rebelliousness and dispute). Don Juan's only *no* is the *no* he delivers to repentance and grace, which are offered to him but which he refuses. His position is not, as some interpretations suggest, that of an enlightened atheist to whom nothing is sacred. As Camille Dumoulié rightly remarked, an atheist demands nothing but to believe, if only we can present him/her with some 'real proofs'.[3] An atheist will always 'grab' firmly the first 'material' evidence of divine existence and thus become an enthusiastic believer. Yet this is not what Don Juan does. Heaven literally bombards him with all kinds of 'substantial evidence' confirming God's existence (a statue that moves and talks, the apparition of a woman who changes her form and becomes Time), evidence that would convince even the most hardened atheist, but in the face of which Don Juan remains unshakable. One is thus compelled to ask if there is not a misunderstanding involved in the 'communication' between Heaven and Don Juan. Don Juan never says that he doubts the existence of God. What he does say is that 'all he believes in is that two and two make four and two fours are eight'. This famous statement is usually perceived as the clearest expression of his atheism and his cynical attitude. Yet, in the Cartesian universe – which is undoubtedly also Don Juan's universe – to say that we believe that two and two make four is as good as saying that we believe in the existence of God. Only a truthful God can guarantee that this 'mathematical truth' is eternal and unchangeable. We also know that it is essential to Don Juan that it stays unchangeable, for he (as Don Giovanni) has quite a calculation to make: 640 in Italy + 231 in Germany + 100 in France + 91 in Turkey + 1003 in Spain. Don Juan's attitude could best be described as follows: 'I quite believe (or even, I know perfectly well) that God exists – but so what?' This is what makes his position so scandalous, intolerable, unthinkable and radically evil. All the parties in the play (including Heaven, which is undoubtedly one of the dramatis personae and intervenes directly in events) are persuaded that Don Juan acts as he does because he does not believe (or know) that the Judge really exists; that he has only to be convinced of His existence, and everything will change. What is utterly unthinkable in this universe is that someone who does not doubt the existence of God should live his life *regardless of Him*. Yet this is the very stance that Don Juan assumes. This is why his attitude becomes really unbearable (for the community) only at the moment when he – in spite of all the substantial evidence and grace that is offered to him – utters his final '*No and no!*' What is at stake here is the idea that for Don Juan, as well as for any other 'atheist', the smart thing to do would be to repent before death, saying: 'After all, one never really knows what may be ahead, let's do it just in case.' Don Juan knows only too well what is ahead of him; the point is that despite this knowledge, he refuses to repent and 'play it safe'.

Rumour has it that somebody once saw Voltaire (another notorious 'atheist') touch his hat in salute when passing a church. Later this witness mockingly asked Voltaire how it happened that he, a sworn atheist, should take his hat off in front of a church. Voltaire looked surprised and answered, 'Well, it is true that God and I are not on speaking terms. But we still greet.' This story could also be said to describe Don Juan's attitude. The episode that takes place in the woods, where Don Juan and his servant Sganarelle come across a poor man, is most instructive in this respect. The following dialogue ensues:

POOR MAN. Would you care to help me, sir, with a little something?
DON JUAN. So your advice wasn't disinterested!
POOR MAN. I'm a poor man, sir. I have lived alone in this wood for the last ten years. I will pray to Heaven for your good fortune.
DON JUAN. Hm. Pray for a coat to your back and don't worry about other people's affairs.
SGANARELLE. My good man, you don't know my master. All he believes in is that two and two make four and two fours are eight.
DON JUAN. How do you employ yourself here in the forest?
POOR MAN. I spend my days in praying for the prosperity of the good people who show me charity.
DON JUAN. You must live very comfortably then.

POOR MAN. Alas, sir, I live in great penury.

DON JUAN. Surely not? A man who spends his days in prayer cannot fail to be well provided for.

POOR MAN. Believe me, sir, I often haven't a crust of bread to eat.

DON JUAN. Strange that you are so ill repaid for your pains! Well, I'll give you a gold piece here and now if you'll curse your fate and blaspheme.

POOR MAN. Ah, sir, would you have me commit a sin like that?

DON JUAN. Make up your mind. Do you want to earn a gold piece or not? There is one here for you provided you swear. Wait – you must swear.

POOR MAN. Oh, sir!

DON JUAN. You don't get it unless you do.

SGANARELLE. Go on, curse a bit. There isn't any harm in it.

DON JUAN. Here, take it, I tell you, but you must swear first.

POOR MAN. No, sir, I'd rather starve to death.

DON JUAN: Very well, then, I give it to you for your humanity's sake.[4]

What is especially interesting about this episode is that it allows two completely opposite interpretations. According to the first, Don Juan comes out of the encounter with the poor man utterly *defeated*. The poor man does not yield and thus proves to Don Juan that Good, which he despises and does not believe in, nevertheless exists. From this perspective, Don Juan's final gesture – the fact that he gives the money to the poor man regardless – functions as the desperate gesture of a humiliated master by means of which he strives to save what is left of his dignity and pride. Only a master can afford to be so generous, to give away his money whenever he pleases to whomever he chooses. So, in the above scene, the only thing that distinguishes Master from Slave (the poor man) is this gesture of 'charity', which only a master can afford.

On the other hand, the same scene can also be understood as a *triumph* for Don Juan, as a consecration of his own attitude. One must not overlook the fact that the poor man is not simply the opposite of Don Juan, but that the two speak the same language. Don Juan encounters his equal, he encounters his 'positive' (in the purely photographic sense of the word). What occurs here is an encounter between radical good and radical evil in which both speak the same language. This uncanny resemblance has to strike us if we compare Don Juan's and the poor man's respective arguments with Sganarelle's exhortation, 'Go on, curse a bit. There isn't any harm in it', which is a perfect example of the customary logic of the (common) good. According to this logic, excessive insistence on something – be that something ever so good in itself – is automatically perceived as evil, as something disturbing which destroys the harmony of the community. While swearing is evil, to prefer to die rather than to 'swear a little' betrays an element of the 'demonic', the 'dangerous', the destabilizing.[5] Thus we have, on the one hand, Don Juan who has 'palpable' reasons to repent but refuses to do so, and, on the other, someone who does not have any 'palpable' reason not to swear yet refuses to do so. In other words, both are in a position where everything 'palpable' (God's signs in Don Juan's case, a complete absence of such signs in the poor man's) speaks in favour of an act which they both reject with the same stubbornness. Don Juan's final gesture, his charity, thus has an entirely different impact: he does not give the money to the poor man *in spite of* his perseverance but *because of* it; his is no longer an act of charity but rather the gesture of the master who recognizes and acknowledges in the slave his equal, a master.

In relation to this master-and-slave dialectic it is possible to offer yet another explanation of what is so scandalous about Don Juan's attitude. Where, and between which parties, does this dialectic feature in the play? On closer examination it becomes clear that it actually takes place between Don Juan and God (Heaven, the Commander's statue). This is especially true in Molière's *Don Juan*, which leaves out the scene that usually begins the story: the scene in which Donna Anna mourns her father (the Commander, who died in a duel with Don Juan), and cries for revenge. Many interpreters suggest that by cutting this opening scene, Molière committed a dramaturgic error, since the finale of the play (Don Juan's confrontation with the Commander's statue) thus loses its proper motivation. Yet one might also argue that with this cut Molière accomplished something else, that he shifted the centre of the drama. The Commander's statue no longer represents someone who has personal reasons for revenging himself on Don Juan; instead, we recognize that the horrifying statue is the envoy of Heaven, of the beyond. In this way, another drama is brought to the fore: that which takes place between Don Juan and Heaven, and in which Don Juan paradoxically occupies the position of the slave. The struggle between master and slave (with the 'absolute master', Death, in the background) thus becomes a struggle between master and 'absolute master' (incarnated in the Commander's statue). From this perspective, Don Juan's position is that of the slave who does not back down before the absolute master (Death) and refuses to accept the symbolic pact (repentance that would lead to absolution) that would allow him to avoid *real*, as well as *symbolic* death (the eternal curse). Even though he knows that 'the blow directed to the other is a blow to oneself',[6] he nevertheless perseveres with his stand till the end. By doing so, he provokes what we may call a hystericization of the beyond, of the big Other, God. The finale of the play stages this hysterization most clearly. Messengers from Heaven emerge one after another, all reminding Don Juan of where he is heading, and offering him a chance to repent, which he persistently refuses. The spirit of these 'interventions from beyond' could be best described by the question '*Che voi?*' (What do you actually want?). It is when confronted with the question of Don

Juan's desire, its enigmatic character, that Heaven becomes powerless and falls
from its position as master. The finest expression of Heaven's powerlessness is
the 'hysterical outburst' that finally puts an end to Don Juan's scandalous life.
'(*Rolls of thunder, flashes of lightning. The earth opens up and swallows him up. Flames
rise from the pit into which he has vanished.*)' Fire, thunder, yawning earth – several
interpreters have already pointed out the comical effect of this spectacle. In fact,
one could establish a connection between this comical effect and one we know
from our everyday experience. When, for instance, a schoolteacher can no
longer manage to maintain order in his/her class by the usual subtle means and
starts yelling at the students, he/she instead usually provokes laughter rather
than fear or respect. Likewise, we can say that in *Don Juan*, thunder, infernal fire
and a yawning earth are not so much manifestations of authority, as signs of its
breakdown.

One of the features that distinguishes Molière's *Don Juan* is the way the hero
sees his relationship with women. Don Juan's argument concerning this point
could best be described as follows: 'They all have a right to a share of my *agalma*,
and they all have a right to make me appreciate theirs.' Or, as Don Juan himself
puts it:

> All beautiful women have a right to our love, and the accident of being the first comer
> shouldn't rob others of a fair share in our hearts . . . the fact that I am in love with one
> person shall never make me unjust to the others. I keep an eye for the merits of all of
> them and render each one the homage, pay each one the tribute that nature enjoins.
> . . . I feel it is in me to love the whole world, and like Alexander still wish for new
> worlds to conquer. (p. 202)

In short, Don Juan's language is a distortion of the language of pure practical
reason, the universal language of moral law. Why do we find Don Juan's
argumentation perverse? Because what he proposes as an object of universal
distribution is the one article which is exclusive by its very definition, namely the
'gift of love'. Don Juan offers to share what Lacan calls the object *a* or, in his
interpretation of Plato's *Symposium*, *agalma*: the mysterious treasure, the secret
object that the subject has in him/herself which provokes the love and desire
of the other. Molière's comic genius displays most brilliantly this logic of the
'distribution of the substance of enjoyment'. The play begins with Sganarelle's
praise of tobacco, which sums up most accurately the discourse of his master.
What Sganarelle says about tobacco could be used, in every detail, to describe
the 'homage and tributes' that Don Juan offers to women:

> Aristotle and the philosophers can say what they like, but there's nothing to equal
> tobacco. . . . Haven't you noticed how, once a chap starts taking snuff, he behaves

politely to everybody, and what a pleasure he takes in offering it right and left wherever he happens to be? He doesn't even wait to be asked or until folk know that they want it! (p. 199)

This is precisely how Don Juan handles his *agalma*: he happily administers it all around him, 'offering it right and left', even before anyone asks him for it.

The inexhaustible character of Don Juan's *agalma* is also pointed out by Kierkegaard: 'What wonder, then, that they all crowd about him, the happy maidens! Nor are they disappointed, for he has enough for them all.'[7] Kierkegaard proposes to solve the paradox of Don Juan's 'inexhaustible spring' by interpreting the hero as a 'force of nature', as the *principle* of sensuousness. He therefore dismisses those who view Don Juan as an individual, suggesting that this perception of the hero is absurd, since such a condensation of sensuousness into one person is unthinkable. This is also the reason why Kierkegaard is convinced that the only appropriate medium for the Don Juan myth is music, and its only acceptable version Mozart's opera. Consequently, he dismisses Molière's play as entirely inadequate, even silly. Yet the question arises whether the interpretation of Don Juan as a *principle* (of sensuousness) does not actually avoid the very dimension of Don Juan that is most disturbing, scandalous and 'unthinkable': the fact that the principle itself appears *as Don Juan*, as a concrete individual; that the universal takes the form of the singular. According to Kierkegaard, it is only in so far as we understand Don Juan as an abstract principle that we manage to avoid seeing his story as some sort of burlesque, especially when it comes to the famous *mille e tre* (thousand and three). This is, however, the weak point of Kierkegaard's interpretation, for it fails to perceive how the very thing that it considers to be the problem is actually a solution of a problem. A burlesque solution, perhaps, yet one that, through its very incredibility, bears witness to the difficulty it tries to resolve. In other words: if we take *mille e tre* as an answer, the final outcome of an impossible task, then we will be able to see that the fundamental impossibility lies elsewhere. For, *mille e tre* presents only an empirical impossibility, while the fundamental impossibility it resolves is structural. It is only this perspective that enables us to account for a fact that is not usually given much attention, but which is nevertheless crucial to the myth of Don Juan.

The myth of Don Juan is in fact a composite of two myths that existed separately long before the first version of *Don Juan*. The first is a myth or legend about a dinner with Death. Versions of this legend differ in their details, but its basic outline is this: a young man, usually a farmer, finds a skull by the road or in the fields. He does not cross himself or see to it that the skull gets to the place where it belongs, instead he kicks the skull and prankishly invites it to have dinner with him (this can be an ordinary dinner or some kind of feast, a wedding feast for example). One of the living dead (often in the form of a skeleton) actually shows up for this dinner, not to eat or drink but merely to return the invitation. The second feast, the feast of the living dead, customarily ends with the intruder's death or on a note of amnesty, accompanied by a moral lesson: in the future, you will respect the dead.[8] The second myth or legend is about an inconstant seducer, a ladies' man or libertine. Before Don Juan, in France, the popular hero Hylas was just such a seducer.[9]

It is interesting that when we hear the name Don Juan today, we automatically think of this second component of the Don Juan myth. Indeed, it would be difficult to find anyone who, when asked what associations the name of Don Juan calls up, would answer 'disrespect for the dead', or 'dinners with the living dead'. But rather than explore the reasons for this eclipse of one of the components of the myth by the other, we will have to satisfy ourselves here with the observation that this double structure is an essential and constituent element of *Don Juan* and gives it a kind of weight that neither of its constituent legends has in itself. From this perspective, a series of fundamental questions arises: how is it that these two seemingly divergent stories come to be joined? What legitimizes this fusion? What do the profanation of the dead and the serial seduction of women have in common.

We can answer these questions, as I indicated above, only if we view the daisy-chain seduction of women as a solution to a certain impasse. A solution which, precisely because of its reprising failure, only reveals the true scandal: the fact that one half of the human race is actually composed of the 'living dead', that is, beings with no signifier of their own that would adequately represent them in the symbolic. It is well known that Don Juan sleeps with all kinds of women: blonde or brunette, tall or short, fat or skinny, old or young, gentlewomen or peasants, ladies or maids. As some interpreters, Kierkegaard among them, have pointed out, we would be wrong to understand this as Don Juan's preference for a 'variegated menu'. What makes Don Juan's attitude possible is rather his indifference to all differences. Don Juan's paradigm is not variety but *repetition*. He does not seduce women because of what is special about or unique to each of them, but because of what they have in common: the fact that they are women, even though his perception of himself seems at first to contest this reading. In Molière's play he says that 'all the joy of love is in the change'. Yet one has to bear in mind that pursuit of change for the sake of change is one of the purest instances of the automatism of repetition. Don Juan himself points out that the change he seeks is not a new woman but a 'new conquest'. One could say that the object of this conquest is of minor importance here. In the core of perpetual change there is a repetition of one and the same gesture.

To sum up: Don Juan seduces women regardless of their looks, their 'appearances', that is, with no respect for imaginary criteria; and regardless of their symbolic roles (it doesn't matter whether they are mistresses or maids, married or single, daughters or sisters of important men, wives or fiancées). The question is, what else remains? Does anything remain at all? The whole of Don Juan's existence testifies to the fact that something remains, though what this something is is completely undetermined.

At this point, one needs to recall Lacan's famous statement that 'the woman does not exist'. To grasp the feminist impact of this statement it is important to realize that, contrary to what others have argued, this is not a mark of the patriarchal nature of society, but rather of something that threatens to throw this society 'out of joint'. One has often heard the following objection to Lacan: 'If "the woman does not exist", this is because patriarchal society has for millennia oppressed women; instead of trying to provide a theoretical justification for this oppression, one should do something about it.' Yet Lacan does not argue that the nonexistence of woman is a result of patriarchal society and centuries of oppression; he argues, on the contrary, that patriarchal society (with its oppression of women) is a 'result' of the fact that 'the woman does not exist'. This makes patriarchy an attempt to deal with and 'overcome' this fact, to make it pass unnoticed.[10] For, after all, women seem to exist perfectly well in this society as daughters, sisters, wives and mothers. This abundance of symbolic identities disguises the lack that generates them. These identities make it obvious not only that the woman does indeed exist, but also that she is the 'common denominator' of all these symbolic roles, the substance underlying all these symbolic attributes. This functions perfectly well until a Don Juan shows up and demands this substance *in itself*, not a wife, daughter, sister or mother, but a *woman*.

One must pay attention to the fact that men, and not women, are most offended and disturbed by Don Juan's actions. It is no coincidence that the play takes place in Sicily, which is – even today – considered to be the cradle of patriarchal values. Nor is it a coincidence that Don Juan is persecuted by two *brothers* (of the 'dishonoured woman'). The best way to insult the typical male chauvinist is to make allusions to his sister's sexual activities. The mere thought that his sister isn't just his sister but possibly something else (unsurprisingly, but significantly, this something else usually comes down to only one alternative: being a whore) drives him mad. What is especially interesting about this kind of insult is that although on the level of content they offend women, they actually always function as a 'knife through the heart' of the man (and, indeed, they are always addressed to men). Seeing the insulted man's response, we have the feeling that this kind of insult affects him in the very core of his being. Insults such as 'your mother (or sister) is a whore' are vulgar reminders of the fact that 'woman does not exist', that she is not 'all his' (*toute à lui*), as Lacan put it.[11] The point is that the dictum 'woman is not-all' is most unbearable not for women but for men since it calls into question a portion of their being. This is best proved by the extreme, utterly disproportionate reactions which these insults occasion, up to and including murder. Such reactions cannot be accounted for by the common explanation that man regards woman as his 'property'. It is not simply his property, what he *has*, but his being, what he *is*, which is at stake in these insults. Let us conclude this digression with another dictum. Once we accept the fact that 'woman does not exist', there is only one way to define a man: a man is, as Slavoj Žižek put it in one of his lectures, a woman who believes she exists.

There are only two ways of dealing with this situation, and they both rely on a symbolic register. The first follows the logic of what Hegel called *das Ungeschehenmachen*, 'retroactive annihilation'. The one who 'took the woman's honour' (that is, her place in the symbolic) and thus 'opened the wound', has to heal it by marrying her. If she becomes his 'lawful' wife, the 'horrible thing' that happened between them retroactively becomes subsumed by the law and loses its disturbing aspect. If he refuses to marry her, he deserves to die, but his death alone is not sufficient to 'heal the wound'. This is taken care of by the institution of the *convent*. The convent is usually the only refuge for women who have lost their honour, their place in the given configuration of symbolic roles, and thus have nowhere to go. In its symbolic function, the convent is equivalent to funeral rituals. In both cases, the main objective is to make real death coincide with symbolic death – otherwise ghosts appear. Yet if the role of funeral rituals is to accompany real death with symbolic reference points which enable us to cope with it, the role of the convent is precisely the opposite. A woman who has to enter the convent because she has lost her honour is already dead in the symbolic, but is still alive in reality. This is why she functions as an 'unbearable sight', as a spectre. She has thus to be removed from circulation (immured in the convent), to stop her from appearing as a *loose woman*: a creature who is symbolically dead (that is, with no symbolic attachments that would define her), but who continues to wander around. A woman who has 'sinned' (who has slept with Don Juan, for instance), but does not go into the convent, is like the living dead, a spectre, a being with no place in the symbolic. Besides the Commander's statue, the other figure who visits Don Juan in Molière's play is '*a spectre in the form of a veiled woman*'. The finale of the play is structured so that both apparitions visit Don Juan one after the other. First the woman (who still wants to save him), then the statue (who leads him to death). This is how Molière stages the connection between profaning the dead and seducing women.

The exposure of women as the 'living dead' in this sense is not specific to the Don Juan myth. This constellation is abundantly present in much eighteenth-century literature.[12] But while the terrifying aspect of these women has faded since the eighteenth century, we must not accept too quickly the optimistic conclusion that things have improved, that women have finally been allowed to exist without being viewed as disturbing sights. We should rather consider the possibility that a new signifier has been invented to cover what was left out by the previous *mother, daughter, sister, wife.* This new signifier is that of 'the woman in love'. In romantic literature, it is love that reconnects loose women to the symbolic order. As long as she is really in love with a man, she can live outside the realm of the law without disturbing it. This is because the core of her being becomes her lover, who, as a man, finds himself 'within' the law. This is why 'real love' demands that if her lover dies, she has to die also; with her lover's death she, too, ceases to exist in the symbolic and becomes once again a spectre. Since the days of Don Juan, the basic frame has shifted, but its structure and logic remain unchanged.

The replacement of the 'law of marriage' by the 'law of love' (that is, the replacement of the *law* by a *legal emotion*) has another important consequence which allows us to illuminate some aspects of what Freud called the discontents of civilization. This shift parallels the replacement of symbolic law by the superego's law. Once love begins to play the role of the substitute for marriage (law), the subject finds him/herself in a kind of deadlock. For this substitution to function as it should, one has to be *constantly* in love, which is not an easy task. Otherwise, as the saying goes, there is no point in two people living together. Whereas it is not considered odd for two married people to live together although there is no 'real love' left between them, an unmarried couple who fall out of love are obliged to reconsider their living arrangement. It is now a common experience for couples who live together for some time to have sudden attacks of conscience and guilt: is this really it? Is this real love? Do I still love this person or is it just habit that keeps us together? These are clearly questions raised by the superego. Or, in Lacan's words, 'love demands love. It never ceases to demand it. It demands it . . . *more* [*encore*]. *More*, this is the name of the rift in the Other in which originates the demand of love.'[13] It is probably not necessary to point out that, for Lacan, this 'rift in the Other' is essentially related to the 'fact' that the Other, or the woman, does not exist.

So it is not simply a joke to say that people marry in order not to have to be constantly in love. (Although whether the institution of marriage can still provide relief from the pressure to love remains a question, considering the fact that, in Western culture, marriage was itself 'contaminated' by the imperative that we should marry for love.) One is tempted to say that suppression (which inhabits the realm of paternalistic law) and depression (which is common to the domain of the superego) seem to exhaust what Western society has invented so far in order to deal with what Lacan formulates so straightforwardly: there is no sexual relationship.

Let us return to Don Juan. If the exposure of women as the 'living dead' is not specific to the Don Juan myth but to a whole genre of literature, what is it that distinguishes Don Juan in particular? We have already said that Don Juan's variegated and colourful collection of women testifies above all to his indifference to difference. We can add that, for Don Juan, all women are '*as one*', except that this *one* does not exist – she exists only as *mille e tre*, hence the quest of the hero. Here, we must avoid a double misunderstanding. On the one hand, what Don Juan illustrates is not the metonymy of desire, the eternal elusiveness of the 'true' object (of desire). He is not looking for the right woman, his constant moving on to another woman is not motivated by disappointment or lack, by what he did not find in the previous woman. On the contrary, for Don Juan each and every woman *is* the right one, and what drives him further is not what he did not find in his previous lover, but precisely what he *did* find, and what he must find in all women if his mission is to be successfully performed. On the other hand, Don Juan does not operate according to the logic of metaphor, of the substitutability of one woman by another. His motto is not *così fan tutte* (they are all the same), one can replace the other. The basic problem and, at the same time, the motive of its actions is to be found on a more fundamental level: to be able to assert '*così fan tutte*', to make a statement about *all* women. Don Juan would be unemployed if there were a signifier to represent *all* (particular) women for another signifier. It is because this signifier does not exist that he has his hands full, for he is confronted with the classic problem of induction. In the same way that the statement 'all crows are black' cannot attain the universality of law (because it is based solely on our past experience and nothing guarantees that, in the future, we will not come across some white crows), the statement 'all women have property x (which distinguishes them as women)' is subject to the same fate. The only way for Don Juan to 'prove' that all women have this x, and thus access to their own signifier, is to sleep with all of them. This is why he only looks in the next one for what he has already found in the previous one, then quickly puts her aside to run to the next next one. He tries to minimize the time of seduction and 'move to the essential' as quickly as possible, never taking the time to enjoy the fruits of his labours. As Kierkegaard wittily remarks in relation to Mozart's opera, Don Giovanni spends less time with a woman than Leporello does writing her name on his list.

This is also what makes Don Juan a different kind of hero from Valmont (*Les*

Liaisons Dangereuses) or Lovelace (*Clarissa*), who put all the emphasis on the process of seduction, of overcoming resistance. The difference becomes most explicit when one compares the respective narrative structures of *Don Juan* and *Les Liaisons Dangereuses*. In the latter, the narrative is focused on the relationship of a libertine with a *privileged* woman (Mme de Tourvel); everything leads up to the seduction of this most inaccessible of women. This is not true of *Don Juan*. If Don Juan were a prototype of Valmont, the centre of his story would be the seduction of Donna Elvira who, as we learn, lived in a convent; Don Juan seduced her after considerable effort, made her leave the convent and marry him, then abandoned her. Yet this Valmontian narrative does not function as the central motif of the play; instead, it appears at the very beginning as a *fait accompli*. In the play itself there is no emphasis on the process of seduction and the enjoyment that it procures. On the contrary, as several interpreters have noticed, we have the impression that Don Juan is *in a hurry*. Only romantic interpretations and versions of *Don Juan* intended to 'uncover' a true love beneath the libertine 'appearance' have stressed the character of Donna Anna and transformed *Don Juan* into a drama of a loving *couple*.

It would be useful to return to the question of what the profaning of the dead and the seducing of women one after the other have in common. In both cases, Don Juan plays with the line that separates the real from the symbolic. He passes from one of the two registers to the other as if there were no difference between them. One could say that, in relation to women, he treats the real body as if it were symbolic, a signifier. The one is the body that woman has as an empirical being (a body of particular form and proportions), the other is the body she has as *woman*. Yet, because this symbolic body, the signifier of the feminine, does not exist, Don Juan always ends up with the real body, which presents an obstacle to the simultaneous inscription of another: this is the logic behind his serial conquests and his substitution of a number 'for the eternal feminine'.

What makes Don Juan's enterprise 'diabolical' and therefore comparable, in some senses, to Sade's, is the fantasy that gives it its frame: the fantasy of a *simultaneous inscription* of all women or of Woman. The failure of this inscription in the symbolic returns in the real as the nightmare of an inconceivable accumulation of bodies. One can say that the Don Juanian and the Sadian fantasies each revolve around one of the Kantian transcendental categories of sensibility. The Sadian fantasy violates the logic of time in that within this fantasy victims are tortured ad infinitum, the moment of death is therefore eternally postponed, while time seems to be frozen. The Don Juanian fantasy, on the other hand, violates the logic of space, of extension (body as *res extensa*), according to which simultaneous inscription of more than one body in one place is impossible. Yet it is this very violation of logic that, in each of the two configurations, makes the 'other' appear as the object of the fantasy. In the Sadian fantasy, the infinite prolongation of one moment of time (the moment just before death) makes extended substance, the sublime *body* of the victim that can be tortured to infinity, the object of desire. On the other hand, the infinite series of seduced and abandoned women in the Don Juanian fantasy aims at an eternal or timeless love. It is precisely time which is most precious to Don Juan.

Fantasy within the Limits of Reason Alone

This comparison obliges us to shift from literary to philosophical questions, specifically to Kant's arguments concerning the 'immortality of the soul as a postulate of pure practical reason'. This move enables us to examine the other face of Achilles, the asymptotic approach to the desired object, and some consequences of it. How is the notion of the immortality of the soul introduced by Kant? It appears as a necessary presupposition of the notion of the highest Good, defined as a *complete fitness* of the will to the moral law. Let us take a look at Kant's 'deduction' of the immortality of the soul:

> Complete fitness of the will to the moral law is holiness, which is perfection of which no rational being in the world of sense is at any time capable. But since it is required as practically necessary, it can be found only in an endless progress to that complete fitness. . . . This infinite progress is possible, however, only under the presupposition of an infinitely enduring existence and personality of the same rational being; this is called the immortality of the soul. Thus the highest good is practically possible only on the supposition of the immortality of the soul, and the latter, as inseparably bound to the moral law, is a postulate of pure practical reason.[14]

A little further on, Kant adds that 'only endless progress from lower to higher stages of moral perfection is possible to a rational but finite being'.

This 'deduction' and its premises involve a noticeable difficulty that strikes the reader most forcibly in Kant's statement that to a rational but *finite* being only *endless* (*infinite*) progress is possible. A question immediately arises: If the soul is immortal, it is – upon the death of the 'body' – no longer a denizen of the world of space and time; and if the soul is no longer subject to temporal conditions, how are we to understand 'continuous and unending progress'?[15] We might also ask why the soul, delivered of all 'bodily chains', would need this progress, for holiness could be accomplished instantly. And if not, if the presupposition of the eternity of the soul included continuous change (for the better), then we would not be dealing with an eternal but with a temporal mode.

The notion of change makes sense only within time. What are we to think of this paradoxical 'deduction' of the postulate of the immortality of the soul? These questions lead us to an inevitable conclusion. *What Kant really needs to postulate is not the immortality of the soul but the immortality of the body.* The presupposition of 'endless progress from lower to higher stages of moral perfection', as Kant puts it, cannot yield an immortal soul, but an immortal, indestructible, *sublime* body. A body that exists and changes through time, yet approaches its end, its death, in an endless asymptotic movement. This is what justifies our saying that the postulate in question is a 'fantasy of pure practical reason', a fantasy in the strictly Lacanian sense of the word. What is especially interesting about the immortality postulate is that in formulating it, Kant provides exactly the same answer to a particular structural impasse that Sade does.

The basic problem that confronts the Sadian heroes-torturers is that they can only torture their victims until they die.[16] The only regrettable and unfortunate thing about these sessions, which could otherwise go on endlessly, toward more and more accomplished tortures, is that the victims die *too soon*, with respect to the extreme suffering to which they might have been subjected. The enjoyment (*jouissance*) – which seems to appear on the side of the victims and which coincides, in this case, with their extreme suffering – encounters here an obstacle in the form of the 'pleasure principle', that is, the limit to what the body can endure. What is implied in the 'too soon' is that the torture ends before the *encore*, which is the imperative and 'direction' of *jouissance*, exhausts itself. In short, the problem is that the body is not made to the measure of enjoyment. There is no other enjoyment but the enjoyment of the body, yet if the body is to be equal to the task (duty) of *jouissance*, the limits of the body have to be transgressed. Pleasure, that is, the limit of suffering that a body can still endure, is thus an obstacle to enjoyment. Sade's answer to the impossibility of surpassing this limit is fantasy, the fantasy of infinite suffering: the victims are tortured endlessly, beyond all boundaries of imagination, yet they go on living and suffering and even become more and more beautiful, or more and more holy. It is important to acknowledge that this Sadian fantasy is not simply a frivolous fancy of some sick imagination, but that it responds to a very specific and, at the same time, general structural problem: the one that articulates the relation between pleasure and enjoyment. This relation extends far beyond its immediate sexual connotations and embraces the relation between pleasure and duty. As is well known, it is the superego (that is, the 'moral agency') that, according to Lacan, inflicts the imperative of *jouissance* on the subject.

Kant is confronted with a very similar problem. For in his work, pathological pleasure (that is, what a subject can *feel*, pleasure and pain) represents an obstacle, a hindrance to freedom. For Kant, freedom is essentially bound to the 'division' of the subject; it is constituted in the act of separation from the pathological. Yet we could say that the pathological takes revenge and imposes its law by planting a certain kind of pleasure on the path along which we follow the categorical imperative. This pleasure could best be described as 'pleasure in pain', pain as a transformation of pleasure, as a modality of the pathological which takes the place of pleasure when the latter is used up. This mode of the pathological is most appropriately expressed by the word *pathos*. Here, the subject's immediate interest is replaced by something else, for example, an Idea or some *cosa nostra* in the name of which the subject is willing to forget his/her immediate interests and pleasure. A subject might be willing to accept pain if he/she knew that it would serve a 'good cause'.

Both Sade and Kant aim beyond this pathos; but in order to specify what this means, we must first distinguish two different types of victim: one who knows why he/she is being tortured and one who does not. We have probably all experienced horror at an image of a tortured animal. Why does such an image evoke such extreme uneasiness? Why is it such an unbearable sight? Clearly the cause of this uneasiness lies in the gaze of the victim – a gaze that animal-rights activists are adept at capturing with their cameras – which reveals that the victim does not know why all this is happening to it, because it has no *cosa nostra* in the name of which it suffers, nothing in which it can locate the sense, the meaning of its pain. We are thus confronted with the image of a victim who simply suffers without understanding why. This is not to say that the torture and suffering of a human being is less horrible than that of an animal. Animals are taken here as a paradigmatic example of the impossibility of making sense of one's tortures and suffering, and there is probably no need to point out that this type of suffering can also characterize man. In aiming beyond pathological suffering, Sade and Kant aim at a 'senseless' suffering that is, however, not that of the dumb animal, but that of a human subject who submits to a torture that surpasses the limits of reason.

For Kant, freedom is always susceptible to limitation, either by pleasure (in the form of any kind of pathological motivation, including pathos) or by the death of the subject. What allows us to 'jump over' this hindrance, to continue to be free beyond it, is what Lacan calls the fantasy. Kant's postulate of the immortality of the soul (the truth of which is, as we saw, the immortality of the body) implies precisely a fantasmatic 'solution'. Its function is to institute the coordinates of time and space *outside* time and space, and thus to enable the infinite, endless progress 'from lower to higher stages of moral perfection'. The introduction of the postulate of the immortality of the soul is often met with the objection that in contrast to the arguments in the 'Analytic of Pure Practical Reason', Kant now seems to promise to moral subjects (some kind of) heaven and happiness. Rather, through this postulate he seems to reintroduce, 'through the back door', that which he previously excluded so rigorously, namely a possible 'pathological motive' for our actions. Yet, in the light of our argument concerning the immortality postulate, this promise (or encouragement) proves to be a very curious one. For this is what it says: if you persist in following the categorical imperative, regardless of all pains and tortures that may occur along the way, you may finally be granted the possibility of ridding yourself even of the pleasure and pride that you took in the sacrifice itself; thus you will finally reach your goal. Kant's immortality of the soul promises us then quite a peculiar heaven. For what awaits his ethical subjects is a heavenly future that bears an uncanny resemblance to a Sadian boudoir.

We must point out, however, that the infinite progression towards moral perfection is not Kant's only answer to what seems to be the inherent, structural impossibility of accomplishing a pure ethical act. In his texts on morality it is possible to discern another line of argument which goes in the opposite direction, and is most explicitly formulated in the following passage from *Religion within the Limits of Reason Alone*:

> But if a man is to become not merely *legally*, but *morally*, a good man . . . *this* cannot be brought about through gradual *reformation* so long as the basis of the maxims remains impure, but must be effected through a *revolution* in the man's disposition. . . . He can become a new man only by a kind of rebirth, as it were, a new creation.[17]

It is this second perspective that brings Kant's developments close to Lacan's conceptualization of an ethical act. Let us borrow here Slavoj Žižek's outline of this conceptualization. An act differs from an action in that the former radically transforms its bearer (agent) while the latter does not. After an act, I am 'not the same as I was before'. In the act, the subject is annihilated and subsequently reborn (or not); the act involves a kind of temporary eclipse of the subject. The act is therefore always a 'crime', a 'transgression', namely of the limits of the symbolic community to which I belong.[18] It is in relation to these features of an act that Lacan claims that suicide is the paradigm of every (successful) act. Yet we must be very careful in our understanding of this statement, because what is at stake is not simply the (voluntary) death of the subject, but rather the *living* beyond one's symbolic death.

It might, then, be instructive to draw a distinction, with Kant's help, between two different logics of suicide. There is first the suicide that obeys a logic of sacrifice. When duty calls, I sacrifice this or that and, if necessary, even my life. Here, we are dealing with a logic of infinite 'purification', in which sacrificing my life is just 'another step' forward – only one among numerous 'objects' that have to be sacrificed. The fact that it is a final step is mere coincidence; or, to use Kantian terms, it indicates an empirical not a transcendental necessity. It is this logic that governs the Kantian postulate of the immortality of the soul and it serves to preserve the consistency of the big Other (qua symbolic order), the highest Good. According to this logic, it is the subject who has to separate her/himself infinitely from everything that belongs to the register of the pathological (or pathos). At the same time, (the position of) the big Other gets stronger and stronger, its 'sadism' increases with each new sacrifice that the subject makes, and it therefore demands more and more of the subject. We can point to examples from popular culture, which seems to be more and more fascinated by this superegoic side of morality. Consider, for instance, *Terminator 2*. The Terminator first helps people wipe off the face of the earth everything that could lead, in the future, to the invention of machines such as the Terminator (and thus to catastrophe, and the eruption of radical evil). In the end only the Terminator him/itself remains to threaten the totality of its destruction, since he retains the knowledge of how to produce such cyborgs. He/it therefore throws him/itself into a pool of white-hot iron in order to save the human race from catastrophe. The same type of suicide occurs in *Alien³*. Ripley first exterminates all aliens, only to find out in the end that the last one resides within herself. In order to eliminate this last alien, she has to kill herself, she has to destroy the 'stranger' in herself, to cut off the last remains of the pathological in herself.

The second type of suicide is less popular, for it serves no cause, no purpose. What is at stake is not that in the end we put on the altar of the Other our own life as the ultimate sacrificial gift. The point is that we kill ourselves through the Other, *in the Other*. We annihilate that which – in the Other, in the symbolic order – gave our being identity, status, support and meaning. This is the suicide to which Kant refers in the famous footnote from *The Metaphysics of Morals*, in which he discusses regicide. 'Regicide' is not really the right term, because what preoccupies Kant is precisely the difference between the murder of a monarch (regicide) and his *formal execution*. It is in relation to the latter that Kant says that 'it is as if the state commits suicide',[19] and describes it as a 'radical evil'. What reinforces Kant's distinction is the difference between the 'king's two bodies'. Were the monarch simply killed, murdered, this would strike a blow only at his 'empirical body', whereas his 'other body', incarnated in his symbolic mandate, would pass more or less unharmed. Yet his *formal* execution, which Kant – in spite of his almost obsessive insistence on form, or more likely because of it – describes as outrageously useless, is precisely what strikes a blow at the monarch's 'symbolic body', that is, the given symbolic order. Why is it that for Kant this act of the people has the structure of suicide? Because people are only constituted as People in relation to this symbolic order. Outside it, they are nothing more than masses with no proper status. It is the monarch (in his symbolic function) that gives people their symbolic existence, be it ever so miserable. A very audible undertone of Kant's argument implicitly poses this question: if the French people were so dissatisfied with their monarch, why didn't they simply kill him, why did they have to perform a formal execution and thus shake the very ground they were standing on ('commit suicide')? As I have argued elsewhere,[20] there is another reason for Kant's being so 'shaken' by this act of 'radical evil'. He is compelled by his argument to describe it in exactly the same words that he used to describe an ethical act, in that:

1. It is a purely *formal* act, it complies with the form solely for the sake of form, which is, as we know, the very definition of morality: what distinguishes morality from legality is precisely a surplus of form, the fact that we act not only in accordance with the law, but exclusively because of the law.
2. The feeling of horror it provokes is not aesthetic but is instead a *moral feeling*.
3. It cannot be explained as arising from a sensible impulse, but arises, rather, *from a maxim*.
4. 'It cannot be explained, since only what happens in accordance with the mechanism of nature is capable of being explained' – it is thus an *act of freedom*.[21]

Thus, on the one hand, the possibility of the absolute coincidence of the will with moral law (or the highest Good) relies on the paradoxical postulate of the immortality of the soul, whose truth, as we saw, is the immortality of the body. On the other hand, the highest Good is 'realized' here, but always in a 'perverse' form, as an act of radical evil that bears an uncanny resemblance to the pure ethical act, an act that follows the logic of suicide via the Other (in Kant's example, the French 'commit suicide' because they have annihilated what, in the Other, gave them their symbolic identity).

In relation to these two ways in which Kant envisaged the possibility of an act, it could be said that his ethics confronts us not with the choice between good and evil, but rather with the choice between two radical evils. Between the infinite or asymptotic approach that would enable the will to coincide with moral law, and the suicidal gesture that – because it implies our death in the symbolic – compels us either to lead the existence of the living dead or start from the beginning, *ex nihilo*, again and again. Kant defines the first choice as that of the Good, yet, as we saw, its paradigm most strikingly resembles the Sadian fantasy of infinite suffering, which strives to accomplish the 'greatest evil'. The second choice is discarded by Kant as 'radically evil', yet it strikingly resembles his own description of the pure ethical act.

To sum up, the reading of Kant with Sade only covers one part of Kantian ethics, whereas the other part still waits to be read – with Don Juan. This reading would stress the discontinuity involved in every ethical act (committing acts one by one, starting over and over again), as opposed to continuous and uninterrupted progress (which stems from the requirement that the *whole* of our existence should fit the moral law). This Don Juanian side of Kant's ethics opens up an interesting perspective: if we were to follow it, our whole existence could not be considered ethical, though we might succeed in accomplishing some ethical acts 'one by one'. This path would ultimately lead us to the anti-Kantian conclusion that: *Ethics does not exist*; there is no such thing as Ethics in general.[22]

Notes

1. Jacques Lacan, *Encore* (Paris: Seuil 1975), p. 13. The English translation of this passage is borrowed from Joan Copjec, *Read My Desire* (Cambridge, Mass.: MIT Press 1994), p. 60. Copjec's most inspiring interpretation of Lacan's reading of this paradox is very much related to the concerns of this paper.
2. Ibid., p. 116.
3. See Camille Dumoulié, *Don Juan ou l'héroïsme du désir* (Paris: PUF 1993), p. 106.
4. Molière, *Don Juan or The Statue at the Feast*, in *The Miser and Other Plays* (Baltimore, Md.: Penguin 1966), pp. 224–5. All further references will be to this edition and will be made in the body of the text.
5. This disturbance, brought about by an excessive insistence on the good, has already been pointed out by Slavoj Žižek: 'Suffice to recall Thomas More, the Catholic saint who resisted the pressure of Henry VIII to approve of his divorce . . . from a "communitarian" point of view, his rectitude was an "irrational" self-destructive gesture which was "evil" in the sense that it cut into the texture of the social body, threatening the stability of the crown and thereby of the entire social order. So, although the motivations of Thomas More were undoubtedly "good", *the very formal structure of his act was "radically evil"*: his was an act of radical defiance which disregarded the Good of community.' *Tarrying with the Negative* (Durham, N.C.: Duke University Press 1993), p. 97.
6. See Mladen Dolar, 'Lord and Bondsman on the Couch', *The American Journal of Semiotics*, nos 2–3, 1992, p. 74. Dolar also points out that not only the bondsman, but 'the lord as well did not pursue the struggle to the end: he left the bondsman alive, satisfying himself with a "symbolic" recognition'. The life-and-death struggle, which is the starting point of this dialectic, must not end with death of either of the two parties, for this would make impossible their mutual (symbolic) recognition. Yet what distinguishes Don Juan is precisely that he is determined to pursue the struggle to the end.
7. S. Kierkegaard, *Either/Or* (Garden City, N.Y.: Doubleday 1959), vol. 1, p. 100.
8. See Jean Rousset, *Le mythe de Don Juan* (Paris: Armand Colin 1976), pp. 109–13.
9. Mareschal, *Inconstances d'Hylas* (Paris: 1635).
10. We can substantiate this reading of 'la femme n'existe pas' by following remarks that Lacan makes in *Television*: 'Freud didn't say that repression [*Verdrangung*] *comes from* suppression: that (to paint a picture) castration is due to what Daddy brandished over his brat playing with his wee-wee: "We'll cut it off, no kidding, if you do it again." . . . [W]e have to reexamine the test case, taking as a starting point the fact that it is

repression that produces suppression. Why couldn't the family, society itself, be creations built from repression. They're nothing else. . . . The familial order is nothing but the translation of the fact that the Father is not the progenitor, and that the Mother remains the contaminator of woman for man's offspring; the remainder follows from that.' *Television: A Challenge to the Psychoanalytic Establishment*, ed. Joan Copjec, trans. Denis Hollier, Rosalind Krauss and Annette Michelson (New York: W.W. Norton 1990), pp. 27–30.

11. Lacan, *Encore*, p. 12.
12. See Roseann Runt, 'Dying Words: The Vocabulary of Death in Three Eighteenth-century English and French Novels', in *Canadian Review of Comparative Literature*, Fall 1979, pp. 360–8.
13. Lacan, *Encore*, p. 11.
14. Immanuel Kant, *Critique of Practical Reason*, trans. Lewis White Beck (London and New York: Macmillan 1956), p. 126.
15. This question was posed by L. W. Beck in his *Commentary on Kant's Critique of Practical Reason* (London and Chicago: University of Chicago Press, Midway reprint 1984), pp. 170–71.
16. My discussion of the Sadian paradigm follows arguments made by J.-A. Miller in his (unpublished) seminars 1, 2, 3 and 4.
17. Immanuel Kant, *Religion within the Limits of Reason Alone*, trans. Theodore M. Greene and Hoyt H. Hudson (New York: Harper 1960), p. 43.
18. See Slavoj Žižek, *Enjoy Your Symptom!* (London and New York: Routledge 1992), p. 44.
19. Immanuel Kant, *The Metaphysics of Morals* (Cambridge: Cambridge University Press 1993), p. 132.
20. See my 'A Perfect Place to Die: Theatre in Hitchcock's Films', in *Everything You Always Wanted to Know about Lacan (But Were Afraid to Ask Hitchcock)*, ed. Slavoj Žižek (London and New York: Verso 1992), pp. 90–95.
21. Kant, *The Metaphysics of Morals*, p. 132.
22. For more on the question of the impossibility of ethics in general, see Alain Badiou, *L'éthique* (Paris: Hatier 1993) p. 28.

6 DECIDING ON EVIL

GÉRALD SFEZ

Machiavelli posed the question of evil as the essential
question of politics, the question that one cannot seek to
avoid without leading to an evil even worse than evil. One
must not seek to exempt oneself, not from evil – for no one
can be exempted from experiencing it – but from the
thought of evil and from taking it into consideration.
Machiavelli insists on the right of power either to praise or
blame evil, two attitudes that are equally proscribed by
Christian tradition. With him evil in all its forms ceases to
be something about which we are forbidden to think.[1]
Machiavelli writes,

> All writers on politics have pointed out, and throughout history
> there are plenty of examples which indicate, that in constituting
> and legislating for a commonwealth it must needs be taken for
> granted that all men are wicked and that they will always give vent
> to the malignity that is in their minds when opportunity offers.
> That evil dispositions often do not show themselves for a time is
> due to a hidden cause which those who have no experience of the
> opposite fail to perceive; but in time – which is said to be the father
> of all truth – it reveals itself. (*Discourses*, I, 3, pp. 111–12)

Even though Machiavelli is here making both real and
fictional allusion to many writers, the way in which he
appropriates the statement bears witness to a philosophical
gesture that is peculiar to him. The affirmation not only
defines a regulative condition of the founding of a state, it
signals the constitutive nature of man and the duty to face
up to it constantly, without any hope of changing it.

Machiavelli's philosophical gesture here is hyperbolic but not methodologically provisional. He affirms the truth of the fundamentally wicked character of man as a matter of fact. Evil is there in its undeniable opacity, and wickedness is a shared fact. In this respect, the *Discourses* formalize what was to be found in *The Prince*:[2] a transformation of wickedness from one quality among others, even if it was already decisive, to the essential quality, and a shifting from the realm of generality to that of universality. On these two accounts, evil is radical. It is not so as a possibility inherent in freedom, but as a fact that is both unplumbable in its foundation and universal in its reality. This *fact* stems simultaneously from experience and from presupposition, something that can be verified but that does not necessarily await complete verification in order for a decision on it to be made. The argument put forward – if wickedness remains hidden, it must be attributed to some unknown cause, and it must be believed that the occasion for it to show itself has not yet presented itself – suspends all possibility of falsifying the statement. One can no more prove this statement than its contrary. It is a petition of principle and a metaphysical constatation. Metaphysical because evil has no cause and we do not really dispose of any experiential proofs of its universal character. This indirectly attributes a regulative role to the idea of evil, not only for the foundation of a state, but for the entire course of human relations.

The status of metaphysical constatation confers an extreme character on the Machiavellian affirmation of the radicality of evil. No possible sublation (*relève*) of evil can be imagined, not only with respect to its possibility, to the universal predispositions of men, but with respect to its reality, or to the actions of men themselves. Evil is not a vicissitude of freedom; it is inexorable. Likewise, evil is not dialecticizable and cannot be completely taken up in a chain of events, converted or changed into good by the very fact that it is outside of causal sequences. If politics aims to pre-empt evil by removing most occasions to commit it, one cannot hope to disarm the wickedness of men by means of institutional dispositions. And, just as it is not a question of accepting guarantees, or calculating for the worst, it is also not a question of making up for a lack by recourse to laws or of getting around the disposition to evil by the positive and immanent regulation of politics. The establishment of the state – and here the term takes on an indefinite value – neither transcends nor changes the character of man's wickedness. Whether he adopts the mask and cunning of the fox or the force and majesty of the lion, or makes himself into a centaur by adding the force of laws to that of arms, man does not cease to be wicked. All he accomplishes is a raising of his deformity to a new power, other and superior.[3]

Thus the power of Machiavelli's thought is to construct the possibility of a common way of life – the general good of a given state – on the express condition of the radical and unsublatable character of general evil. The great question of politics would then be: How can a happy course be conferred upon the handling of evil, given that evil is inflexible, that it cannot be sublated, that it always returns to its place and that the fact of human wickedness must be taken as proven? How can one constrain men to be good without changing their nature? How can the general good of a state be established when evil will never be overturned and the negative can never be fully put to work? How can good pass through evil, even though evil will never pass? How can one find a way of working with evil without succumbing to the illusion of fooling it and without believing oneself capable of an affirmative dialectic that would seek, by the intermediary of immanent arrangements or transformers of energy, to make evil conspire to do good unbeknownst to itself? What does probity in politics mean in the face of evil?

Since the radicality of evil is an unsurpassable condition of human relations, one must know how to anticipate evil, and, in this preventive attitude, how to accept the least damaging evil in opposition to all others. Political choice then is a policy of deciding which evil least reinforces the extremity of evil, and neither hopes to attenuate its abrupt character nor seeks to be excused by the pacified image of a political realism.

These considerations on the general character of the extremity of evil might lead one to believe that good exists only empirically, by default or by a negative path, by chance (chance not always furnishing the occasion) or as a result of the capacity to contradict this predisposition to evil and perturb its course, to insert between this predisposition and its realization some sort of reason to abstain from it. Politics would then be the power to prevent as far as possible the meeting of the predisposition and the occasion for its realization. But this cannot be the case for several reasons. First of all because the disposition to evil is not man's only disposition. This does not imply that there is a disposition to the good, nor that at the very root of the possibility of evil there is an ability, a freedom, to choose between good and evil. What exists is a heterogeneity of dispositions. All that can be said is that the disposition to evil is preponderant in so far as it is found at the intersection of these dispositions, that it is in the disposition to evil that the largest number of dispositions are most frequently bound together. Next and above all because the statement of the radicality of evil is formulated in detailed terms that should awaken our attention and orient us toward another way of handling evil rather than eternally seeking new ways to avoid it. Time, the father of all truth, unmistakably brings everyone's disposition to evil to the light of day. Man has a disposition to evil that some day will find the occasion to manifest itself, even if this disposition can be hidden for an indefinite period for some reason – it does not much matter what – that intervenes and, by its perturbation or interference, prevents it from taking effect. What is remarkable here is the inexorable character of the appearance of evil in time determined by the figure of Time as the father of all truth, that is, determined by contingency and the figure of Chronos. Every time Machiavelli speaks of time in these terms he appeals to the figure of Chronos and to the complex determination of a destiny in the very fabric of contingency, an inexorability in the aleatory itself. One day, in an unpredictable fashion, man will fall, as into a trap that closes upon him. Man abandoned to time is man abandoned to evil in all its forms. Thus Machiavelli writes of Cesare Borgia, at the moment Borgia's fortunes have turned and his destiny is truly sealed: 'I cannot say anything more about his affairs nor make up my mind about their necessary end. We must wait for Time, who is the father of Truth.'[4] Under the two faces of evil – evil to be committed and evil to be suffered – man abandoned to time is man bound hand and foot and turned over to the father of all truth and to malignant Fortune. This allows us to understand that the man who sooner or later gives in to the occasion for evil is not seizing the occasion and approaching time under the dimension of *kairos*, is not capable of distinguishing and choosing the *kairos* of evil. He does not *decide* upon evil. Where the man abandoned to the destiny of evil (to Fortune and to the father of all truth/to his ineluctable inclination) commits exactions lacking in all rightness and justice, the man who decides on evil, whether he seizes the occasion or creates the event, finds the just balance. An example of this difference in posture is strikingly exemplified by Giovampagolo Baglioni's decision *not* to kill Pope Julius II. Although the Pope, who gave in to his disposition to evil every time he had the occasion, was at Baglioni's mercy, Baglioni shrank from deciding on murder even though it would have delegitimized the domination of the Church.[5] It is not a question of forbidding evil or finding the means to invalidate its effects, but of making a *leap* from evil committed in indecision to a decision upon evil. This leap is that from the apprehension of time as *chronos* to time as *kairos*: not two different times but time relinquished and time seized again.

Now, this reversal from passivity to activity in the commission of crime, which draws another relation to time and reveals the formula of correct political judgement (*justesse politique*), is parallel to a judgement of the greatness of evil. The man abandoned to his penchant for evil and handed over to time takes the negative path of wickedness in so far as he follows a middle path (*via del mezzo*) in evil; he is all the more wicked because he is only so in halftones. Thus, Machiavelli writes about Giovampagolo Baglioni: 'Most men prefer to steer a middle course, which is very harmful; for they do not know how to be wholly good nor yet wholly bad' (*Discourses*, I, 26, p. 177). Judging the greatness of evil means knowing how to be 'wholly bad' and choosing the extreme of evil, which

paradoxically allows one to be less bad. It must be understood that this judgement is an economical use of evil (entering into evil if there is a necessity) and
carries both the sense of a determinate evaluation and that of a relation to
supreme evil. Machiavelli retranscribes the idea stated above in another way in
the following chapter, adding a displacement of meaning: 'So they concluded
that it must be due to men not knowing how to be either magnificently bad
or perfectly good; and that, since evil deeds have a certain grandeur and are
open-handed in their way, Giovampagolo was incapable of performing them'
(*Discourses*, I, 27, p. 178). The quantitative evaluation of the extreme rejoins the
qualitative evaluation of what is great, absolutely speaking, from the point of
view of aesthetic judgement. Giovampagolo's failing is not knowing how to
judge evil and, consequently, not judging it correlatively to the good, and,
absolute judgement being equally comparative, not judging evil in terms of
greatness. He therefore failed to commit a crime 'the greatness of which would
have obliterated any infamy', procured him an immortal glory and protected
him from 'any danger that might arise from it' (ibid.). Judging evil at its correct
value means confronting the insoluble and making the decision of extreme
evil that is a decision on the lesser evil in such a way that it can be said that one
must aim at evil in its absolute character (as *telos*) if one wants to attain a lesser
evil (as *scopos*). Deciding on evil means seizing the event of evil, beginning with
the resolution to relate to its greatness, thereby committing a political act and
working towards the constitution of a common way of life.

The formulation of the limitative statement on the radicality of evil thus
allusively gives us the solution and defines a spirit of the conditions of correct
political judgement. It constructs a policy of the lesser evil which confers on evil
a happy course without in the least effacing the abrupt character of its radicality
in the sense in which Machiavelli understands it.

Now, this spirit can be confirmed by the fact that the statement of principle
about the radicality of evil – its generality and extremity – is answered by
another limitative statement of principle that is subject to a similar metaphysical
character, partially verifiable and partially unverifiable: the statement according
to which 'there is always just as much good and evil' (*Discourses*, II, preface,
p. 266). This regulative statement delimits both the possibility of a politics (it
limits in principle the extension of evil and tears us away from the suspicion of
disaster) and that of an audacious policy of the lesser evil (it limits all ambition
to be forever done with evil). Machiavelli writes,

> When I reflect that it is in this way that events pursue their course it seems to me that
> the world has always been in the same condition, and that in it there has been just as
> much good as there is evil, but that this evil and this good have varied from province to

province. This may be seen from the knowledge we have of ancient kingdoms, in which the balance of good and evil changed from one to the other owing to changes in their customs, whereas the world as a whole remained the same. The only difference was that the world's *virtù* first found a home in Assyria, then flourished in Media and later in Persia, and at length arrived in Italy and Rome. And, if since the Roman empire there has been no other which has lasted, and in which that the world's *virtù* has been centred, one nonetheless finds it distributed among many nations where men lead lives of *virtù*. (Ibid.)

What is affirmed here is not necessarily the existence of a constant parity between the quantity of good and the quantity of evil, but the existence of a constant relation between the two quantities, at the same time as there is an equal probability of good and evil. This affirmation both rests upon and goes beyond the historical data. Historical experience furnishes us only with cases or with examples that are so many signs of this truth. The affirmation binds together this theory of a globally insignificant difference between ages (and of the horizon of a probably null sum of good and evil) with a theory of a cycle whose duration is indeterminate and tendential, and whose periodicity is aleatory and, on this account, very different from the widely accepted versions of cyclical history. This renders a determinate policy possible, first of all on account of the fact that the sum of good that moves about in time and space is positively defined despite the quasi-universal disposition of men (that which binds and holds their relations) toward vice, and second on account of the fact that the movement of the sum of good is designated in terms of the *translatio* of *virtù*. This signifies that the incessant transfer and redistribution of the sum of good is not the doing of Fortune but of glory, and that where one had expected the migration of Fortune as a new translation of the transfer, one finds instead the migration of *virtù*. *Virtù*, following a quantitative relation that does not originate in the generality of men's behaviour, confronts evil, understood here in the sense of bad things that happen. The affirmation of this constant relation between *virtù* and evil confirms the excessive character of the assertion with respect to any verifiable experience. At the same time it indicates that what comes to respond to the actuality or effectivity of evil – towards which every man is nonetheless oriented – is a *positive* quality that transcends any exhaustive determination, the quantity of which has an unassignable origin, *virtù*. Thus, on the one hand, the statement constitutes a regulative safety guard that *defines in right the possibility of an economy*, or poses its condition of possibility and comes to limit the statement of principle regarding the radicality of evil, limit against limit.[6] On the other hand, it defines what comes to respond to evil in the positive terms of an unassignable excellence, in such a way that in this essential respect what answers back to evil is not what effaces it, circumvents it or inhibits it, but what acts *with and against* evil, *virtù*. Thus the character and the nature, the distinguishing mark of politics is found to be drawn according to general ontological considerations about the problem of evil in the world. Its configuration is bound up with these two statements that can be called transcendental, in so far as they partially escape the demand for accountability and are only partially induced from experience or verified by it. Their role is to give a sense of orientation in the space of politics. The two statements limit one another in so far as they complete one another. The formula of the equality of the sum of good and the sum of evil of the ages of the world confirms even as it limits the idea of the inexorability of evil and opens the path to the idea of different compossibilities – to the fiction of a figurable calculus and to the thought of its unfigurable character and of the limit posed on all possible calculations.

The affinity between *virtù* and evil, which relates them to one another as allies, or as face-to-face adversaries, is given a distinctly different accent in *The Prince* and in the *Discourses*. The definition of evil is not the same in the two texts, and the problem of the economy of politics, that is, of the management of the proportion between good and evil and its regulation in time, its course, is not presented in the same way. Nor is that of the economy of evil – the least cost – or that of the nature of its radicality, the form of wickedness. *The Prince* defines evil as a vicious disposition fundamentally connected to the ability to go back on the rule to which one has publicly consented, the ability not to hold to one's promises. Lying, fraud and the betrayal of one's word define men's wickedness, the point that must be regulated and upon which one must act to avoid becoming its first victim, the very thing that makes all human relations, those of internal as well as of external politics, a relation of war. Man is at war, which is to say that he lives according to the given word and its betrayal, what is promised in words and not kept in fact. Wickedness appears with the cunning borrowed from the fox; it is not attached to the force borrowed from the lion, except in the aftermath or to the extent that the borrowing is itself, considered retroactively, an act of simulation. Cunning, or simulation, is what is given in the speech act that defines wickedness and requires that the prince take it as his guide and pre-empt it. Machiavelli writes:

> Those who simply act like lions are stupid. So it follows that a prudent ruler cannot, and must not, honour his word when it places him at a disadvantage and when the reasons for which he made his promise no longer exist. If all men were good, this precept would not be good; but because men are wretched creatures who would not keep their word to you, you need not keep your word to them. (*The Prince*, pp. 99–100)

This cunning is linked to the general regime of dissimulation as such, the same as that which is secretly at work in the speech of counsellors and that a prince who is forewarned and who exceeds his counsellors in cunning and dissimulation listens to without being taken in. All the other qualities of wickedness are to be understood on the basis of the feature of cunning, beginning with that of cruelty. If, in the relation between states, it is necessary not to keep one's promises, in the relation of the prince to his subjects, who are divided into the two forces of the nobility and the common people, the requirements are more complex. Certainly it is appropriate to begin by disappointing, on account of the fact that any seizure of power raises hopes on the part of the allied party that cannot be satisfied immediately. If the absolute beginning of this time is like a promise of happiness, it is due to the state of grace which it elicits (the power of innovation or the public favour of the *status nascendi*) and not to verbal promises; whereas the beginning as such, the time that follows the absolute beginning, represents precisely a time in which it is appropriate to disappoint by refusing to promise, in order not to have to keep promises that cannot be kept, and to gain the favour of all, starting with the party of internal enemies, by keeping promises that have not been made, thereby astonishing them. It should be said that the distinction between good and bad cruelty opposes the figure of the prince who keeps promises he has not made (begins with evil and continues with good) to that of the prince who does not keep his promises (begins with good and continues with evil), on account of the very fact that the beginning *is* a promise, not only from the point of view of innovation but also from that of the formation of a habit. An acquired habit is a given word. The problem of cruelty in the internal political relations of a state, central to *The Prince*, can also come down to a para-doxical treatment of the promise that does not entirely agree with characteristic relations between states. Still, the general economy of the relation to the promise is entirely paradoxical with respect to the formula of 'keeping a promise' and, in all the forms of paradox it implies, constitutes a gap with respect to the ideal of proper action. For it is at one moment a question of not keeping a promise made and at another of keeping a promise that was never made, in a relation which is always one of distortion and dissymmetry. All these inversions obey a principle of dissimulation.

This is because it is a matter of calculating or of following the right economy in the administration of the dose of good and evil, of choosing the opportune moment to commit evil (the good kind of cruelty), of knowing when in the whole causal chain of actions and events to inscribe the time of what is outside of any causal chain, and when to inscribe disconnection in connection itself. Not making a decision, refusing to use cunning and even lies with a view towards the choice of the right chain of events, resisting the notion of a good kind of cruelty, 'if it is permissible to talk in this way of what is evil' (*The Prince*, p. 66), means capitulating to weakness in face of evil (the bad kind of cruelty, the highest price to be paid, evil committed by constraint and not by a sense of political decision) and clearing the way for what can be called sovereign evil. Sovereignty of evil here signifies the totality of evil as a maximum evil, whereas the economy of evil implies the principle of a minimum evil, it being understood that the general economy of good and evil – the principle of the sum – is particularly valid here, at the level of the microcosm (every good has a drawback proper to it, the converse obviously not being true), just as it is valid globally, at the level of the macrocosm. This minimum evil, however, is a supreme evil – an unavoidable cruelty and an accursed share – and, on this account, it remains sovereign. One must know how to distinguish the *kairos* for the extremity of evil and for acting gloriously, if one does not want to get caught in the trap of being forced to have recourse to the greatest evil, or of having to give in to evil by weakness and cowardice, by surrendering to the occasion. A single gesture distinguishes the political use of evil both from the practice of vice and from political weakness, for on both sides it is a question of an evil that escapes decision as it escapes any principle of economy. Political decision-making does not thereby allow one definitively to escape from the impossibility of deciding on evil or from being carried away by sovereign evil, and it is in this that the corruption of every regime and every exercise of power consists. Deciding upon evil puts off the tragic for as long as possible; it is what constructs the best possible argument on the combined basis of the tragic and the aleatory. In this line, deciding on evil does not limit itself to taking into account the evil to be committed in a chain of events. It must include the ability to grasp the unpredictable occurrence of what presents itself unexpectedly as an evil to be committed, or to reinscribe disconnection in a chain of events whose connections have been ordained. It conjoins a principle of economy and an anti-economical principle of the limitation of any power of calculation, reimplying the incalculable in calculation and judging calculation on the basis of the incalculable, and vice versa.

The thought of *The Prince* thus defines evil in terms of dissimulation, particularly verbal dissimulation, and describes a symmetrical economy of good and evil, and an economy of evil in itself, by integrating the notion of disconnection in a chain of events and of the incalculable in calculation. The question of the handling of evil in *The Prince* is essentially that of the relations between cruelty and decision-making, based on this consideration of the relation to the given word. It is a question of answering back in advance thanks to the very practice of dissimulation, for it is dissimulation that makes possible a whole parachronism of political time. Politics, in all its dimensions, is war pursued by means of cunning, and it is only in cunning that all the uses of evil are in play, where the best defence is a good offence. The general relation is a relation of antedated symmetry. In the same movement, a certain economy of evil takes on its full value from the good use of cruelty and from its correct distribution in time. Since there is no way to escape committing evil, it is a question of pre-empting evil with respect to oneself and with respect to others, and thus beginning with evil if one wants to diminish its burden and give it the accent of greatness. To begin with evil is to take the initiative with respect to it, and in this initiative to diminish evil's share by reason of the affective logic of passional intersubjectivity. This logic implies that an evil deferred makes the imminence of the threat weigh more heavily (and fills men, the prince's subjects as well as the prince himself, with distrust and terror) and thereby indirectly increases the quantity of evil (for the fear of the threat has all the weight of evil; as a promise of violence, it is violence), even as it directly increases the quantity of evil in a vertiginous and incalculable manner, since this quantity can no longer be managed, the prince having to surrender to it in uncontrollable proportions, even while retroactively marking the good previously done with the sign of cowardice or of evil in effect. The affective logic of the passional intersubjectivity of politics makes evil deferred a considerably heavier evil according to all dimensions of time, in every respect. The alternative is thus between being 'always forced to have the knife ready in [one's] hand' (*The Prince*, p. 66), and passing for never having accomplished any good, or for having always been cowardly and passive or, on the contrary, committing evil all at once and never having to do it again. Even if it *were* a question of the same quantity of good and evil in formal terms, it would not be the same quantity in fact on account of the repercussions of the act in time and the change that occurs in the order of time in the two cases. Deciding on evil means responding to the causal chain that implies that evil exercised suddenly and in its totality is less painful, and that good, on the contrary, can be more fully savoured when it is done bit by bit. Thus cowardice in the face of evil, far from attenuating it, aggravates it, all the while diminishing good's power of repercussion, its intensity, even effacing all trace of this good by a sort of retroactive anaesthesia and amnesia.

In the *Discourses* the problem of evil takes on another relief, or rather the very depths of the problem envisaged by *The Prince* are set against a different backdrop. If the problem is still closely correlated to dissimulation, despite Machiavelli's discursive feints, its initial form here does not oppose a *virtuoso* use stemming from a greatness of dissimulation, like that of the new prince, to a cowardly and weak use, obeying the inclination to vice, weakly dissimulating, characteristic of most men. Instead the question of terror and not that of cruelty is placed at the heart of the problem, and two different courses of terror are opposed. In *The Prince*, the question of awe (*stupeur*) is subordinated, and this is

marked by the fact that the figure of the lion, force in its majesty, represents the
figure of fear with respect to the wolves and does not in the least define the nature
of wickedness, whereas in the *Discourses*, wickedness is primordially an affair of
the use of terror, and consequently is directly involved in a genealogy of force
rather than a genesis of the broken word. Thus the problem of deciding on evil
no longer engages so much the question of cruelty as that of terror, which gives
all the more depth to the treatment of awe. Very strangely, at first glance, it
appears that the legitimate use of evil is no longer defined by a difference in the
level of dissimulation and in the economy of cruelty, but by an absolutely new way
of making the most general possible use of terror. There, where those who do not
understand politics generally practise a specular terror, the truly political man
generally responds with a terror of another order that escapes the attraction of
specular terror. Generally, for he continues to practise specular terror, it only
defines the major mode of political relations between states and no longer of
internal politics, where it is henceforth only a minor mode. The *Discourses* thus
proceed to make some astonishing divisions: the wrenching of a practice of terror
away from the ordinary and primordial one; the distinction between two courses
(the course of the relation between states, which broadly obeys a relation of
symmetrical terror, and the course of the relation between political forces, which
becomes the essential problem and broadly obeys a dissymmetrical terror); and
the repercussions of one course upon the other and of the two inverted hier-
archies that the courses are arranged in as to which predominates, the specular
terror or the terror which tears itself away from it. Likewise, the relation of war
between homogeneous instances is no longer the essential point; what counts is
civil struggle between heterogeneous instances, and this has repercussions upon
the nature of war between states and vice versa. It is in the *Discourses* that
Machiavelli discovers the great scene of politics and thus enlarges the theatre of
the uses of evil as much as he deepens the stage by returning to the thought of
the primitive scene and of the arch-scene. Machiavelli thus reflects more pro-
foundly upon the question of the origins of evil and conceptualizes the form of
deciding on evil not in terms of the relation between decision-making and cruelty,
but in the strikingly different terms of the relation between law and terror.

Machiavelli in fact thinks the question of the interwoven origins of evil.
The truth of relations of power takes place on the basis of two origins: that of
the commonality of desires and competitive rivalry in the appropriation of the
same goods occurring under the sign of rarity (honour and wealth);[7] and that
of the primitive and primordial communication of fears. Even though it is not
possible to trace the exact genesis of these two origins, it is the latter that is more
primordial and primitive. Everything begins with an exchange of terror:

And the sequence in which these events occur is such that men seek first to be free
from apprehension, then make others apprehensive, and that the injuries of which
they had ridded themselves, they proceeded to inflict on others. It was as if it were
necessary either to treat others ill or to be ill-treated. (*Discourses*, I, 46, p. 224)

This scene of exchange of offence and fright is played 'in an instant'. It can be
visualized according to a slight diachrony (hardly has one escaped from fear
than one sends it off in a reflection in order to escape the imminence of its
return) as it presents itself with a certain recurrence in history, but it is itself
primitive and transhistorical, synchronic and like a single stroke. It is a sort of
primitive scene of politics. I have just escaped from fear, a fear of being attacked
which is not necessarily well-founded, an a priori fear, a fear that I decipher by
reading a threat in the other's face. Instantaneously, I live my violence in the
violence that I grasp in his features; I send the imminent threat back to him in a
reflection. But the other's face is like a tangent. I read fear and threat in the
other's face simultaneously, indistinctly – the threat he holds over me and the
fear that my face inspires in him. It is impossible to know who began to frighten
and who began to be afraid. This scene of projection and reciprocal anticipation
condemns the two parties to a sort of race against the clock. Hardly – but this
instant is subliminal – have I escaped fear by freeing myself from its grasp than I
seek to take the initiative and, not content to find myself free and safe, seek to
bring the other down. The two moments – escaping the other's grasp and taking
the initiative; gaining my freedom and establishing my domination – are
contiguous rather than successive, and the desire for self-preservation is tied, in
the blink of an eye, to the desire to destroy the other; escaping the other's grasp
and pre-empting him are as if one and the same act. 'If I don't do it first, he
will.' This primitive scene of politics is the foundation of the relation between
oppressor and oppressed. The relation can moreover be set forth in several ways:
at the same instant, I live my violence in the fear the other inspires in me and I
live my fear in the fear I inspire. Merleau-Ponty writes in his commentary: 'It is in
the same moment that I am about to be afraid that I make others afraid; it is the
same aggression that I repel and send back upon others; it is the same terror
which threatens me that I spread abroad – I live my fear in the fear that I
inspire'.[8] This test is non-negotiable: it is completely without verification of what
happened at the origin or the initiative of the relation; it is abyssal; it does not
forgive.

But for Machiavelli, one cannot liberate oneself from the relation of specular
terror at the foundation of the whole relation of the race for domination by a sort
of conversion of identification. The chiasmic discovery that 'by a counter-shock,

the suffering that I cause rends me along with my victim; and so cruelty is no solution but must always be begun again', is insufficiently liberating. One cannot escape it by the fault line present in the relation of symmetry when, in what Merleau-Ponty calls 'a Communion of Black Saints', I discover that 'the evil that I do I do to myself, and in struggling against others I struggle equally against myself'. This fault line in the specular relation makes the cruel man, upon seeing in the other's face a word, a word of anxiety and defeat, discover, even if only minimally, the truth of the alter ego, the fact that there is (an)other myself. The opening of this breach does not make us progress from a relation of force to a relation between subjects, from pure difference and pure identity – animality – to the play of difference and identity, of the common measure – humanity.

Machiavelli cannot agree with this kind of sublation by access to the human. His thought seeks to hold itself upon the threshold between the human and the inhuman, and not to cross the threshold. Given that evil is unavoidable, it is not so easy to liberate oneself from the originary specular terror; evil does not lift like fog at the advent of language. The economy of human relations, which is founded on rivalry and whose essential basis is the exchange of terror, will never cease to persist and to haunt every human relationship. Henceforth, the practice of evil will always be that of pre-emption, of not keeping one's promises, of inscribing within the mix of action and speech a sort of riposte or reply to the exchange of terror that does not take us out of the realm of that exchange, but pursues it by elaborating it. The transmission of offence is what founds war as the definitive paradigm of politics. This negativity will never give rise to any conversion or elevation of evil to dignity. No mobilization of fear will be able to put an end to the exchange of fears, exactly as no sharing of a common good can allow us to be done with rivalry.

But the interest of Machiavelli's thought is to introduce, in addition to this way of taking the question into account according to the logic of homogeneity, a way of taking it into account according to the logic of heterogeneity, and a way of reinscribing the vicissitudes of the disagreement within this latter logic. It is a question of avoiding a certain course of the common evil. This course is that of violence under the condition of the One (or of the double), on the level of both the foundation of the state and the on-going course of political relations. This violence haunts the state from its foundation and threatens to ruin the regime of the greatest good and the least evil. Another model delivers to us, in effect, *the key to political difference*; it introduces politics itself and confers a happier course upon evil. This model demands that the condition of disconnection be maintained and that public space be fixed as dissymmetrical. It presents itself in different ways according to the essential moments of politics.

It is first of all necessary that the state not be self-founded. Self-foundation is the first form of the domination of the One, a 'left' sense of autonomy, an exorbitant pretension to self-sufficiency and to doing without the other, as if matter had to give itself form, to be both matter and form, the bronze and the sculptor, a mute violence of self upon self, an impossible demand. *There must therefore be foundation*: foundation introduces the condition of minimal heterogeneity and paradoxically makes possible the emergence of freedom as independence or as emancipation. The founder should come from the outside and the relation should be between a lawgiver/founder and a dispersed people. The gesture of foundation coming from the exterior or *as if* from the exterior of the dispersed people emancipates from foreign domination, fulfils the condition of independence and delivers one from the illusion of pure autonomy.[9] A lawgiver/founder thus must impose a form upon the matter of the state. But this is a first form. This notion of a first form or of the beginning of a form is essential. This is why Machiavelli does not conceive of foundation (for example, the foundation of Rome by Romulus, if the regression is stopped at that point) and praise it as a foundation/fabrication.[10] For Machiavelli it is not a matter of giving the state its whole form or creating the entirety of the state. Foundation/fabrication, on the contrary, is an attempt to create the unity of the state at a single stroke and in a single gesture, to accomplish the state's task according to the affirmation of a beginning that is also a completion. By this very fact, it ties the foundation of the state very closely to the gesture of the founder, in such a way that the state will never be able to gain an independence with respect to its founder: their fates are absolutely bound together. In foundation/fabrication, the state is tied too closely both to itself (its hands are tied) and to its founder. Foundation can only succeed if it does not take place in this way. Foundation is rather of the order of an encounter between a man and a people, in which the founder's *virtù* communicates with that of the people by a reciprocal impulsion, more of the order of an establishment of a relation than of the fabrication of a reality. The mosaic motif is ever present in order to mark and fuse together the foundation of a people in the mode of a double election (alliance and oath) and the foundation of the state, according to an operation that takes place in both directions and an exchange of the values of the two acts brought together as one. Nor does the founder entirely mark the body politic with the seal of the One. If it is indeed a question of giving a form to a new matter, it is in a quite particular mode. The unformed must be led to take hold of itself in a form, and in an uncompleted form. Moreover, the problem is only one of technique, of working out a relation between the unformed's potential for action and a form that escapes the technical relation. This relation does not create a definitive and irreversible order, a natural inclination, because it is not a question of making a body out of matter, of forcing it to take on a physical unity. There is indeed a violence done in this act, and of the highest degree, but this violence is not a dissolution of disconnection. This is why Machiavelli praises so the foundation of Rome. At the foundation of Rome, there is terror; Machiavelli praises the effect of awe present in the murder of Remus: 'when the effect is good . . . it always justifies the action' (*Discourses*, I, 9, p. 132). A relation of means to end is present there, or so it would seem, but it would be wrong to believe that from this moment onward any sort of dialectic of means and ends is put into place; it stops there, and it is not a watchword. Terror is a silent event; it is not the putting into place of a regime and the putting into circulation of a political arrangement that can run all by itself. Silent awe allows the event of foundation by one man alone: a foundation that relatively unifies the Roman people. This operation does not eradicate the plurality or the dispersal of the people it unifies, and could never resemble the foundation of a unitary state (a unified Italy or France), a nation-state; the configuration of unity is minimal. What makes this foundation exemplary is what could be called the condition of disconnection, of incompleteness and of exposure to Fortune, and it is thus that the greatest good and the least evil are primitively realized. This terror that relatively unifies has hardly any relation to the project of radical foundation assigned to the gesture of revolutionary foundation, and if Machiavelli demands that it be made one of the exemplary sources for conceptualizing the task to be accomplished, it is under conditions which prevent the foundation from being saturated. It is thus in a form that is neither that of harmony (politics is originarily what does not form a concert and what does not accord without violence) nor that of the violence of the One, that the gesture of foundation finds a legitimacy from which inspiration can be drawn.

Beginning with this point, in a second moment, the body politic can take the more just path, the preferable path, that of political division. The *différend*[11] is the only way to construct the common good on a foundation other than the suffocation of political forces, to give life to the law, for it is the best way to get around this sharing of evil that extreme terror and specular fright represent. The solution to specular terror (and once again, the word 'solution' is not entirely appropriate, and perhaps it would be better to speak of attenuating an ever-present risk of precipitation into specular terror), disengagement from this terror here depends on the existence of a *différend* between the humours of the two parties:

> if we ask what it is the nobility are after and what it is the common people are after, it
> will be seen that in the former there is a great desire to dominate and in the latter

merely the desire not to be dominated. Consequently the latter will be more keen on liberty. (*Discourses*, I, 5, p. 116)

This is something like a political nature and a de facto political difference that opposes two heterogeneous humours or desires, the desire to dominate and the desire not to be dominated/not to dominate. This opposition no longer rests upon the division of a common goal, a common good, that of power, wealth and honour, nor on the form of a desire for freedom in the mode of comparative appropriation, but on the divergence of goals between the desire for power on the one side – which is infinite because it is always a desire for more power, and which seeks to impose its goal in a hegemonic fashion – and, on the other side, the desire for absolute freedom – which is every bit as infinite in its own way because it requires beyond measure the freedom not to be oppressed/not to oppress/not to govern, a desire for nonpower that equally seeks to impose its goal on the whole of the social. This political *différend* – there is a *différend* because each of the two parties does not share the other's goal even while recognizing it and experiencing it in a minor key, in recognition of misrecognition – makes it possible to get over or get around the scene in the mirror, even though one is always rubbing up against it, and allows one to avoid the bad solution of unity conquered or acquired on the basis of a shared attraction for a common good and a shared repulsion for a common evil. Political difference makes it possible to avoid the impoverishment of public space and precipitation into a crime committed in the name of the One (reason of state or terror).

This political difference, which is a difference in nature or which is situated somewhere between nature and culture, is not of itself enough for a disengagement from specular terror. The role of the state is to institute the division and to inscribe evil along this fold. To institute means above all to sanction the political difference or the difference of destination of the nobility and the common people, a difference of destination that is a difference of postulation or desire and a difference in fear. But, at the same time as it sanctions and confirms this orientation, institution also limits the ambition or weakens the realization of each one of these desires, in their absolute character and their pretension to political hegemony. Juridical and political institutions are there in order to confirm and inform political difference, in order to reinscribe the *différend* and to regulate it relationally. At the same time, the institution can have no possible power, and this quarrel of rights can have no possible vitality without constantly drawing on the source, the inexhaustible reserve of the uninstituted and the uninstitutible. Furthermore, one could say that the more the institution reinforces itself, the more it leans upon this reserve, which is also its reserve of possible institutions. The quarrel of rights is indissociable from the disorder of tumults and of what does not present itself in argumentation or in language, but in silence or in a cry, the inarticulate character of sharp violence. The conflict which gives rise to this violence is the very life of the republic and presents itself in these tumults,[12] a conflict that comes to institute itself even as it preserves that which in it is a resistance to institution. The institution as an inscription and regulation of the *différend* signifies that the self-governance of society is what makes possible the quarrel of rights and the negotiation of disputes, and what does not prohibit violence or close public space to the possibility of the emergence of a savagery, the violence of silence or of a cry, that is, to the conflict that bears with it the strongest portion of heterogeneity between the two parties in the relation. The republic is the best formula for politics on account of the possibilities it offers on all levels and the dimensions of this capacity to reinscribe and to regulate the *différend*. Thus, politics is the ability to confer upon public space its problematic *nature* by constituting it as a dissymmetry, that is, by authorizing a new form of the condition of disconnection in relatedness, that of dissension among political forces. The self-governance of society is most powerful when the polity maintains the whole spectrum of its division, from radical heterogeneity to hard-won agreement, without ever dissolving into the disparate and without ever forming a body. Machiavelli's invention does not so much consist in conceiving of a better arrangement of organized institutional space as in offering the possibility of an exposition of the whole spectrum of the *différend*, from the sharpest heterogeneity to the agreement that proposes a settlement. Disengagement from the specular terror does not occur by a policy of avoidance of violent conflict in its acuity, whether the formula for avoiding it be that of the perfect constitution, or of instituted harmony – mixed government – or even of a quarrel of rights that excludes the savagery of humours, or of any form of organicity of the body politic and of the regulation of disagreements.

Thus, under this condition of heterogeneity, a different kind of relation of harmony and conflict, and a different kind of relation of violence can take place which guarantee public space. The republican refoundation cannot be thought on the model of fabrication, because here too, in analogy with the problem of foundation itself, it does not take place under the sign of the One. It is no longer a question here of constituting the people's loose bond with itself or with its founder, but of constituting the greatest gap in division, or a division that would not be organized around a common good. One must go further still: it is the whole course of politics, and more particularly the history of the republic, of which Rome is the best example historically, which is placed under this general condition of problematic unity and disconnection and which commands a certain relation to violence from which terror itself is never absent. Terror is present not only at the moment of foundation and refoundation, but at a much higher frequency and periodicity. Terror is like a second language there. This second language of terror is not conjunctural; it is constitutive of the preservation of public space in its dissymmetry.

This language of terror unites the exercise of terror to the example of political virtue. Every form of state, and particularly composite political bodies – such as republics – needs to submit to self-examination in order either to maintain or recapture its original splendour. The impetus for this can be an accidental event arriving from the outside or one's own doing. Machiavelli tells us that the latter can be due to the law itself or to 'some good man who arises in their midst and by his example and his virtuous deeds produces the same effect as does the constitution' (*Discourses*, III, 1, p. 387), a man who has *virtù*. The relation is nonetheless complex, since it appears that even when there is such an institution (the law that created the tribunes of the people, that which named the censors and all the laws against the appropriation of power and the hegemony of power relations), it can only reawaken the body politic if a *virtuoso* man accompanies it with the authority of his *virtù*. The law brings life back to the state, but a man's *virtù* imposes life upon the institution itself. And when this occurs, the event of a man's *virtù* responds to the institutional event and inscribes its example in an uncommon union with terror. He strikes a great blow (*coup*). Machiavelli writes:

> For between one case of disciplinary action of this type and the next there ought to elapse at most ten years, because by this time men begin to change their habits and to break the laws; and, unless something happens which recalls to their minds the penalty involved and reawakens fear in them, there will soon be so many delinquents that it will be impossible to punish them without danger. (*Discourses*, III, 1, pp. 387–8)

What are the essential features of this status of terror?

1. Terror is not exclusively an inaugural fact of the foundation of the state or of the republican refoundation of the state; it is, in a certain mode, constitutive of the regular course of the republic or of its inscription in duration, which cannot take place without periodic ruptures that necessitate a recurrence of the great *coup* of terror. It always occurred in Rome as an event whose intervals could not be defined or programmed; the Roman event was not prescribed, and doubtless the condition of prescription is, in itself, a factor that corrodes the nature of the great *coup*. Independent of the fact that Machiavelli fixes a periodicity, terror is not nor can it be programmed, and it is still as event that it is to be desired. Terror presents itself in the register of the event, and this event is only ever a limited act that does not begin a series or an epoch. It is a unique act that reforms history.

2. This event of terror gives renewed life to the republican law. The law and its institution do not suffice by themselves; terror is necessary, and it is necessary in order to renew the law or so that right can live. It is an awe that accompanies the institution and that depends upon it, so that one cannot oppose the fact of the republican institution to the existence of terror. This terror does not only maintain the institution, it renews it; it is what accompanies and allows the development of republican institutions. If there is a republic that becomes more complex and more perfect, there is a certain recurrence of events of terror. Which is to say that the terror is not present because the republic is absent. This awe accompanies not an institutional void but the institution itself, not the celebration of the institution or its immobility but its innovation and its mobility, not a taking hold of itself (*ressaisissement*) in unity, but in division.

3. This event of terror allows the composite body politic to take hold of itself in its principle. Is it, properly speaking, a question of attacking corruption and remaking the body politic (*refaire du corps*)? It is nothing of the sort. This reprise of refoundation that punctuates the history of the republic corresponds neither to the model of reform (attempting to correct the deformed in order to give it back its form and improve it) nor to the model of revolution (eradicating the deformed). It is rather a question of replunging the deformed into the unformed, and, on the basis of the unformed, of reviving it by giving it a new form. The terror is a moment that cannot be completely inscribed and that acts in the promiscuity of the deformed and the unformed, in the way that they constantly brush up against one another. At this moment, it is not a question of remaking the unity of the body politic (*refaire de l'un et du corps*), but of redividing or remaking the passage from division without principle, pure scission or the disorders of the state, to division according to principle. Terror thus remakes the dissension between the political forces, channels heterogeneity once again and gives voice to the reprise of the *différend* and its margin of possible expression, to its conflict between a supplementary articulation and a relaunching of what cannot be articulated: the invention of the tribunate and the censors. The act does not aim at correcting the deformed in order to give it back its form, for the deformed cannot be corrected and the previous form cannot be re-established. It cannot be a question of correcting corruption by the carrot or the stick. It is not a question of a terror that unifies, but of an awe, close to terror, that redivides. Or rather it unifies the two parties upon the rediscovery of their division.

4. This awe which is sometimes identical with the terror and sometimes close to it is played out simultaneously in the relation of the *virtuoso* man to public

space and in the relation of a rediscovered dissymmetry between the two parties that divide public space. The *virtuoso* man, whether he supplements the law or accompanies it, incarnates or condenses within himself an effect of admiring awe through a double gesture. He unites the public via the fact of its division and turns the two parties over to an awe in the face of the other, an awe that is reciprocal but not specular, since it rests not upon grasping similarity but, quite to the contrary, grasping unsurpassable alterity. He simultaneously unites the public upon the possibility of inscribing this division juridically, on the level of institutional, juridical articulation, of dialogue and debate. He thus operates conjointly on the levels of what can and what cannot be articulated. In this moment and in the intrication of motifs this awe is attached to the person who cast the intrigue of politics back into play and who did so by an extraordinary gesture.

5. This event of terror is tied to *virtù* in its moral and political ambiguity, or rather in the relation between *virtù* and evil, which is one of contiguity and not identity. In the list of names evoked by Machiavelli, that of Junius Brutus is to be found in the first rank, even though the examination of his story marked the proximity of his gesture to royal terror.[13] And this is not the only example. This is because between virtue and terror, there is proximity (and not the subordination of a means to an end) in *virtù*, but if terror is not a means, neither is it the essential feature of *virtù*, as is the case with terrible virtue. *Virtù* does not entertain an immediate affinity with terror, and terror does not follow from it in a straight line. *Virtù* imposes the necessity of terror upon itself. The ability of *virtù* to sustain the conflict between the moral and the political and to confront the moral dilemma involved in the contrariness between the republican law and the symbolic law is clearly illustrated here. What suscitates awe and admiration is the gesture, which is principally a gesture of transgression out of the bounds of the ordinary, of symbolic law (the murder of the father, the son, the friend, of the closest person to whom I am indebted) in defence of the republican law. Such extraordinary transgression can be encountered even in filiation and political alliance. The model of the morality of purity is neither present nor demanded here, for what is present is the model of courage in necessary evil. The act's equivocal character between virtue and radical evil is maintained. Evil here encounters only its majesty: it is political and constitutes the beneficent course of evil; not its facility, vice, but the course which, in a single difficult act, demands political courage and something like a presence of mind to evil. This courage has value only if the act is sober, and, in a sense, minimal, a lesser evil (such as killing the Pope).

6. This terror is silent. It is not capable of giving reasons for itself. It is a

transgression that knows itself to be such, but one whose share of evil is unavowable. If it displays itself in public, it is in silence. The facts will never cease to accuse it, even if the results will fail to excuse it. This is why it most frequently suscitates an admiration that suspends praise and blame. Silent, the event inspires silence. Evil remains opaque: without self-justification, without appeal. Now, this silent terror that allows the redivision of the body politic is accompanied by a pagan religion which does not forgo terror, or which, both on its own account and in its correlation with politics, also allows a taking hold of self in principle by the exercise of terror. Pagan religion is a religion that exists in cunning but also in violence, a religion of bloody sacrifices of animals: 'such spectacles, because terrible, caused men to become like them' (*Discourses* II, 2, p. 278). This is a noteworthy aspect: pagan religion is accompanied by terror or finds itself in an analogy with political terror just as it, too, can accompany political terror, and this proximity is what gives it the vocation of making action possible and of remaking the division. Here the Roman religion allows a sacrificial terror whose vocation, in an act of extraordinary transgression, is to refound the division. It is the spirit that presides over the redeployment of public space in the silence of transgression, and it is as much a factor of men's division as of their unity.

7. This terror is an act of division of political space, but it is conjointly an act of division of political time. This division of political time does not take on the same character and does not have the same intensity when it is a matter of the republican refoundation properly speaking and when it is a matter of the invention of the tribunate, for example. But, in a certain fashion, between one time and the other, it is necessary to inscribe a gulf, and for it to appear that the same language is no longer spoken. The act of terror is what inscribes this gulf. The *coup* of terror that brings us back to the order of division according to the heterogeneity and the *différend* of public space, and to the order of the republic as a body politic or as a mode of treatment of the division, is also what inscribes difference and divorce between the before and the after. It is the inscription of the unformed in the between-two-forms or the impossibility for the previous form to persevere in its being (the deformed), the impossibility to retranslate the new form into the old one and vice versa. It deepens the *différend* between the two times, while the *différend* between the political forces themselves grows deeper still. A language cannot be split, and the new way of speaking makes translation into the old way of speaking impossible, even as it affirms itself as having been there from all time, eternal and shared: it terrorizes. But it can only do so on the basis of the reference to an even more ancient language, as if the

amnesia of the preceding time was possible only on the basis of the anamnesis of an even further-off time.

These essential features of republican awe reveal its nature, in which, as in the case of the terror of foundation, one can clearly see the economic character, the mode of symbolization in dissimulation, and the mode of obedience to what can be called the condition of disconnection. It closely links evil and the law in a relation not only of antagonism, but also of correlation: for evil is as powerful as the law, in a way that makes the law, however severe and inflexible it might be, capable of turning evil back on itself. Such an existence for the law could not be identified with any possible rhetoric of the unconditional, even if the level of the law has the value of a transcendental event. Consequently, republican awe refers back to an economy of evil and the greatest good that is forever exposed to the risk of collapsing into specular terror (the terror of the double). This is all the more true since, while the features of the interior political legitimacy primarily incarnated by the republican model are clearly drawn by the nature of terror in disconnection, this legitimacy exists in a constant correlation with the other model in so far as the relation between states is entirely situated on the side of homogeneity. In this model the alternative is that of oppressor and oppressed, and thus relations between states are haunted by the primitive scene of the specular terror. Here, the *différend* is quite limited, even though Machiavelli evokes the incomparable character of possible models of states such as Italy and France. Now, the exterior scene of relations between states makes itself felt on the interior scene of relations between political forces. But the interior scene resists the exterior scene and reacts upon it by enrolling it in its own mode. The conflict between France and Italy is not only a conflict of homogeneous powers, but also a conflict between heterogeneous powers or between different senses of power (the power of a state that does not judge itself on the basis of the ambition to be One-Body against the power of a centralizing and unified state that does judge itself on the basis of this unity of the Body).

Thus the common affinity of *virtù* and evil engages a strict correlation between cruelty and decision-making or between terror and the law, depending on whether one is dealing with *The Prince* or with the *Discourses*. However the handling of evil might be posed and resolved, it takes place during the opening of the archi-scene of history as a common confrontation between *virtù* and Fortune. This confrontation designates *virtù*'s ability to break with Fortune and thereby impose another end on it. Deciding on evil is a point of both attachment and detachment to jealous Fortune. It is what is disengaged in two senses: what frees itself from Fortune and what comes out of it, a way of getting loose without getting away. It is thereby a politics of the lesser evil that includes the irreducible even as it retranslates it: a politics that declares that one can allow oneself to praise or to blame evil, and which, at the same time, includes a lesser evil which is the minimum of the extreme, whose excess plays such a crucial role in the economy of a common way of life that judgement upon it is suspended to the point that one can say of the act that 'if [it] is not loved, at least [it] escapes being hated' (*The Prince*, p. 97). This is what makes the politics of Machiavelli a politics of the threshold and not of a going beyond, in opposition to every experience of sovereign evil and of the heart of darkness.[14]

Translated by James Swenson

Notes

1. See Niccolò Machiavelli, *Discourses on the First Ten Decades of Titus Livy*, ed. Bernard Crick, trans. Leslie J. Walker, S.J. (Harmondsworth: Penguin 1983), Book III, chapter 1. Citations are given in the text with book, chapter and page numbers.
2. See Niccolò Machiavelli, *The Prince*, trans. George Bull (Harmondsworth: Penguin 1981), chapters 28 and 23. Citations are given in the text.
3. See Machiavelli, *The Prince*, chapter 18.
4. Legation 13.18, 4 November 1503, in Niccolò Machiavelli, *The Chief Works and Others*, trans. Allan Gilbert (Durham: Duke University Press 1989), vol. I, p. 143.
5. 'They could not believe that it was any good motive, or his conscience, that held him back, for the heart of a criminal who had committed incest with his own sister and to gain the throne had put to death his cousins and his nephews, could scarce be influenced by any pious consideration' (*Discourses*, I, 27, p. 178).
6. This is a fashion of opposing one presupposition to another or of making the two ends meet.
7. See *The Prince*, chapter 25, and *Discourses*, I, 37.
8. Maurice Merleau-Ponty, 'A Note on Machiavelli', in *Signs*, trans. Richard C. McCleary (Evanston: Northwestern University Press 1964), p. 212. Subsequent citations are from the same page.
9. See *Discourses*, I, 1.
10. In 'What is Authority', *Between Past and Future: Eight Essays in Political Thought* (New York: Viking 1961), pp. 138–9, Hannah Arendt ties the exercise of terror to the project of foundation as making or fabrication and to the fulfilment of the state in a single creation according to the dialectic of means and ends, and attributes this general conception of politics to Machiavelli (Robespierre and the revolutionary terror are being situated in this filiation). This interpretation does not seem to be correct; on this point see my 'Le risque de l'actuel', *Cahiers de philosophie*, no. 13 (October 1991), p. 64.
11. The legal term *différend* is borrowed from Jean-François Lyotard, who defines it as 'a case of conflict, between (at least) two parties, that cannot be equitably resolved for lack of a rule of judgment applicable to both arguments' (*The Differend: Phrases in Dispute*, trans. Georges Van Den Abbeele [Minneapolis: University of Minnesota Press 1988], p. xi). I have left the term untranslated throughout. — Trans.
12. Machiavelli writes: 'To me, those who condemn the quarrels between the nobles and the plebs seem to be caviling at the very things that were the primary cause of Rome's retaining her freedom, and they pay more attention to the noise and clamour resulting from such commotions than to what resulted from them, i.e. to the good effects they produced' (*Discourses*, I, 4, p. 113).

13. See *Discourses*, III, 3.
14. In his novel *Heart of Darkness* (Harmondsworth: Penguin 1995), Joseph Conrad allows one to hear this passage beyond the threshold and this encounter with 'evil or truth' (p. 44). Evil then presents itself in the sovereignty of its abstraction, in relation to an Idea and a disinterested faith in it, 'something you can set up and bow down before, and offer a sacrifice to' (p. 20); and it is the intimacy of the relation to the sovereign abstraction of evil that suscitates the most irresistible emotion of the most powerful terror: 'The fact is, I was completely unnerved by a sheer blank fright, pure abstract terror, unconnected with any distinct shape of physical danger' (p. 104). Machiavelli's politics of the least evil is resistance itself to this intimacy with terror.

7 SEE NO EVIL, SPEAK NO EVIL
Hate Speech and Human Rights

RENATA SALECL

What is going on when someone utters 'hate speech'? What does a speaker hope to accomplish by disparaging members of another nation or race, by proclaiming the Jews guilty of all kinds of conspiracies, by declaring homosexuals to be social misfits or by publicly denouncing women as inferior human beings? Would someone who publicly blames blacks, Jews or even single mothers for all the troubles of society actually be happier if these people were simply to disappear? Of course not. It is common knowledge, for example, that one encounters a higher incidence of anti-Semitism in those countries where there are very few Jews, such as the Austrian provinces before World War II. If the goal of hate speech is not really to change anything, then what is its intention? And how can we control its effects?

I will address these questions with the help of Lacanian psychoanalysis. Lacan's theory suggests an understanding of the problem of violence and speech which differs from that of structuralist and poststructuralist theorists, primarily because Lacan's notion of the subject does not give way on the issue of responsibility. Additionally, psychoanalysis will help us to reassess the dilemma currently posed by cultural relativism. Every culture understands what violence is in a different way and every culture also has a different under-standing of those universals – human rights, equality, freedom – that motivate its attempts to combat violence.

But the problem with cultural relativists is that they do not see that their tolerance for difference is always only a different form of the tolerance that allows their governments to deal with ethnic and racial conflicts in other nations according to their own interests.

The Violence of Words

Is the subject whose speech hurts a member of an ethnic minority or race responsible for his or her action? Relying on deconstructionist theory, Judith Butler has offered one way to answer this question: the subject who utters injurious speech only quotes from the existing corpus of racist speech; he or she repeats, re-cites, fragments of the discursive environment, of the reasoning and habits of the community. The subject who is perceived as the author of injurious speech is therefore only the effect, the *result* of the very citation; and the fact that the subject appears to be the *author* of the utterance simply disguises this fact.

For deconstructionists, the relevant question is therefore: who should be punished for injurious words? Is it not history itself that should be put on trial instead of an individual subject? The subject as the fictitious author of the words is actually someone onto whom the burden of responsibility has been shifted so that this history can be masked. Since history itself cannot be put on trial or punished, the subject becomes its scapegoat. If those who utter injurious speech merely cite from some pre-existing social and linguistic context and by so doing become a part of the historic community of speakers, society is wrong to impose responsibility for injurious speech on a single subject.[1]

One is tempted to say that in this approach to injurious speech there is no place for individual responsibility. But in fact the deconstructionist position is not so straightforward, for it is increasingly maintained alongside an insistence on 'political correctness', that is, an insistence that language must be changed so that it no longer reflects racial, sexual or ethnic prejudice. One would not be wrong to summarize this insistence on 'political correctness' as the demand that the subject feel guilty and that he or she vigilantly and constantly question his or her identity and motivations. The most popular critical position these days steers an odd and unsuccessful course, maintaining on the one hand that the context totally determines the subject, and on the other hand that the subject must distance him or herself from this context by constantly apologizing for uttering improper words. The shortcomings and inconsistencies of this position lead us to seek fresh inspiration in psychoanalysis.

The Big Other and the Pain of the Victim

Before addressing the problem of responsibility as it is raised in psychoanalysis, let me first explore the matter of the intention of the subject who verbally attacks a member of a religious minority, another race, and so on. It can be argued that the subject who utters a racist slur seeks a response, and that there are two possible types of response. As those American race theorists who favour 'hate speech' legislation correctly point out, the prime intention of injurious speech is to provoke the person assaulted to question his or her identity and to perceive him or herself as inferior.[2] But the speaker also aims at another response: by uttering injurious speech the speaker searches for confirmation of his or her own identity, engaging in race bashing in order to define him or herself as part of the racist community that would grant him or her stability.

In hate speech one encounters the same logic that is found in all forms of violence, which is always aimed at ruining the fantasy scenario that sustains the identity of the person being harmed or even tortured.[3] The target of violence is the unsymbolizable kernel in the other, which Lacan called the object a – the object-cause-of-desire. It is around this object that the subject forms its fantasy, its scenario of provisional wholeness. In the case of hate speech we are dealing with the attacker's demand that the victim question this perception of wholeness, his or her sense of identity. Since one's identity has its root in the object a, the slandered person or race cannot defend itself through recourse to the 'truth' or to a critique of the ideology that underpins the slanderer's attack. Hate speech is so insidious because it is designed to take advantage of the victim's structural 'defencelessness'.

But the goal of injurious speech is not only to humiliate the other, to assign a subordinate place to the person being verbally attacked: it also seeks to assign a special place to the one who speaks. Here Althusser's theory of ideological hailing comes in handy.[4] When a policeman hails an individual on the street, his intention is not only to assign a subordinate place to the addressee (to interpellate him as an ideological subject, as Althusser points out), but also to define his own position in regard to the addressee. Through the act of hailing, the policeman demonstrates that he has authority and can force the person he hails to accept this fact. The violence of the performative is thus defined not only by what it does to the addressee, how it assigns him or her a place in the social-symbolic structure, but by the way it forces the addressee to recognize the speaker's authority. By uttering a performative statement, the speaker primarily expresses a desire for recognition. So, when I as a subject am hurt and humiliated by someone's demeaning remark, I assign, through my very injury, authority to my accuser.

We must, however, be precise about the authority that the sender of the injurious message wants the addressee to sanction. From where does this image of authority emanate? Here one encounters the Lacanian big Other, the social-symbolic structure: it is from the Other that the subject receives its symbolic identity. The subject constantly searches for the point in the symbolic universe from which he or she will appear likable to him or herself, and in racism this symbolic identification plays a major role. The social-symbolic structure within which racism is at work is always already in place, otherwise the racist speaker would have no independent idea that words have the potential to wound. One can thus agree with deconstructionist critics that the subject always quotes from the vast historical corpus of racist vocabulary and that the individual subject never invents racist speech. But with every racist sentence, one must add, the subject reinstalls this symbolic space anew. For the existence of the Other is radically dependent on the subject.

By uttering racist speech, the subject seeks out the Other that would confirm its identity, grant its authority. And paradoxically, it is the addressee of this speech who plays the role of the 'mediator' between the sender and the Other: by recognizing him or herself as the addressee of the sender's words, he or she actually occupies the place in the symbolic structure from which the speaker receives confirmation of his or her identity and authority.

This demand for recognition of authority is not only part of assertive speech but determines the logic of speaking in general. Every act of speaking involves this demand for recognition from the Other: every sentence that the subject pronounces constructs an Other that has to hear it and grant the subject its identity, affirm it as a speaking being.[5] But while every speaking being in some fundamental way constructs the Other and simultaneously charges it with recognizing him or her, the racist goes a step further by making him or herself an *instrument* of the Other, the values of Western civilization, for example. When the racist attacks blacks, he does so as the Other's 'mouthpiece', as it were; he speaks on behalf of the Other, who is really speaking through him. The racist can thus be certain about himself only on two conditions: that the Other exists, and that he is the Other's tool. By what means does the racist acquire confirmation that these conditions are met? Paradoxically, confirmation comes from the reaction of the victim.

As I mentioned earlier, the racist targets in the victim the traumatic kernel around which the victim organizes his or her identity. Words can only injure if and when the victim is so struck by them that he or she cannot immediately reflect them, when he or she is either totally mute or is only able to respond by violence. In sum, the most horrible verbal violence happens when the victim cannot respond rationally, when words hit the very centre of the victim's being.

The famous 1942 case *Chaplinsky v. New Hampshire*,[6] which introduced the notion of 'fighting words', presents an almost Lacanian reading of this phrase. The court ruled that 'fighting words' are not protected by the First Amendment because they have a tendency directly to cause acts of violence by the person to whom such words are addressed. The court also explicitly stated that words count as fighting words when they are 'said without a disarming smile'.[7]

When his injurious words cause the victim to be hurt to the point where the only possible response is violence, when his speech touches the traumatic object in the victim, the racist receives proof of the Other's existence. It is the pain of the victim that constitutes the ontological proof of the existence of the Other for the racist. When the victim is so hurt that he or she cannot respond, the racist needs to convince himself that the injury was justified. The paradox is that the racist first needs some (racist) theory which allows him to perceive the verbal assault against the victim not as injurious malice but as a justifiable act, and yet it is the victim's pain that provides the very validation he seeks. In sum: for the racist, the Other always has to be firmly in place, so that the racist can sustain his perverse fantasy of serving the Other's enjoyment.

This fantasy is also sustained through the formation of a community.[8] Not only does the community vindicate the racist's fears, the fears themselves vindicate the excessive commitment to the community. A simple belief in the danger of foreigners is insufficient to sustain the dread that constitutes racism; what is also necessary is the knowledge that others perceive the same danger. In other words, it is not so much one's own private belief as one's belief in the belief of others that 'justifies' for the racist the violent hatred he maintains toward all foreigners. At the same time, however, it is the foreigner or victim of racism who is the condition of possibility of one's belief in and commitment to one's racist community. The dangerous other invented by racism (blacks, the Jew, and so on) acts as a kind of master signifier to unite the disparate elements and problems of a complex society and give them a clear and coherent meaning. This enemy-other lends consistency to the community in which we dwell by becoming the easily graspable cause of all its ills. It is easy to see, then, that the type of victim 'in vogue' at any given moment goes hand in hand with the ideological definition one gives to one's society. A few short years ago, when the Democrats were in power in the United States, a poll taken by the *New York Times* revealed that the majority of people who lost their jobs blamed not the boss or the owner of their company, but the government, which was running things so badly that their bosses had no alternative but to lay off workers. Now that the political right is in power, new culprits have to be found, and it is already clear that single mothers and their 'criminal' children are best suited to the job of redefining American woes.

This circular relation between the community and its other raises the question of enjoyment and thus of responsibility. If a community's victim can be said to be its symptom, it then becomes evident that the community holds itself together via a vital attachment to an intense negative pleasure – or enjoyment. Psychoanalysis has always held the subject responsible for his or her enjoyment, beginning with Freud, who spoke of one's *choice* of neurosis; the symptom can be said to be a materialization of the subject's forced choice. Consider, for example, the case of Dora. While it remains true that she lived in problematic family and social circumstances – her father was unprincipled, Herr K. was a lecherous family friend, his wife had strange sexual tastes and her own mother was strangely absent – psychoanalysis forces us to observe that none of the 'objective' circumstances explains Dora's investment in the whole affair. The question remains: what did she get out of being the victim of these circumstances; what type of enjoyment bound her to this unpleasant group of characters? Analysis would be forever blocked if this question were never posed, and the situation would be simply incomprehensible.

This taking into account of one's own responsibility for the enjoyment that accrues to one's actions distinguishes Lacanian theory from structuralism and also from deconstructionism. We can very much agree that the subject is determined by a social-symbolic structure, that in the case of hate speech the subject only cites from the vast history of racism. Nonetheless, the subject 'chooses' to speak. Although the subject may lose control of the words and say more in slips of the tongue or between the lines than he or she consciously intended, the subject cannot escape responsibility, even if this responsibility accounts for no more than the mere fact that he or she is a subject.

The Remainder

We cannot, of course, determine what is at stake in the use of hate speech without clarifying its relation to language in general. Psychoanalysis is founded on the fact that something in language always escapes our grasp of it. Some incalculable element is always at work in it and emerges unexpectedly to undermine what we are trying to say. Lacan called this element *lalangue*, and Jean-Jacques Lecercle called it the 'remainder'.[9] The remainder is that something in language that exceeds not only the speaker's control, but scientific inquiry as well.

The science of linguistics is endlessly concerned with delineating *language*, with giving language a coherent form through a series of universalizing propositions, so that it will, in the final instance, be thought to be able to say everything. Referring to Lacan's *L'Etourdit*, Jean-Claude Milner has shown that for this

possibility to be established, something must be left out of language: 'in order for
any All to be said, a limit is needed which, in suspending it, would guarantee it as
an All constructible in a predetermined way'.[10] The limit that totalizes language
and encourages our belief that we can 'say it all' is what excludes *lalangue* – the
remainder, the leftover that insists in language and is thus the condition of its
existence:

> *Lalangue* is made of a bit of everything, of what wallows itself in the gin-mills, and of
> what we hear in the salons. On each side, we encounter misunderstanding, since, with
> a little good will, it is possible to find a meaning in everything, at least an imaginary one.
> Did he say 'dide' or 'Dieu'? Is this 'croate' or 'cravate'? . . . The *lalangue* is the storage,
> the collection of traces which other 'subjects' have left, i.e. that, with the help of which,
> let's say, each subject inscribed its desire into *lalangue*, since the speaking being has to
> have a signifier to be able to desire; and desire in what? in its fantasies, i.e. again in
> signifiers.[11]

Language announces itself as complete and as capable of saying everything by
prohibiting something, by ruling something out of bounds. Take as an example
of *lalangue* a child's babbling or improper words and sentences: one cannot say
that these prattling forms do not issue from language. Yet it is precisely because
these incorrect forms are, in a certain respect, part of language, made up of it,
that they have to be dismissed from it. The domain in which language and
lalangue confront each other, the domain where prohibition takes place, is *speech*.
It is when words are spoken that the prohibition of *lalangue* is set in motion.
Thus, the insistence of linguistics on the delineation of correct and incorrect
forms is determined by the fact that, as Lacan points out, 'saying is of the order
of not-all – "all cannot be said"'.[12] To retain the image of its universality, the
science of linguistics has to insist on a limit; it has to determine what 'cannot be
said', what is improper, in a given language.

Lalangue is thus something that is part of a language at the same time that it
is outside it, prohibited. For Lacan, language is both the result of the exclusion
of *lalangue* and also the source of its construction. Language is thus a scientific
concept invented by a master, or, better, language is a scientific way of dealing
with *lalangue*, a way of understanding it. As Jacques-Alain Miller says: 'language is
the effect of the discourse of the master, its structure is the very structure
of the master's discourse'.[13] The master imposes him or herself on *lalangue*,
captures and articulates it in order to form the body of language so that language
becomes something that can be written. This mastery of *lalangue* is the task of
all the theories of language (grammar, phonetics, logics and so on) 'by means
of which the speaking being paves its way through *lalangue*, conceptualizes it,
even if only by alphabetizing it'.[14]

Lacan's main point is that the aim of *lalangue* is *not* communication, and he thus offers the unconscious as his prime example of *lalangue*. Communication implies reference, which the unconscious does not have; this is made clear by the fact that the effects of the unconscious disrupt the whole body, as well as the soul.[15] The unconscious bears witness to a knowledge that escapes the speaking being. Accordingly, Lacan has described the unconscious as

> a knowledge, or know-how [*savoir faire*] with *lalangue*. And what can be done with *lalangue* goes far beyond what can be encompassed by language. *Lalangue* concerns us first with all that it encompasses as effects that are affects. That the unconscious is structured like a language, can be said precisely because the effects of *lalangue*, which are a knowledge already there, expand beyond all that the being who speaks is able to utter.[16]

The subject can thus be said to understand jokes, slips of the tongue and so on, not because of language but because of *lalangue*.

Through the remainder what is spoken is not only something more than the individual speaker's intention, but something more than the sum of the speech acts of the members of a linguistic community: 'Even if someone invents the words, by the time they become a slogan they have lost their subjective character.'[17] As pointed out by many contemporary theorists, including Deleuze and Guattari, the purpose of language is not simply to inform, communicate or solicit information, but to establish relations of power.[18] Language not only represents the world, but acts in it. In determining just how it acts, what it effects, we must not neglect to consider the struggle between language and its remainder. For if the latter can be defined as '*the return within language of the contradictions and struggles that make up the social, . . . the persistence within language of past contradictions and struggles, and the anticipation of new ones*',[19] then it is not enough to say that through the remainder history speaks in the form of citation. Instead we must say that in the remainder it is the *antagonism* of this very history, the social-symbolic struggle, that is inscribed.

Nor should we neglect the role of the remainder, of *lalangue*, in the functioning of hate speech. The subject understands hate speech as injurious not because he or she knows the meaning of the words uttered, or the structure of the language in which they are uttered, but because there is in language a leftover, a remainder, that disrupts this structure and allows new meanings to be attributed to the words. *Lalangue*, as both lack and excess, is at the same time the point at which the system fails, becomes uncertain, and the point where this lack is cancelled to become a surplus: 'The map of *lalangue* is the map of the "points of poetry" where lack is cancelled, where it becomes excess, and where what is impossible to utter is said in a poem.'[20]

Hate speech could be perceived as another form of this excess, as a violent 'poetry' that temporarily fills up the lack in the symbolic structure. Hate speech simultaneously includes a certain social antagonism and attempts to annihilate it – though, of course, it constantly fails at the latter. This is why hate speech is not simply a form of citation, a repetition of some received idea or historical prejudice, but a 'novel' way of stating some social antagonism.

Let's take the example of the racist attack at the University of Stanford in which two white students hung a poster of Beethoven repainted as a black man on the door of a black student. What was the message of this act? One might answer that it was, 'There has never been a black equivalent of Beethoven, a black genius of his status.' But if one takes into account the current debates about affirmative-action programmes in universities, the poster also implies another meaning: 'You have no place here, since, as a black man, you'll never be a genius.' What is inscribed in this racist attack is, therefore, not only a historical prejudice, but a bitter response to what the white students saw as a limitation of their own freedom and power.

The Violence of Cultural Difference

Since each subject forms the fantasy of its own integrity differently, that is, since every fantasy is specific to the subject who is structured by it, he or she also perceives differently the sort of violence that is capable of shattering such fantasies of wholeness. Similarly, different cultures understand violence in radically different ways. Certain initiation rites (female circumcision, for example) which appear to be essential in non-European countries strike Westerners as forms of torture or mutilation. Differences such as these raise important questions about universal values such as human rights, freedom, equality and so on, which are often invoked against perceived forms of violence. The question is: should these values, inventions of a Western European tradition, be universally applied or should they only be applied to Western nations? What happens when a non-European nation claims to live by different values and challenges the imposition of these others? In short: how should we react when a culture – in the name of its own traditional values, its own understanding of human rights – engages in practices that other cultures perceive as harmful?

In recent years, this dilemma has been exacerbated by various events: in the former Yugoslavia, Serbs have persistently claimed that what outside observers perceive as an aggression against others is only their way of defending the human rights of their fellow Serbs who are being tortured by neighbouring nations; during the famous Rushdie affair, Muslims insisted that they should be free to resort to physical threats in order to protect the integrity of their religion. These transparent attempts to legitimize violence through a contestation of certain universal values have to be considered alongside some current critiques of 'Eurocentrism' that call for an end to all universals in the name of a wide-sweeping particularism.

We are now witnessing the emergence of a cultural relativism that forbids any intrusion into other cultures and confines the notions and applications of universal values to Western civilization. These relativists seem to reason as follows: 'We admit that our culture was imperialist in the past, but we now reject this past and embrace cultural differences; we therefore urge that our so-called "universal" values not be imposed on others.' If one wanted to be truly consistent in defending cultural relativism, then one would also have to claim that we are not in a position to judge or actively oppose totalitarian regimes (fascism, Stalinism, Islamic fundamentalism and so on), since they all emerged in histori-cally different circumstances incompatible with our own.[21] Hearing about the violent practices of other cultures, cultural relativists are forced to take the position: 'We disagree, but we are not in a position to judge others whose culture is so different from our own.' This position is now often taken by Western governments faced with violent conflicts all around the world, from Bosnia, to Rwanda, to the forgotten case of East Timor, to mention only the most brutal cases. When dealing with countries like Cuba or Iraq, however, cultural relativists often become universal defenders of human rights and easily forget the Cubans' or Iraqis' right to determine their own values.

An example of the cultural-relativist perspective is evident in the film *Before the Rain* (1994) by Milcho Manchevski. Moving between London and a village in Macedonia where Orthodox Macedonians and Muslim Albanians engage in violent nationalist clashes, the film offers a 'reflection' on the national struggles in the former Yugoslavia. In the first episode, entitled 'Words', a young Orthodox monk finds in his cell a frightened Albanian girl hiding from Macedonian nationalists who claim that she is a murderer. Once they track her down, the cycle of clashes that permanently shatters this peaceful region begins. The second part, 'Faces', introduces Anne, a picture editor in London, and her lover Aleksandar, the charismatic, Pulitzer Prize-winning Macedonian war photographer who, after sixteen years of living in exile, decides to return to his village in Macedonia. Anne's dinner with her estranged husband in a chic London restaurant is interrupted by a loud argument between a waiter and a customer, both ex-Yugoslavs. The argument ends in a shooting match that kills Anne's husband. The third episode, 'Pictures', takes place when Aleks returns to Macedonia, where all of the senseless violence alluded to in the first two episodes emerges in a new context, this time that of the overt hatred between

Macedonians and Albanians who for decades had peacefully lived together. Aleks's fond memories of home are bitterly shattered and at the end he is shot and killed by his own cousin.

The film is full of symbolism about the regression of peoples into old historical patterns, about their national symbols and the glorification of their religion. A typical Macedonian or Albanian is thus dressed in a mixture of his or her national costume and typical Western clothes (kitschy shirts, sneakers and so forth), ornamented with religious symbols and shown holding a cellular phone in one hand and Kalashnikov in the other.

The story does not follow a chronological sequence of events, but disrupts this temporal logic by mixing elements of life in London with those of life in Macedonia. For example, at a time when Aleks is still alive, Anne is shown looking at pictures that will be taken at the end of the story when he gets killed. The structure of the film is circular: at the end of the first episode, the Albanian girl (who, as we learn later, is a daughter of Aleks's old love, Hana) is killed by her brother, but the last episode concludes when Aleks, in trying to save the girl, is killed by his own cousin's gun. This disruption of the temporal logic and circular structure underlines the timelessness and irrationality of ethnic violence.

Aleks's perception of the national conflicts of his former home is presented as a distanced and distorted vision, seen through a camera. To the village doctor, the war appears as a virus that infects the community, which can potentially spread anywhere and infect anyone: people in Bosnia, in Macedonia and even in Britain. The film, in general, presents violence as simple irrationality, as some deeply seated instinct that suddenly erupts with terrible force. We thus see a beautiful countryside where people live in picturesque old houses and are obsessed with national myths and religion. The film shows no signs of the ugly architecture of the 'real' Macedonia: crumbling socialist apartment blocks, ugly factories, polluted cities, villages composed of rickety shacks and so on. Group identities are deliberately blurred so that it becomes ultimately unclear what idea or ideal drives people to kill: is it nationalism, religion or something else? The final point is that none of these notions is worth dying for.

The 'viral' explanation of violence reveals ideology operating in its purest form. According to this view, society is a body that is infected by a virus carried by fanatic nationalists. First of all, viruses are invisible – one cannot easily detect the carrier – and second, no remedies (antibiotics) can help the body combat them. An infected body heals itself by creating its own antitoxins, no outside intervention will do. In such an explanation of violence, politics, of course, has no place; there isn't any need to analyse the situation that produces the violence.

In *Before the Rain*, the only thing that crosses the division between the two national groups is love: Aleks still loves his former girlfriend, Hana, who is now a widow; however, because of the national hatreds their love cannot be realized. And young Macedonians and Albanians still fall in love, as happens with Hana's daughter, though in the end they may be punished with death. And, significantly, people mostly die at the hands of their own people.

With such a perception of nationalism to sell, the film has been very successful in the West. Its underlying message – people from this beautiful region are incomprehensible to our Western mode of thinking; something in these people, their primordial passions and hatreds, exceeds our grasp – seems to please even the most educated Western film-goers. The extradiegetic audience, in other words, is no different from the diegetic one. And what do they do in regard to this violence? The media publish pictures of killings in Bosnia; the people in the London restaurant become innocent victims of the 'savages' who settle their accounts on the wrong terrain; in general, all the observers can presumably do is be shocked by the unbridgeable differences that separate them from these people, and attend their funerals, if only to make new pictures.

The Difference of Universals

The dilemma of how to think the relation between universal human rights and the right to cultural difference is one of the greatest antinomies of our time. As Cornelius Castoriadis pointed out, this dilemma relates to the fact that 'we [Westerners] at the same time claim that we are one culture among others *and* that this culture is unique, since it recognizes the alterity of the others (which wasn't the case before, and what other cultures do not acknowledge to us)', yet we have, in addition, invented values we claim as universal.[22] To show how this dilemma becomes not only a theoretical issue, but one that must be dealt with in everyday life, Castoriadis cites the following example: let's say that you have a colleague, a member of an African Muslim nation, whom you value highly, and you learn that this person wants his daughter to undergo a ritualistic circumcision. What should you do? The dilemma is this: if you do not say or do anything, you are not helping to protect the girl's universal human right not to be submitted to mutilation. But if you say something and try to change the father's thinking on this matter, you are robbing him of his culture, and, by doing so, transgress the principle which says you must respect the incompatibilities between cultures. Castoriadis concludes that in such a case Westerners cannot give up on the values they have invented and which they believe to be valid for all people, regardless of their cultural backgrounds.[23]

Another conflict between universalism and particularism in the domain of human rights stems from the fact that they not only guarantee the rights of the individual, they also open a space for collective group rights. Both liberals and communitarians believe that most conflicts can be resolved by prioritizing these rights: for liberals, individual rights take priority; for communitarians, group rights do. Yet in neither case does the choice serve to prevent violent collisions between the two or outright abridgments of seemingly fundamental rights. Let us take the famous American case *Santa Clara Pueblo* v. *Martinez*.[24] This case deals with the tribal custom and law according to which the children of women who marry men outside the Pueblo tribe lose their tribal status. This custom does not pertain to men: if they enter an exogamous relationship, their children retain their tribal status and thus their rights to tribal property. The Pueblo tribe claimed that patrilinear descent was essential for the preservation of their cultural identity; the woman bringing suit, Julia Martinez, challenged this law by arguing that the identity of the tribe had not always been founded on patrilinear order and that the traditions of kinship had changed throughout the history of the tribe. In this case, the group rights of the tribe eventually prevailed over the individual rights of one of its members.

There are many similar conflicts worldwide: in the US, the Amish community refused to send their children to public school; in France, Muslim women insisted on their right to wear headscarfs in school; and women of African-Muslim descent were denied the right to female circumcision.

And how are we to decide between the competing claims of individual rights and group identity when one's *group* identity accounts for a substantial part of one's *self*-identity? In other words, since the two kinds of rights are not mutually exclusive, a choice of one often diminishes or harms the very thing that was chosen.

A liberal response to these dilemmas is to argue that one has the right to submit oneself to whatever ritual mutilation one likes as long as one has been properly informed of one's choices and been given information that will allow the choice to be made. This, of course, raises the issue of 'proper information', since there is and can be no neutral space of knowledge. The very space (a school, for example) we perceive to be a place for the distribution of knowledge about alternatives to existing practices may be perceived by some groups as a place for the violent erasure of their own knowledge and identity. (The Amish case clearly shows this.) In short, many of these dilemmas have no definitive answer; they simply cannot be finally resolved. And yet to throw up our hands in despair, as though there were nothing to be done, is to miss the point that the very invention of the notion of rights opened the possibility of these ongoing debates and made these various conflicts visible.

Moreover, the fact that the notion of universal values was a product of

European culture does not mean that it can be interpreted by a historical, genealogical approach or that its validity can be limited to this culture. For the fact is that this notion cannot be historicized. We cannot account for the existence of human rights by pointing out that it emerged at a specific time in European history. As Castoriadis wrote,

> Contemporary Europeans ['European' here is not a geographical expression, it is an expression of civilization] do not take account of the enormous historical improbability of their existence. In relation to the general history of humanity, this history, this tradition, philosophy itself, the struggle for democracy, equality, and freedom are as completely improbable as the existence of life on Earth is in relation to the existence of solar systems in the Universe.[25]

This is true in a general sense; that is, no matter how we try to find the source of society's institution in God or in various gods, in the laws of nature or reason or among its ancestors, this source remains a necessary 'self-occultation of the self-institution of society'.[26]

But there is another, more specific sense in which certain aspects of European culture cannot be historicized. The moment universals such as equality and human rights were established, they lost their foundation by retroactively transforming their own history. Again, Castoriadis reminds us:

> The exigency of equality is a creation of *our* history, this segment of history to which we belong. It is a historical fact, or better a *meta-fact* which is born in this history and which, starting from there, tends to transform history, including also the history of *other* peoples. It is absurd to want to found equality upon any particular accepted sense of the term since it is equality that founds us insomuch as we are Europeans.[27]

The search for particular historical foundations of universal notions, their relativization, presents a danger of profound absolutism since in doing so, I posit myself as observer in a presumably neutral position from which I can judge history as I please. I thus take it for granted that everyone accepts the same rationality that I do. I also presuppose the equality of humans as reasonable beings, which is not an empirical fact but a hypothesis of all rationalist discourses. Castoriadis points out that in the history of philosophy, the most totalitarian of theories were not those that spoke about abstract principles, but those that were searching for objective empirical facts: it was usually empiricists who put themselves in the position of abstract neutrality from which they then judged the supposedly objective facts.

An essential attribute of democracy is its 'active forgetfulness': for democracy to be established on the grounds of the empty space of power, one has to disregard its contingent origin. Democracy is usually established through some violent act, and can easily be brought to an end through nonviolent, democratic means, through elections, for example. This active forgetfulness is also at work in law, where, as Walter Benjamin pointed out,[28] the violence through which the law emerges is forgotten once the law is established. And the same goes for universals: for human rights, for example, to have any political purchase we have to forget that at the time they were established they pertained only to white male Europeans. In our understanding of universals traces of racism and male domination often remain, but since universals are in themselves empty, we have to engage constantly in the struggle for their meaning and for their expansion, so that they do not exclude groups of people. The active forgetting that pertains to universal notions simply means that their exclusionist history does not diminish the inclusionary character that they have in contemporary democracy.

It is essential that universal notions such as human rights and freedom remain open projects whose full meaning and power are not historically determined, and that they open up the possibility for questioning the very society from which they emerged. Such universals emerged at the moment the subject lost its rooting in nature, at the moment it became an empty substanceless subjectivity marked by an essential lack. As Ernesto Laclau notes: 'The universal is part of my identity insofar as I am penetrated by a constitutive lack (insofar as my differential identity has failed in its process of construction).'[29]

Different cultures perceive universals differently, since universal notions are always in a specific way incorporated into the fantasmatic structure through which a particular society deals with its own inherent antagonism, its own inability to constitute itself as a coherent whole. Emerging in this way, as a means of filling out the structural gap in the organization of society, they are always in a specific way inscribed in the symbolic organization of society.

How can we, therefore, understand the way another society perceives its universals? For Castoriadis,

[W]hat is different in another society and another epoch is its very rationality, for it is caught each time in another imaginary world. This does not mean that it is inaccessible to us; but this access must pass by way of an attempt (certainly always problematical; but how could it be otherwise?) to restitute the imaginary significations of the society in question.[30]

So what is at stake here is our willingness to put ourselves in another's skin and try to understand the logic of his or her reasoning. Castoriadis's recourse to imaginary creations for describing the structures through which other cultures reason should be supplemented with the Lacanian concept of fantasy, since fantasy is something other than a merely imaginary creation in so far as it touches the unsymbolizable real. And here the problem begins, since it is the very core of society that we are dealing with when we try to understand the real, the unsymbolizable kernel around which society structures itself. The problem therefore is that another culture structures itself differently around some central impossibility. That both our culture and the culture of others are crossed by an antagonism is what makes the cultures similar; but the way they deal with this antagonism is different.

Let me return to the problem of hate speech, which, as I pointed out earlier, very much touches on the real, the kernel that causes us pain when we are submitted to verbal violence. Contemporary societies perceive this issue in radically different ways. Most lawmakers would agree that it is an issue that has to be dealt with somehow, but the legislation and what this legislation protects vary so widely from country to country that international human rights organizations cannot establish any general rules regulating hate speech. With the exception of the United States, the majority of other countries, especially the European states, have some kind of legislation as part of their penal code that deals with hate speech. Yet this legislation has different intentions in different countries. For example, in France and Germany, 'hate speech laws' deal primarily with anti-Semitism and the denial of the Nazi Holocaust. In the past, in the Communist countries in Eastern Europe, defama- tion laws were mainly used to protect the Party elite from the criticism of the masses, and today such laws re-emerge in some post-Communist countries (Romania, for example), where the ex-Communists are back in power. However, in other countries, such as Indonesia and India, 'hate speech' prosecutions tend to involve those who criticize a dominant religious group.[31]

What actually regulates injurious speech in society is not so much existing law as what Hegel named *Sittlichkeit* – the system of mores, ethical life.[32] *Sittlichkeit* is what holds a community together; it is what envelopes the national substance. But it is essential that *Sittlichkeit* remains contingent in relation to the law: the law cannot encompass ethical life. Ethical life always eludes legal regulations, but at the same time it grounds our understanding of the law, or the submission to the law by the public. For *Sittlichkeit* it is crucial that it 'enjoin us to bring about what already is':[33] it concerns 'the norms . . . of a society . . . sustained by our action, and yet [which are] already there'.[34] It could also be said that *Sittlichkeit* functions as an ego ideal, the instance with which we identify in the symbolic order, the point from which we appear likable to ourselves and thereby obtain our symbolic identity. This instance is not, however, the same as the law itself.

In the United States, the lack of a unified national substance gives *Sittlichkeit* a different status than the one it has in Europe. A melting pot or a salad bowl, the US – the mixture of nationalities that form the nation – has replaced the uniform national substance with the Constitution, the word of the founding fathers. The Constitution works in America according to the same logic as the notion of the nation in European democracies. And the way Americans express their love for their country and respect for the founding fathers is not through national identification or nationalism, but through patriotism, devotion to the father. The Constitution, especially its First Amendment, thus replaces the national substance and becomes the thing around which American *Sittlichkeit* forms itself.[35]

To exemplify how differently *Sittlichkeit* operates in various countries, let us compare Sweden and the United States with respect to their attitudes towards violence and pornography on public television. Sweden, which is perceived as one of the most liberal countries in terms of sex, has a very liberal approach to pornography, but it also has very strict rules regulating violence on television, especially as it affects children. Thus, many American films are not allowed to be shown on Swedish television, while pornographic films are freely exhibited. In America, things are exactly reversed: on public television there are lots of violent films and no pornography. This example shows us not only how contingent society's reaction to violence is, but also that no general rules can be made regarding the way a society perceives its *Sittlichkeit*.[36]

For that reason, there are also no clear answers as to how to regulate hate speech: language simultaneously can and cannot be controlled, and the results of its control cannot be planned. But both the supporters of the legal prohibition of hate speech and its opponents think that clear answers exist and that the question is only whether one is for or against control. The dilemma of hate speech is one of the antinomies of our society, for which no resolution exists once and for all. One can only hope that the very debate that surrounds this issue produces as a side effect more tolerance, since it is only through this debate that people will be able to confront the fact that words cause harm to others.

What we are witnessing today is a constant struggle about who will define universals and who will define what injurious speech is. The law is only one battlefield, although one of the most important ones. The fact that even totalitarian regimes must invoke human rights and freedoms, if only to legitimatize violence, is proof of the power of universals. Universals are, however, essentially empty, which is why we have to engage in the struggle for their content. And this struggle has to work towards expanding universals, not limiting them to only some cultures. This very expansion is the only way for the universals to acquire new, hopefully democratic, meaning.

Notes

1. See Judith Butler, 'Burning Acts: Injurious Speech', in *Deconstruction is/in America*, ed. Anselm Haverkamp (New York: New York University Press 1995). Here is an example of the ambiguity of Butler's position: 'If the utterance is to be prosecuted, where and when would that prosecution begin, and when would it end? Would this not be something like the effort to prosecute a history that, by its very temporality, cannot be called to trial? . . . This is not to say that subjects ought not be prosecuted for their injurious speech; I think that there are probably occasions when they should. But what is precisely being prosecuted when the injurious word comes to trial and is it finally or fully prosecutable?' (p. 156).

2. See *Words that Wound: Critical Race Theory, Assaultive Speech and the First Amendment*, Mari J. Matsuda, Charles R. Lawrence III, Richard Delgado and Kimberle Williams Crenshaw, eds (Boulder, Co.: Westview Press 1993).

3. On the ruining of fantasy in war, see chapter 1 of my book, *The Spoils of Freedom: Psychoanalysis and Feminism after the Fall of Socialism* (London: Routledge 1994). See also Elaine Scarry, *The Body in Pain* (Princeton, N.J.: Princeton University Press 1989) for a different but insightful approach to the 'unmaking' of the victim's word by the torturer.

4. See Louis Althusser, 'Ideology and Ideological State Apparatuses', in *Lenin and Philosophy and Other Essays* (London: New Left Books 1971).

5. As Lacan says: 'What I seek in speech is the response of the other. What constitutes me as subject is my question. In order to be recognized by the other, I utter what was only in view of what will be. In order to find him, I call him by a name that he must assume or refuse in order to reply to me.' Jacques Lacan, *Ecrits: A Selection*, trans. Alan Sheridan (London: Tavistock Publications 1977), p. 86.

6. *Chaplinsky* v. *New Hampshire*, 315 US 568 (1942).

7. *Chaplinsky* v. *New Hampshire*, 315 US 568, 573 (1942).

8. See Etienne Balibar, 'Is there a "Neo-Racism"', in Etienne Balibar and Immanuel Wallerstein, *Race, Nation, Class: Ambiguous Identities* (London: Verso 1991).

9. See Jean-Jacques Lecercle, *The Violence of Language* (London: Routledge 1990).

10. Jean-Claude Milner, *For the Love of Language*, trans. Ann Banfield (London: Macmillan 1990), p. 101.

11. Ibid., p. 129.

12. Ibid., p. 106.

13. Jacques-Alain Miller, 'Théorie de lalangue – (Rudiment)', *Ornicar?*, no. 1, 1975, p. 30.

14. Ibid., p. 31.

15. See Jacques Lacan, *Television: A Challenge to the Psychoanalytic Establishment*, ed. Joan Copjec, trans D. Hollier, R. Krauss, A. Michelson (New York: Norton 1990).

16. Jacques Lacan, *Le Seminaire Livre XX: Encore* (Paris: Editions du Seuil 1975), p. 127.

17. Lecercle, *The Violence of Language*, p. 44.

18. Gilles Deleuze and Felix Guattari, *A Thousand Plateaus: Capitalism and Schizophrenia*, trans Brian Massumi (Minneapolis, Minn.: University of Minnesota Press 1987).

19. Lecercle, *The Violence of Language*, p. 182. 'If the remainder has one rule to impose on the speaker, it can be only a form of double bind: I order you to disobey' (p. 137).

20. Ibid., p. 40. 'Language is material not because there is a physics of speech, but because words are always threatening to revert to screams, because they carry the violent affects of the speaker's body, can be inscribed on it, and generally mingle with it' (p. 105).

21. If one were a cultural relativist at the time of Hitler's regime, one could consistently have reasoned: 'Hitler and his neighbouring nations have had a long history of disputes; as horrible as his crimes might be, they are part of the culture of nations in conflict.'

22. See Cornelius Castoriadis, *Philosophy, Politics, Autonomy: Essays in Political Philosophy* (Oxford: Oxford University Press 1991), pp. 37–8.

23. Ibid.
24. *Santa Clara Pueblo* v. *Martinez*, 439 US 49 (1978). I rely here on the unpublished paper by Marty Slaughter, 'Preserving Cultural Communities: Group Rights and Multiculturalism in the American and Canadian Context'.
25. Castoriadis, *Philosophy, Politics*, p. 135.
26. Ibid., p. 133.
27. Ibid., p. 135.
28. See Walter Benjamin, 'Critique of Violence', in *Illuminations* (New York: Shocken Books 1967).
29. Ernesto Laclau, 'Universalism, Particularism, and the Question of Identity', *October*, no. 61, p. 89. 'The universal emerges out of the particular not as some principle underlying and explaining it, but as an incomplete horizon suturing a particular identity. The universal is the symptom of a missing fullness and the particular exists only in the contradictory movement of asserting a differential identity.'
30. Castoriadis, *Philosophy, Politics*, p. 67.
31. See the Human Rights Watch Policy Paper: '"Hate Speech" and the Freedom of Expression', March 1992. 'Indonesia's criminal code provides for the imprisonment for up to five years of "anyone who publicly and deliberately expresses a feeling or undertakes an act of enmity, abuse or insult towards a religion followed in Indonesia." This statute was used to prosecute Arswendo Atmowiloto, editor of *Monitor*, a Christian-owned newspaper, for publishing the results of a poll of its readership in which the prophet Mohammed ranked 11th (just after Arswendo) among most-admired leaders. Arswendo began a five-year prison sentence on April 8, 1991' (p. 6).
32. See *Hegel's Political Writings*, trans. T.M. Knox, ed. Z.A. Pelczynski (Oxford: Oxford University Press 1964).
33. Charles Taylor, *Hegel* (Cambridge: Cambridge University Press 1975), p. 376.
34. Ibid., p. 382
35. The Constitution is read differently by different political groups. It is not only that political discourse very much determines what counts as free speech and that this interpretation changes significantly over time, but the meaning of the Constitution itself emerges out of the hegemonic struggles that go on in American society. Usually, the left claims that one has to explain the Constitution by taking into account the historical situation in which it was invented, while the right insists on the literal meaning of the Constitution. But in contemporary political struggles it sometimes happens that the left starts insisting on the letter of the Constitution and the right insists on analysing its context, arguing that its interpretation changes with historical circumstances. This happened in California in the debates around Proposition 487, which limited the rights of immigrants since they are not US citizens. Some leftist lawyers opposed this proposition, claiming that the founding fathers did not use the word *citizens* but only the phrase 'the people of the United States'.
36. As Kenneth Lasson points out: 'Swedes are far more interrelated with (sometimes dependent upon) their government than Americans. They appear to have great trust in their democratic process and look to it for protection of their civil liberties. . . . Thus the Swedish laws prohibiting defamation of race are, to the people who live under them, innocuous, particularly when contrasted with the oppression exercised by Nazi Germany which threatened all of Europe in the name of race superiority. History, as well as philosophy, shapes society's degree of toleration for laws.' See Kenneth Lasson, 'Group Libel Versus Free Speech: When Big Brother *Should* Butt In', *Duquesne Law Review*, vol. 23, no. 1, p. 89. 'It has been suggested [by David Riesman] that libel is more important in America than in other Western democracies because an individual's reputation is considered akin to a property interest. Similarly, the role of the group in the American social process has been subordinated to the role of the individual' (p. 117).

8 THE POLITICS OF MEMORY IN CONTEMPORARY GERMANY

MICHAEL GEYER

The standard account of the Germans' relation to the Nazi past is that the Germans have forgotten the history of the Third Reich, the Holocaust, their genocidal past.[1] No doubt there is some truth to this assertion. Many, perhaps a majority of Germans, want neither to remember their role in this history nor to be reminded of its existence. But the claim that Germans do not remember is also a myth which has helped to mobilize a politics of memory; that is, the deliberate use of memory toward refashioning the German body politic.

This politics is predicated on the assumption that public knowledge about the Third Reich and the transparency of a reckoning with the past will have a cathartic effect; and that remembering the Holocaust will prevent the recurrence of National Socialism and of the attending evils of racism and anti-Semitism.[2] It will remake German identity and thus sever relations with the past. As a politics, the myth of a German amnesia has motivated German academics and intellectuals to explore the history of the Third Reich during the past twenty-five years. Driven by a fusion of passion and reason that is not normally associated with German intellectual culture, the individual and collective initiatives of this project would have been unimaginable without a deliberate politics of memory. The result of this sustained politics is that there is now in Germany after twenty-five years a culture of memory.[3]

Notwithstanding this outcome, there is also good reason to suggest that the emphatic project of combating radical evil with enlightened knowledge is in jeopardy. It is not that memory has suddenly faded with German unification, as many proponents of a politics of memory feared it might.[4] What happened instead is that the culture of memory continued to expand, reaching a high point first with the surprising popularity of Steven Spielberg's film *Schindler's List* and then with the innumerable commemorations that accompanied the fiftieth anniversary of the end of World War II. While these memorial efforts were overwhelming in their own right, they did not follow the path of enlightenment. What can be discerned, above all, is a return of memory without the effects that once were presumed to follow in its wake. The result has been a veritable *crise de conscience* among all those who had fervently hoped and fought for a new and enlightened Germany. The problem, then, is that while the Germans continue to remember, they (not all of them, but a significant public) do not do so in the way a politics of memory intended, nor with the desired effects. We find ourselves in a puzzling and, in a way, frightening moment. What the conditions for the success of a politics of memory were and how its unravelling came about are the subject of the following reflections.

The eventual success of a politics of memory is surprising if one considers the first two postwar decades. During those years the quest for recollection of the still very present Nazi past was the affair of a small minority of contemporaries who broke the generational code of a self-serving mutual attestation of innocence and honourable conduct – the code of a generation which had actively participated in the German pursuit of war and genocide. At that stage, the very act of recovering the past, which manifested itself as naming names, exposing crimes and attributing guilt, cut through a veil that shrouded the overwhelming presence of the past in benevolent oblivion.[5] This revolt of 'angry men' quite literally exhausted itself in running up against a solid wall of lies. The smug rejection of any responsibility for Nazi crimes by even the most obvious perpetrators and the wholesale denial of any participation in any but the most upstanding activities by the majority of German contemporaries gave the controversies of the day an extraordinary degree of bitterness. The trial of the members of the *Einsatzgruppen* (SS murder squads) in the small city of Ulm (1958) and the Auschwitz trial in Frankfurt (1964) encapsulated these confrontations.[6] These trials were punctuated by recurring debates about the statute of limitation for Nazi crimes; that is, whether Nazi crimes should fall under the statute of limitation for first and second degree murder. The debate was finally settled in 1979 with the abolition of the statute of limitations.[7] Occasionally, these clashes also surfaced in the deliberations over what to do with the physical remnants of the Nazi state, its monumental ruins in Berlin, Nuremberg and elsewhere.[8] This early debate had little of the moral baggage that the politics of memory was to acquire later on. It faced up to the physical, personal and mental continuities of the Nazi past and, indeed, to a recovery of Nazi elites, insisting that a lack of exposure and dissociation would lead to a continued poisoning of the body politic.

In a sense, this was a debate among contemporaries which should have taken place twenty years earlier during the Third Reich or, even better, during the Nazis' rise to power. With hindsight, it has been characterized as a form of *nachholender Widerstand*, or after-the-fact resistance.[9] Yet the results were rather mixed. Apart from Chancellor Adenauer's official politics of *Wiedergutmachung* (literally, politics of making up), there were egregious cases of former perpetrators remaking themselves as staunch proponents of a politics of memory.[10] Others gained their distance from the Third Reich by publicly disassociating themselves from their pasts.[11] As important as it is to recall that the latter group had been silent in the 1930s and 1940s (and, indeed, had in varying degrees participated), it remains crucial that they eventually spoke up in the 1950s and 1960s. For, in raising the issue of memory against an overwhelming desire to bury the past, they pushed West Germans out of their forgetfulness, setting apart the West German experience from both the East German and Austrian ones, as well as from the Italian or, for that matter, the common experience of occupied Europe.[12]

With hindsight, one wonders what is more surprising: the slowness with which the process of 'digging up the past'[13] initially took hold or its acceleration in the 1970s. When in 1978 the then prime minister of the state of Baden-Württemberg Hans Filbinger was 'outed' as a Wehrmacht judge who had condemned a deserter to death after the signing of the capitulation, the success of the public case against Filbinger was surprising and even shocking.[14] For one thing, there was little precedent for such 'muckraking' journalism in Germany. Investigative journalism had never really attained the legitimacy in postwar Germany which it had once possessed in the Weimar Republic. The same is true for literature and the stage: Rolf Hochhuth or Peter Weiss seemed to invent a whole genre of investigative plays while, in fact, they were recuperating a tradition which had been destroyed by the Nazis with a great deal of popular support.[15] Exposing the past entailed, above all, the recovery of a language of critical inquiry which had been wrecked and lost; it also required the creation of a public. Such a public clearly had not existed during the postwar trials against Nazi crimes that culminated in the Auschwitz trial(s). Public reception of the trials was, for the most part, noncommittal, if not outright hostile. The Mitscherlichs' discussion of the German 'inability to mourn' pointed this out,[16] but it took some time for their message to be heard, and when it finally was, it had become dated.

The small opposition of the first two postwar decades succeeded only in so far as it was able to generate a literary and media publicity which attracted the more rebellious minds of a younger generation. The politics of memory took off only when it captured the hearts and minds of this generation, who in turn captured the attention of a lively and heterogeneous educated public that was the product of the opening up of higher education in the 1960s. Thus, a generation of youngish teachers and university professors rose to prominence in the context of the arrival of an only slightly younger, postwar, baby-boom generation of students. The bond between a wartime (Hitler Youth) cohort and a postwar generation proved to be an emphatically West German and historically bounded, 1970s and 1980s, phenomenon.[17] Matthias Greffrath has described this political alliance with some malice, but not altogether inaccurately, as a fusion of 'humanism and efficiency'.[18] Linked to the renewal of a (left)liberal, progressivist, urban and cosmopolitan culture in Germany, this generational alliance came to be politically identified first with Willy Brandt, then with the New Social Movements, and eventually with the red-green coalitions in various state diets and municipal governments. Sociologically, its centre of gravity can be found among knowledge professionals and in the service sector. Very distinctly, its political orientation emerged from the turmoil of 1968. But it took shape as a progressivist liberalism only after lengthy confrontations between extremists tending to terrorism and hedonists fleeing to Tuscany. The progressivist centre eventually garnered a broad-based backing in the late 1970s and early 1980s, attracting an even younger generation of teenagers born in the 1950s and 1960s in conjunction with pacifist and environmentalist politics – both underwritten by a deliberate politics of memory.[19]

At this late point, memory turned into an 'issue' that nobody could avoid. While the general awareness of the issue was still driven by those who had pioneered its politics, memory was now political capital for everyone to use – impossible for anyone with some public stature to ignore. The fortieth anniversary, in 1985, of the end of World War II proved to be the watershed. A variety of discourses about the German past congealed into a prominent theme of public life. This moment was seized, on the one hand, by Jürgen Habermas's initiation of the *Historikerstreit* and, thus, his renewal and consolidation of the old politics of memory against its real and imagined enemies. Quite unwittingly, it seems, the Frankfurt School went popular. On the other hand, the then president of the Federal Republic, Richard von Weizsäcker, also captured the moment. He picked up on the themes of German guilt and responsibility which had been political currency for some time, but had not been in the mainstream of politics. Weizsäcker's honest and hazardous wager was – in opposition to Helmut Kohl, who advocated 'drawing a line', *Schluβstrich*, as a new politics of forgetting for the masses – that the public recognition of guilt would enhance German prestige and would, in fact, carry popular (mass) appeal. He was right on both counts. His high-political sanction of the issue carried enormous appeal both at home and abroad. It put an end to the time when a politics of memory served as the main marker of opposition against high politics.[20] The very idea that the memory of the Third Reich could be used in this fashion suggests the distance that had been traversed between the 1960s and the 1990s and, all protestations to the contrary, attests to the power that the politics of memory had accrued in the West German public sphere.

Popular or not, remembering continued to be hard labour. It never came naturally nor did it flow easily. As Jenninger's case (1988) – the president of parliament, Philipp Jenninger, was forced to resign after a speech that could be read as sympathetic to Nazi anti-Semitism[21] – suggests, the margin for error was extraordinary, because what exactly the politics of memory comprised shifted kaleidoscopically. It developed in a process of accretion in which slivers of remembrances (one's own and fictional and real others) and ways of publicly recollecting the past were piled on top of each other in a contradictory and tension-filled process. It soon became evident that the process would also be an unfinished and incomplete cultural and personal affair. One wonders how it could have been otherwise, since it was from the beginning the story of a half-hearted, repeatedly interrupted, frequently timid, always circumlocutory approach to German mass murder and genocide.

The politics of memory lived off an insistence on the special responsibility of intellectuals to counter the pervasive forgetting of the past. In its initial phase, this was a debate among contemporaries, but forgetting was increasingly attributed to the older generation as a whole. The 'silence' of the 1950s came to be read as the amnesia of a guilty generation that paralysed and stymied present German society. Disclosures about the Nazi past of leading officials, revelations about secret ties between state institutions, for example, between the *Bundeswehr* and old Nazi officers, leaks about the survival of 'brown' networks in the new state, publicity about the annual meetings of SS veterans groups, creating awareness about the continuation of Nazi language and thought, were the pragmatics of a politics that was a curious combination of several factors. It contained strong, sometimes overwhelming elements of youthful *Angst*, the effort to escape the long shadow of present or absent parents.[22] It was also in equal measure a fear of missing out on the present and its newly available opportunities. The young were not only rebelling against their parents, they were also finding their way in a mobile consumer society of which their parents had no more understanding than they had. To compare this phenomenon to the rock and roll rebellion elsewhere is not to belittle it. The politics of memory was also inspired by an antifascism which at that point had become thoroughly monopolized by the East German regime.[23] Yet the youthful German flirtation with East German *antifa* discourse was rather like the fashion for gangsta rap among white, suburban teenagers. It was good enough to scare the hell out of parents whose fear of the 'East' (of communism and the Soviet Union) was part and parcel of the unsettling memory of the past. But the ham-fisted antifascism of East German functionaries, while retaining its moral valence, never quite managed to hold the attention of Westerners or, for that matter, of a younger generation for very long. The East German antifascism was even more an act of repetition, replaying the past with a vengeance, than the politics of the 1950s 'angry men' in West Germany had been. It got stuck in the moment of defeat of the German Communist movement, whereas the politics of memory became a very presentist affair aimed against those who represented the past.

The pained exploration of the Nazi roots of a Hitler Youth generation became the most fraught expression of this instance of memory. Novels like Christa Wolf's *Kindheitsmuster* (1967) suggest genuine moments of transcendence in an otherwise quite mad scene. At the time, though, her excavation of a childhood and adolescent memory bespoke the bond between the Hitler Youth and the postwar generation exceptionally well.[24] It recalled the troubles of growing up (and of growing up in the 1930s in Landsberg an der Warthe, at that), while making sense of the present. Only Günter Grass came close to her, although his literary career and his political engagement were never quite as tightly integrated as the East German Wolf's.[25] Uwe Johnson, whose *Jahrestage* is possibly the starkest account of past meeting present in East and West, has only slowly gained recognition for his work because he stayed away from Germany and from politics.[26] While a closer scrutiny of these memory works would indeed suggest a great deal about the difficulties of approaching the German 'heart of darkness', such readings are only moderately helpful in approaching the unfolding politics of memory. We come closer to what happened if we keep in mind that this politics of memory gathered steam in a shift of generations. It was the receptive audiences of a Wolf, Böll, Grass, Hochhuth or Lenz who made this politics, turning the memory of the past into a public concern with considerable mass appeal. This was, above all, a postwar generation talking back to their elders, talking not so much about their own memories (although the latter soon became a subfeature of this genre) as about the ones their fathers and mothers did not have but should or could have had, as these writers testified.[27] If Christa Wolf set out to explore her past in order to see what could be salvaged of her own life (and on a grander scale, of German life), the postwar generation set out to recover the past as a way of cutting off and cutting loose from the past. The bond of the Hitler Youth and the postwar generation was conditioned by this slippage. It afforded both an exploration of the past and a wholesale distantiation from it.

The postwar generation is just now beginning to emerge as a subject of reflection. The phenomenon of its emergence cannot be subsumed under the students' movement (the *Außerparlamentarische Opposition*), but the latter came to express more loudly and, in some ways, more consciously than anything else the trepidations this generation felt growing up in the late 1950s and 1960s.[28] Theirs was, above all, a trying out of all kinds of new masks on a tabula rasa that was bulldozed clean by the suspicion of fascism and its conflation with capitalism. Re-reading the theories of fascism produced at the time, *Faschismustheorie*, one is struck less with the poverty of their formulations than with the compulsion with which they obliterated whole swaths of the German past because of their association with Nazism. These texts will be remembered more for their conspiratorial overtones than for their analytic insights.[29] Inasmuch as they contained and furthered a politics of memory, it amounted to a lobotomy which afforded the patient his or her wholesale remaking as 'new man', the 'new woman' being a rather more tenuous creature. Revolutionaries and proletarians populated the streets, much as billboards of one or the other Marxist orientation occupied university seminars, battling it out with each other and with more scholarly types who fought for the pure rendition of Karl Marx or Horkheimer and Adorno – so pure, in fact, that Adorno fell short when confronted with his own absolute image.

The zeal of the student movement's antifascism suggests ghosts that were not evident to its protagonists. If 'theory' was the name of the game, stability of meaning was the far more pressing and troubling concern. Both the Nazi past and the materialism of the 1950s were experienced as utter corporeal and mental constriction twenty years after the regime had collapsed. They were imminent and suffocating threats to identity. The drama of distantiation from this past/present was played out in countless different ways, but German terrorism eventually came to stand in as its most radical solution.[30] The biography of Ulrike Meinhof, who turned from a provincial Roman Catholic into the most wanted and, at the same time, most revered and charismatic terrorist, is a telling example of both this sense of constriction and the violence of liberation. Her life story amounted to a wholesale rejection of the past to the point of self-destruction.[31] This history suggests that the deliberate 'post-fascist' subject was a highly tenuous and artificial creature – the rootless personality that post-structural theory ascribes to modern capitalism.

For most people of Meinhof's generation, the alternative to violence was a politics of memory that put a wedge between past and present and thus afforded a safer and, above all, less violent transition to a postwar German identity. They went on what they perceived as a 'long path through the institutions', which amounted to a balancing act between abandoning traditions and inherited customs and building a life in an increasingly prosperous Federal Republic. The personal, the intellectual and the political were closely imbricated in this process. Mores changed with lifestyles, and political orientations were refashioned as a new habitus. The new (West) German humanism, a novel leisure culture (exemplified by the Tuscany faction of mostly southern German intellectuals who bought their second homes in Italy) and the emerging New Social Movements, commonly treated as separate developments, had more in common than any one of them would admit. The resulting fusion of 'humanism and efficiency' was the eventual outcome of the learning process in which a wartime and a postwar generation began to settle into the cosmopolitanism of the Federal Republic.

The key to the volatile mobilization of memory was the refashioning of the German intellectual classes in a postwar identity. The coming to terms with the past was a tool for the 'construction' of the good life that was free of the ballast of the past. There was always a strong sense of the 'constructedness' of this process – a wilful departure and a break with the past that set the present free. But while the 'post-fascist subject' was an artifical construct, it cannot be explained via the aestheticist theories of a Paul De Man, for example. The German politics of memory was always a moral politics – and it laboured, above all, under the constraints of the radical destruction of knowledge in the Third Reich. Traditions of critical thought had been eradicated, and it took an extra-ordinary exertion of the imagination to recover what was once present, but was now invisible and lost. In a culture in which the Frankfurt School and its knowledge was not simply absent but had been destroyed, the recovery and, indeed, remaking of that tradition amounted to a deliberate leap. Oddly, it was, as Jürgen Habermas has suggested, a leap into an enlightened, pre-Nazi past, as prerequisite for the future.[32]

Progressive Germans of the educated class believed firmly in the possibility of improving the nation, for which a working through of the Holocaust became the cornerstone. Their conviction was, and to a point still is, that a full and truthful account of the evils of the German past would lead to a more conscientious and more enlightened present and serve to guide future-oriented action. This recovered and recuperated modernity, in contrast to the creative and generative modernism of the 1910s and 1920s, was highly normative. It delineated right from wrong, and separated a false (premodern) German identity from a correct postnational one. Individual introspection, public tribunals to assure collectivity, critiques of hidden motives and intentions – all made up a culture of guilt and salvation, and a remarkably Protestant culture of guilt in a country that, at the time, was predominantly Catholic.[33] The acknowledgement of guilt under the watchful eye of the norms of Western modernity became the measure of progress, individual and collective, in the West German politics of memory.

It is difficult to say whether politics was fuelled by historiography or historiography by politics. Each profited from the other. Historiography managed at this point to escape the confines of the guild of national-liberal and nationalist historians that had predominated well into the 1960s with the help of a nascent politics of memory. In turn, the politics of memory depended on the hard-nosed objectivism of maverick historical scholarship. This scholarship found its most prominent articulation in a social-scientific historiography: *Gesellschaftsgeschichte.* The rise of a generation of scholars influenced by Hans-Ulrich Wehler's combination of social scientific history and political engagement is perhaps the most impressive instance of this turn.[34] Yet *Gesellschaftsgeschichte* also tended to stay away from the subject of the Third Reich. This seemed puzzling at first, since the historians repeatedly circled around the origins of what they did not study in the end. Only when it moved from a critique of 'premodern elites' as the causes of twentieth-century evil to a history of the German bourgeoisie did the project's logic become transparent. Much as in the recovery of the Frankfurt School thought, the pre-Nazi past became the battleground for a better future, the object of *Gesellschaftsgeschichte* being to distinguish between 'good' and 'bad' traditions in the German past. Even then, it took a while to discover that the German bourgeoisie could be seen as a 'good' tradition.

Initially, *Gesellschaftsgeschichte* imagined the past as a negative horizon of the present. This past accounted for the difference between a process of modernization, encapsulated in the Western experience, and the incomplete or failed modernity of Germany.[35] If only the roots of the German failure could be shown, disaster could be undone, and Germany brought back on track. This historical imagination persisted long after a scholarly critique of the German exceptionalism had raised doubts about the validity of this historical concept. It remained present as the cultural practice that informed a historical politics of memory. The Western present became the substitute for a German past that could safely be discarded.

Then again, the past could not so easily be made to go away. Too many contemporaries were alive and too many of them had actively or passively been involved in the Nazi regime. Their presence was not conjured away by the appeal to a logic of modernization; it took a different historiography to make that happen. In 1978, a young historian, Christian Streit, published a thesis on the treatment of Soviet prisoners of war by the German *Wehrmacht,* in which it was claimed that roughly three million POWs died from mistreatment or neglect by the German army. The thesis was a solid professional achievement, well-researched and documented.[36] While it was understood that the book dealt with a 'sensitive' topic and, as a result, would raise objections (which it did), it was very much part of the professional mainstream – so much so, that Andreas Hillgruber, later the cause célèbre of the *Historikerstreit*, together with Ernst Nolte defended both the book and the student against criticism from the old guard of Nazi officers. Eventually, these efforts would result in something like the (yet to be completed) ten-volume series *Das Deutsche Reich und der Zweite Weltkrieg* (1979–), with individual volumes ranging well over one thousand pages each.[37] The investigative practice of this historiography would be instrumental in the Waldheim affair – the former UN secretary general and Austrian president who was accused of having participated in, supervised or, at least, known of the deportation of Jews from Saloniki and who was, in the end, caught in an obvious cover-up of his wartime past.[38] In different circumstances the sheer length of the volumes in the series might have been a deterrent against sales, much as tedious investigations into the documentary evidence of Waldheim's activities during the war would dampen sensationalism. But the volumes have become bestsellers and the investigative results of the Waldheim affair have left a dent in the Austrian self-perception as innocent victims of the Third Reich. We can see here the practice of distantiation, which occasionally took on a hyperrealist quality. The more detail one amassed about the real working of the regime (as opposed to the claims of participants), the more evident the evil nature of the regime became. This kind of history was never particularly good at explaining what happened, but it convincingly ascertained that evil did happen. It claimed 'truth' against falsification and facticity against interpretation. It set the empirical record against 'narratives' (the stories of contemporaries) about the past, and it used that record as self-evident moral indictment of the past and its actors. It supplied sufficient evidence to prove the criminality, the barbarism and the inhumanism of the Nazi regime. Moral judgement and empirical proof happily coincided.

The extreme 'archivalism' of this historiography sharply contrasted with the subjective narratives which had depended in large measure on the recollections, written and oral, of contemporaries, including those used in criminal investigations and trials after the war. The effectiveness of this tool increased over time. While historians by and large insisted on the primacy of the written record, journalists-turned-historians soon learned the power of images. Once photographs and images came into play, the last and decisive protection broke down. When murderers became plainly visible in the act – in fact, they had a proclivity to take photographs that has yet to be fully explained – the remaining authenticity of recollections by contemporaries was undercut.[39] The images they took of the slaughter devastated their own efforts to hide or distort their pasts. The photographs taken by perpetrators as mementos – in order to prove to themselves (against all orders) that they had actually committed these crimes, or in any case had been present – evidence a *Schaulust* (a pleasure in watching enemies being hanged or shot), but also an element of disbelief, the sense that they could not quite believe what they manifestly saw (and did). The hard surface of these photographs was the ultimate and most uncontrovertible evidence of an investigative history. Empiricism, and photographic empiricism at that, proved to be the wedge with which the past was split from the present.

But if historians discarded memory as an evidentiary base, others recovered it through what would eventually become *Alltagsgeschichte*, everyday-life history. This is the third and most recent development in the formation of a West German politics of memory. While everyday-life history had roots in older explorations of 'alternative' German traditions, particularly working-class and radical democratic ones, it only came into its own in the 1980s when it moved toward an experiential history of the Third Reich. Historians such as Lutz Niethammer or Alf Lüdtke relied on ethnographic approaches and the new techniques of an oral, interview-oriented history. In short, they had their own scholarly apparatus as well as a distinct methodology. But they were fiercely attacked by those who seemed to be their natural allies, the empiricist as well as the analytic social historians.[40] The fog of controversy only begins to clear if we take into account the very different relationship of *Alltagsgeschichte* to the past. The historians of everyday experience took seriously the notion that 'the past' is a living memory in the present. Moreover, they were less hesitant in seeing themselves as part of the very process of remembering. The resulting subjectivism ground hard against the objectivism of the progressive histories of the 1970s. With *Alltagsgeschichte* the careful fencing-off of the past in a distant country came to a halt. Worse, the experience of the historians themselves, as they were affected by the Nazi regime, became part and parcel of their analysis. Guilt could no longer be safely deposited with premodern classes or in a foreign past.

The resulting controversy constituted a major juncture in the politics of memory. Previous histories had exorcized the past as tainted heritage. *Alltagsgeschichte* took on the whole of that past, occasionally to a fault. The 'guilty' were no longer 'out there'; they were 'among us'. They existed not in a different time, but in 'our' life. This turn inserted an element of instability in what had been a clear-cut distantiation of the Third Reich as the 'wrong' modernity. Too much of the present was imbricated with the past, and too much of the past with one's own present. As a result, some everyday histories drifted into a puzzled appreciation of the experience of Nazism and war – an empathetic re-evaluation of the past. Written histories were, perhaps, less susceptible to this temptation than were documentaries provided for television and cinema.[41] But the difficulties remained the same for both written and visual forms. Once the politics of memory engaged the actually existing memory of the German people (rather than setting 'evidence' against 'memory'), there was no self-evident pivot from which to evaluate the past and no preconfigured distance to be maintained toward the experience of the Third Reich. The division between past and present, the assessment of evil, had to be generated in the process of historical interpretation, and there was no automatic guarantee of a cathartic outcome, because there was no longer an ideal 'West' that would salvage the present. In the end, it was not methodology that saved this history, by and large, from abandoning its critical stance. Rather, it kept faith with the critical project, in some small part because of the corrective publicity of memory work, and for the most part because of the belated discovery of the victims of Nazi genocide and of their memories.

The role of the public in 'memory work' is exemplified by the case of a courageous student, Anna Rosmus, who began to uncover piece by piece the history of her Lower Bavarian home town, Passau, during the Third Reich.[42] It is a story that was repeated all over the country in the context of a nationwide history-workshop movement. Initially, Rosmus could count on the support of family networks, but increasingly she had to work against efforts to silence her. What is interesting about this case is not simply the result of the study (which showed how deeply the town and, especially, its notables had been implicated in the history of the Third Reich and how well they were aware of the fact) or, for that matter, that this study saw the light of day. Rather, what is remarkable is that this local study went national and, eventually, global. Contrary to its image and its self-proclaimed goals, the nascent microhistory gained momentum from tie-ins with regional and even national publicity. As soon as the national media picked up the issue, the silence in Passau was irrevocably broken. The feature film, *The Nasty Girl* (1990), that was eventually made about the whole incident got the story of the local girl who stood up to the town notables right, but missed this peculiar feature of the German politics of memory in the 1980s – its imbrication of the local and the national. Local efforts depended on a national politics of memory, which gained its evidence from local cultures of memory. It is difficult to see how this spillover could have happened without the support of the print media, be it local newspapers reporting on everyday history or national newspapers and weeklies discussing the 'new' history favourably, or television networks presenting their results in a rapidly increasing number of documentaries, docudramas and talk shows. Everyday history generated memory for a national symbolic space that grew from the margins to the centre with the help of the national media. Although everyday history had a tendency to extoll the virtues of authentic memory and insisted on the local, it succeeded when and where it captured print media and television.

However, the animosity of Passau only partly stemmed from the fact that Rosmus had deprived some notables of their good consciences. In Passau as everywhere else in Germany the threshold of tolerance lay somewhere else. It came with the naming and the recognition of the victims of the Third Reich. German memory work crossed an invisible line when it began to trace the memories and the voices of those who were silenced by expulsion or mass killing. Only when the history of the Third Reich became a history of Jews (or, for that matter, Gypsies, Poles, Russians and homosexuals) in Germany and Europe did the National Socialist 'topography of terror' become apparent.[43] Time and again and in place after place, this recovery of an extirpated memory was a shocking and fearsome moment. It took forty years to realize that the absence of the memory of the victims was 'the silence' that made a difference.

Only when this politics of memory uncovered 'killing fields' everywhere did it discover the absence of the murdered. Ever since, this absence has been one of its main concerns, expressed, to some extent, in efforts to recover lost and extinguished pasts. German-Jewish life, in particular, has become the subject of an astonishing number of grass-roots projects that have made visible the many places all over Germany where men, women and children were persecuted and murdered.[44] These projects have laid bare the social fabric into which the camps were fitted; have explicated the camp system, its effects and the displaced memories of those who encountered the camps and their inmates every day.[45] This has led to protracted conflicts because no place, no community wanted to be reminded of or associated with slave labour, persecution and annihilation. The experience of Dachau was repeated over and over again.[46] Yet by the same token these sites of persecution and destruction have become German places of memory. They have been visited by countless people, especially young ones, so that one might well say that the Germans have, at long last, encountered their past.

But this discovery proved to be a strange gift, for it created a manifest tension between German 'memory work' and the history and memory of 'others'. It remains unresolved how this past can be brought back into German history without taking away from the fullness of past life on the one hand and its *shoah*, its utter destruction, on the other. Behind this tension lies another and even bigger conundrum. Did the memory work of the Germans appropriate a past that was irretrievably separated from their present as a result of the Nazi genocide? There was and is no ready answer, as the inconclusive search for a 'German' representation of the Holocaust suggests.

*

The proponents of a politics of memory most commonly felt that they had to fight against a world of Germans who wanted nothing more than to forget. The former understood themselves as outsiders with no influence at all, contrasting their genuine and enlightened politics of memory with a mass culture of consumption which they identified as a culture of oblivion. This opposition has become part of German identity and has entered the scholarly and journalistic debate on the burden of the past. In contrast, the critics of an enlightened politics of memory have insisted that the danger of this politics consisted in the fact that it had made inroads into public consciousness and had begun to form a public culture of memory. Castigating the 'national masochism' of the West German elites, the shackles of *Vergangenheitsbewältigung*, these critics suggest that the intellectual subcultures have spilled over into society and begun to affect a widespread mass audience.[47]

While we may not share the values of these glaringly biased interventions, they have a point to make. There has been in German mass culture a remarkable efflorescence of memory work which has no roots in enlightened politics. Still, it does amount to a coming to terms with the past in its own right. As with the politics of memory, one must be careful not to overstate its reach; it has always had its popular detractors, who may well form a majority. But I tend to think that it is a genuine mass public that crosses class, gender, regional, denominational, generational and even 'ethnic' lines. This assertion, however, will require further research into little-known territory. For the time being, it may suffice to point to its existence and the basic contours of its activities.

From the start, there was a countercurrent to the father-son and mother-daughter drama that emerged so prominently, at the urging of sons and daughters, during the 1970s. Just as a younger generation broke away from an older one in order to liberate themselves from the past, fathers and mothers had begun to extricate themselves from the clutches of their lived pasts by themselves. There is virtually no literature on this subject, but the phenomenon is sufficiently widespread, if one trusts hearsay, to merit attention. For the moment, an anecdote concerning my own family may help to illustrate what I mean. Rather to my surprise, in the early 1980s, my father and uncle had a reconciliation, after a long, quite unfathomable estrangement and became the best of friends, experiencing what amounted to self-therapy regarding their own father and the impact, they felt, his tempers and beatings had on them. I do not know how they began this conversation, but since numbers of other people began to have similar conversations, one would assume that they had seen something about this on television. They surely had not read Alice Miller and would have loathed Theweleit, although they reached some of the same conclusions as these authors.[48] Their father's beatings had traumatized them for life and they were just now getting over them, as far as that was ever possible. One might add that neither of them had, in the past or in the present, developed the armoured personality that Theweleit mythologizes as the persona that comes with this kind of upbringing, although both had sympathized, in different and age-specific ways, with the National Socialists. Now, in the early 1980s, they were very openly talking about the latter in the context of the former, their upbringing. They were talking about their past allegiances as something they had shed a long time ago politically, but were now leaving behind personally. There is no reason to believe that this effort was any less 'honest' and 'heartfelt' than that of their sons and daughters; and there is no reason why it should have been less critical than the much more self-consciously enlightened politics of memory.

The separation of intellectual and popular culture is highly artificial, in any case. Both sides shared in the same public space, and there was much more overlap between the two than the distinction between 'high' and 'low' culture would allow. In order to be heard and seen – that is, to gain publicity – intellectual cultures took to the multiplier of the mass media despite some very principled reservations. And people watched television and talked intelligently about 'the past'. While they were set to prove that they themselves did nothing wrong, many acknowledged that 'things' had gone terribly wrong. This was not much of an acknowledgement of Nazi crimes and surely not what the politics of memory had wanted, but it was a fissure that lay bare for some time, ready to crack wide open, if personal or other circumstances intervened. There is, I am quite convinced, a long history of private occasions when this happened. As the story of my father and uncle – and, in a different way, that of Albert Speer – suggested, these could be very personal moments and very individual circumstances.[49] But it was only through film and television that a memorializing culture finally took hold.

The moment of recognition that this was happening can be specified with some precision. It came in 1979 with the airing of the television miniseries *The Holocaust*, which had the peculiar effect of stunning the academic caste that was rallied in front of television cameras, poised to set the record straight. The German network and the intellectual public had expected to encounter a popular Holocaust scepticism and wanted to be ready, typically, to prove wrong through hard evidence anticipated lapses of popular memory. But instead, television audiences saw a group of academics overwhelmed, incapable of handling the emotional outbursts of memories that took place. People from all walks of life jammed the telephone lines to talk. This overflow, however, was the exact opposite of *Erinnerungen* or interiorizations. The past had stuck with these audiences, and now, long-buried internal tensions erupted through the aid of electronic images which helped them identify their own memories. These memories found expression in the television docudrama; that is, the soap-opera quality of *The Holocaust* had a predictable and commonly observed effect, although the subject was highly exceptional.

It was not the fact of genocide that upset viewers. The Holocaust remained incomprehensible, beyond representation, although – and this is what mattered – it was the irreversible conclusion of the story. Once this ending became evident, the attitudes that facilitated the separation of Jews and Germans began to falter. The audience's memories were in this sense part of a specular imagination; in the image of the other (the Jewish family as the victim of Germans) the audience discovered a part of itself that had been lost – and that, indeed, had been betrayed by them. Betrayal and lies surfaced as tangible accusations. They were the small change of dictatorship and they were the things people remembered. They saw it all on television and many people in the audience saw themselves for the first time in the double of the fictional image.

This image world was, as far as the contemporaries of the Third Reich were concerned, a part of their own identity which they had wilfully or through silent complicity destroyed: a world of memories resurrected and thrown in their faces by their sons and daughters. For a much younger generation of teenagers, the images presented an alien culture, a past about which they knew nothing. Out of this television series a novel generational configuration arose, quite different from the one that had championed a politics of memory. Grandparents talked to grandchildren while parents stood by in dismay. The parents insinuated that old and young spoke of 'the war', revising their former stances toward it and toward violence; the truth of the matter is that they also spoke of the Holocaust – with unpredictable effects leading both to moments of catharsis and to a bond between old and young in an acknowledgement of the past.

Neither the force of the past nor the emotional rendition of the Holocaust as melodrama, but the market-driven interplay between representation and receptive audience is responsible for the outpouring of sentiment that followed the airing of the series. The power of this 'society of the spectacle' is commonly overlooked,[50] following a long genealogy of indictments. These indictments were strongly reinforced by Adorno's revindication (and secularization) of the Jewish *Bilderverbot* and powerfully translated into aesthetic practice in Claude Lanzmann's documentary *Shoah*.[51] But notwithstanding the cultural and moral authority of the prohibition on visually representing the Holocaust, we do have a twenty-five-year record of what images have done and can do. In Germany, they have recaptured and brought into the open a memory that had been excised from public life.[52]

Thus, the main popular form of remembrance of the Nazi past has been industrially produced by radio, television, and the movies. It is a public memory that is almost impossible to escape because of the sheer volume of output and the repetitive nature of its features. Television formed *Erinnerungsbilder*, but they were images of a peculiar kind: not interior recollections, but mementos of a disastrous past that gained visibility as moving pictures. If a politics of memory found its *lieux des memoires* in sites that were marked by genocide,[53] the televised and broadcast *Erinnerungsbilder* formed what one might call electronic sculptures of remembrance for a memorializing culture.

One of the clearest proofs of this argument is the sudden readiness to make amends – not merely on the part of the state, as was the case in the 1950s, but on the part of communities and individuals as well. There have been several instances of a veritably national remorse: the otherwise inexplicable outburst of sentiment after the showing of *The Holocaust*, or the highly emotional readiness of Germans, in 1990–91, to come to the aid of Russia. There have been equally stunning blunders that suggest limits to this effusion. The tenacious resistance to owning up to the murder of the European Jews, reflected in the absence of the Holocaust in the widely popular *Die Heimat* (1984); and the enduring vacillations in the relations with Poles and Czechs are two of the more prominent cases. But equally noteworthy are the many efforts to revive the memory of Jews in Germany and to establish a new bond with survivors of the Holocaust and their children, a community project that was impossible without the participation of dedicated volunteers and the tacit approval of local publics. In this kind of activity popular memorializing and the politics of memory intersected, creating the memory culture of the 1980s.

These invitations and the subsequent meetings were occasionally embarrassing and often clammy and clumsy, the most egregious fumbles becoming the subject of lore among the invitees and, especially, their sceptical children. Tragicomic stories revolve around Jewish fears of returning and, in some cases, outright refusals; the uncomprehending eagerness of the German hosts to welcome their Jewish guests to their beautifully rebuilt and, to their guests, completely alien cities; the painful evidence of the destruction of Jewish culture in Germany, which no amount of goodwill could undo. Despite these embarrassments, the long-standing efforts to establish a Christian-Jewish dialogue have made substantial advances as a result of a growing self-awareness and the growth of small Jewish communities in Germany due to the influx of Russian Jews after 1991. Altogether, one would have to say that it took a great deal of patience and tolerance on the part of individual guests and Jewish communities to make this German memorializing effort work.

Some communities have begun to build synagogues for even very small Jewish communities, as in Darmstadt; or memorial institutions, archives and research institutes, as in Essen and Frankfurt; or to restore and publicly name Jewish sites where, at best, there had been only a commemorative marker. It is, of course, significant that public markers are being placed where synagogues once had been, Jewish community centres are being built, that a didactic centre to perpetuate the history of the Holocaust has been erected in a German locality,[54] but it also important to note that these sites had to be instantly protected by the police, that the presence of Jews in history and actuality has also unleashed a new anti-Semitism.

To return to our main argument, however, we must reiterate that the memories of the Nazi regime did not return as *Erinnerung*, as the sages of post-war enlightenment would have had it. They were, instead, mass-mediated. Their return had little to do with the recovery of earlier high bourgeois forms of subjectivity and publicity. Irrevocably, the individual labour of remembering had taken a back seat to the mass production of memory, which facilitated a very different mode of recall. Memories were not summoned up by an individual and interior process of self-examination, nor were they subjected to a tribunal of conscience in a culture of guilt. The televized articulation of the past set the individual free. It implicated no one in particular, but merely represented actions and non-actions, attitudes and behaviours which everyone remembered, and whose bitter consequences were now summed up in a story that led inescapably to annihilation and catastrophe. This televized past functions like a kind of secular morality play; it exposed the evil that resulted from certain ideologies, attitudes and behaviours in such a way that they could no longer be thought without their attending historical consequences.[55] This did not have the emancipatory effect the 'angry old men' and their sons and daughters who had pioneered a politics of memory had hoped to achieve.

Less evident and much more difficult to explain is another feature: the industrial mass production of memorial images was, from the very beginning, a strangely dual affair. It was never only the memorialization of exclusion, expulsion and genocide; in fact, it might well be argued that genocide was the smaller, although never insignificant, part of the nascent memorializing culture. The film *Hitler: A Career* (1977) and the television broadcasts of the TV miniseries *The Holocaust* (1979), *Heimat* (1984) and, a decade later, although with much less acclaim, *Die zweite Heimat* (1992) and *Stalingrad* (1992), as well as *Schindler's List* (1993) were stages in a rich and diverse development. Each memorializing production moved Germans – I would argue, the same Germans – deeply. This was taken by many as an indication of the insincerity of the whole effort – an assessment that is not entirely off the mark, but falls short of making sense of the tension that characterizes the German memorializing culture of the 1980s. For although each of these films tried to move Germans in different and, indeed, opposite directions, they all had the same effect. Together they managed to transform the German interest in the Third Reich from a pursuit of memory to a pursuit of history.

There is no evident strategy separating the recollections of the Nazi regime and the acknowledgement of its terror and its genocidal politics. Obviously, there were groups that wanted to separate these two issues sharply, appealing either to an outright appreciation or an outright condemnation of the Third Reich. But the memorializing public did both; and while this runs counter to historical and moral insight, it is difficult to see how it could be otherwise for a memorializing public. The abandonment of an earlier distance from the past gave way to a quite manifest nostalgia for *Heimat*, the nation and its past, which also entailed a reassessment of the Third Reich. This sentiment was expressed in a new historical consciousness that was articulated quite faithfully in the plans for a German historical museum.[56] Above all, this sentiment was expressed in the TV series *Heimat*. At the same time public recognition of the Holocaust as a German crime and of Nazi rule over Eastern Europe as a savage and brutal regime was also increasing. This recognition accompanied the search for a national identity. Jenninger's disastrous speech in front of the Bundestag in 1988 is a good indication of the imbrication of the two developments and of the strictures against them.[57] It is one of the best examples of the peculiar dual reckoning of the past in a German memorializing culture.

The memorializing culture of the 1980s came at a quite extraordinary moment in West German life, when old realities, old perceptions and old habits rapidly began to lose hold. Everyday life in a prosperous and mobile consumer society simply could not be navigated with the postures, behaviours, and norms of the interwar years. Withdrawal into 'alternative' lifestyles or into the past were possible responses. Value change was another;[58] and while the notion of value change was heavily biased toward the New Social Movements, there is no reason to think that it should not include such things as the yoga practices of my mother, which she undertook with like-minded locals in a small town in the provinces. A new regime of beliefs, values, behaviours and body practices emerged. It was a popular regime, even when it was championed by the urban avant-garde. Memorializing was used – take my father's story as an example – to shed a past that had weighed on individuals and the nation. Television, the recognition of sameness in an electronic public, replaced the authentic *Volk*. And television, while mostly presenting its American-made wares, went in for history on a grand scale.

The desire to unburden oneself of memories of the Third Reich came at a price. Memory could not be thrown out like furniture was in the 1950s, although it occasionally seemed that way. It was too important an individual mark and too important a collective experience to be discarded. In order to unburden themselves of memories without entirely abandoning themselves, individuals and the national electronic public had to negotiate conflicting emotions, to struggle between pride and a desire for absolution; a hesitancy to acknowledge involvement and a willingness to make good; an insistence on their own identity and a desire to acknowledge that of others whose presence revived the memory of mass murder. These tensions were not resolved. They were, instead, articulated in a culture of shame – which is, I think, the most appropriate rendition of the popular version of German *Betroffenheitskultur.*

This culture was sentimental and, as some of its critics suggested, it was also a 'feminine', moralizing culture. It was, moreover, a Christian culture that built on an implicit understanding of repentance as a means to assuage past evil. 'Reconciliation' (*Versöhnung*) emerged as its main theme. It was a culture that capitalized on the general well-being of the Germans and their remarkable security. It relied on the fact that the 'new', postwar Germans lived in a different world. That is, those who took on the responsibility for the German past also felt that they were under scrutiny, continuously watched over by others – 'foreigners', especially 'Americans', who appropriated the Holocaust in their own way, and, most difficult of all, by Jews who were regaining a voice in German affairs. This sense of being watched also produced a sense of victimization which could easily be exploited, making the Germans into the victims of memory.[59] The ever-present 'eye' of the other, the prominence of rituals of *Wiedergutmachung,* the insistence on visible social effects of coming to terms with the past, the anxiety about behaving incorrectly – all served to transform the German memorializing culture into a distinct culture of shame.[60] This process remained very German indeed, and as such was not exactly the ideal vehicle to facilitate the memory of Judaeocide and genocidal war, although it did so in the end through the insistent presence of victims in images and memorials. Unstable as this culture was, it maintained, in all its ambivalence, the popular reality of the memory of the Third Reich and of the Holocaust.

How popular was this reality? Surveys and opinion polls do not give an unequivocal answer; while they register the persistence of its themes, they also suggest that many people turned off their televisions and radios and skipped the relevant items in the newspaper. More content-oriented analyses suggest that memorializing had become sugar-coated, appealing to a sense of the basic innocence of the Germans and to their sense of pity in relation to the victimized.[61] There was a tendency to identify with the victims in lieu of recovering their own memories of events. If it must ultimately remain undecided 'what the Germans actually thought', we can nevertheless draw a clear picture of the reactions of those affected by this memorializing culture, that is, of the Jewish congregation in Germany on the one hand, and those like Chancellor Helmut Kohl, who set out to create a counterpolitics of memory, on the other.

The growing publicity given to the Jewish communities in Germany can be traced to many sources. The fact that some municipal administrations came to support them more actively is probably more significant for the gentiles that it is for the Jews in Germany. The wider public recognition of the very fact of the Holocaust was far more important, because the memories of survivors were finally given a voice.[62] This was a very tense process, not least because there was and continues to be tremendous resistance against allowing Jewish identity to be defined by the fact of survival rather than by an active participation in the diaspora community. A more self-conscious Jewishness and a more deliberate involvement with German politics and culture emerged when Ignaz Bubis became the president of the Central Council of Jewish Communities. That this growing self-consciousness did not translate into a growing self-confidence about the status and place of Jews in Germany was due to the fact that the novel publicity also generated a new anti-Semitism.[63] That it also resulted in a decline of 1950s 'philo-Semitism' is an indication of the changes that had taken place, since support for the Jews had depended on the absence or, in any case, the silence of Jews in Germany.[64]

The efforts of Chancellor Helmut Kohl to gain control over and roll back the politics of memory are equally telling, since as a populist politician he bet on the desire of the masses to forget. His effort to absolve himself and the entire wartime generation from the labours of memory with reference to the absolution of a *Gnade der späten Geburt* [mercy of late birth] was a well-rehearsed and well-calculated strategy that took advantage of an enthusiasm for *Schlußstrich*, a conclusion of the memory debate. In addition, *Bitburg* – the joint German-American effort of Kohl and President Reagan to declare Germans, even SS soldiers, victims of Nazi tyranny – came to signify a whole array of strategies to bolster German national consciousness and create a new sense of pride in German identity, implicitly challenging the politics of memory as negative and ill-tempered.[65] If a calculation of German sorrows against the suffering of Germany's victims had been a deliberate apologia, under Kohl it turned into a strategy of moralizing about the evils of history. Both the *Schlußstrich* debate and the *Bitburg* spectacle served to underscore the normalcy of the (national) present as opposed to the aberrations of the past and eventually led to the dedication of the *Neue Wache* in Berlin to the victims of tyranny.[66] Inasmuch as Kohl was successful, it was due to the sense that a different postwar world had emerged; but despite extraordinary political and monetary expenditures he succeeded neither in shutting down the debate on the past nor in giving it a distinctively national turn, notwithstanding unification and the national(ist) revival in its aftermath. For so cunning a politician as Kohl, this was quite a defeat. In 1985 he was overshadowed by Richard von Weizsäcker, who had pleaded for a politics of memory in clear contradistinction and in an open challenge to Kohl. And in 1995 he was eclipsed by Roman Herzog, the new president, who established the tenor of the fiftieth anniversary of the end of World War II by making it into a manifestation of the German memorializing culture.[67]

Somewhere between twelve and fourteen thousand public events were mounted to memorialize the end of the war. The publicity of memory, particularly in May 1995, was impossible to escape. While these commemorations were accompanied by some nasty altercations among intellectuals and politicians over the evaluation of the war's end ('defeat' v. 'liberation'), they did not produce the kind of frictions that were expected by the advocates of a politics of memory. The old ploy of weighing the pain of the victims against German suffering had largely lost its meaning. While it was not entirely absent, it had none of the power it once possessed and did not preoccupy the national debate or, for that matter, the many documentaries that were made. The prevalent sentiment rather harked back to *The Holocaust* (with its melodramatic emphasis on Jewish suffering) and to *Heimat* (with its emphasis on the sorrows and joys of being German). As far as one can tell, people were moved and, indeed, afflicted by both, noting quite lucidly the difference between the German genocide of the Jews and the pain it caused and the suffering which those who defeated Nazi Germany inflicted on the Germans.

All of these gestures, however, pale in comparison to the event that put the culture of memory in the spotlight: Steven Spielberg's film *Schindler's List* (1993). The German reception of Spielberg's film was overwhelmingly positive. There is some scepticism about the reasons for its popularity, which may in part have to do with the fact that it casts a German as the redemptive figure in a film about the Holocaust. But another element was equally important: Spielberg set up the plot as a cathartic experience in which the shame of the past becomes the source of a new identity. Unwittingly, he thus regenerated two parallel identities: his own post-*shoah* Jewish identity and the German post-Holocaust identity. Surprised by the German response to his film, Spielberg put this point this way: 'If the German reaction to my film should indeed be shame, then it is important for me that the audience understands that it was shame which has motivated me to make this film. It was the shame of having felt ashamed that I was a Jew.'[68] He was right. 'Shame' was part of the response to the first showing of the film in Frankfurt at which Spielberg and Weizsäcker were present, Kohl was absent. At the end of the film the audience started to applaud the filmmaker, but then quickly fell silent and left the cinema. This gesture was subsequently repeated all over Germany. 'Shame' was also the response of high school student audiences, among whom *Schindler's List* was most popular in Germany. Finally, at the fiftieth anniversary of the liberation of Auschwitz, the new German president, Roman Herzog, spoke of the 'shame' of the German past. The Catholic Church spoke of the 'shame' of the Church as an institution and of its members as practising Christians for not having come to the rescue of the Jews.

So Germans did remember after all, despite loud differences of opinion; memory is not a single, homogeneous artifact. There have been a range of activities: one might best speak of memory as a performance, even though the newest wave of remembering has centred around 'sites of memory' and monuments. There has been hostility. In fact, remembrance has created and revived old hostilities: anti-Semitism is clearly more articulate than ever. A strong desire to slip away from the responsibility for genocide and the Holocaust has continued as an undercurrent. But no amount of passing time has diminished the stigma of mass murder. Shame emerged not simply as rhetoric, but as a public and quite broad-based emotion attendant on recalling the past. Above all, there was a strong sense (and a strong desire) that this history was past – not forgotten, but no longer present. Yet some new feeling has also recently emerged, as the German reception of *Schindler's List* clearly demonstrates.

The film's favourable reception revealed an eagerness to become acquainted with a past that had most definitely ceased to exist. The film was most successful among the youngest generation, which insisted (against all reality checks of high school curricula) that they had encountered, in Spielberg's film, the history of the Holocaust for the first time.[69] In some sense they were correct, since they encountered the past not as a lived experience, within the communities of those who had been there, but as the retelling of a powerful and moving story of something that had happened before their time. In this context, the fact of salvation, the hopeful message of the film, was far more important than the fact that the 'saviour' in the film was a German. The survival of Jews is the only guarantee that life continues after the catastrophe. Younger Germans read the ending of the film in their very own way: even for the victims and their descendants the Holocaust was over. This does not make a coming to terms with German Judaeocide or, for that matter, with Jewish communities in Germany easier, and it considerably alters the process and meaning of memory work.[70] *Schindler's List* is the first indication of things to come.

The tension generated by this transition is evident in two Berlin projects: the Steglitz Holocaust memorial, which has now been completed, and the national Holocaust memorial, which was started with great fanfare, but has run into extraordinary difficulties. If the debate accompanying the Steglitz monument resembles the old confrontations aroused by a politics of memory, the controversies over the national German memorial of the Holocaust suggest some of the new fissures that have emerged in the wake of the memorial boom.

The Steglitz memorial is a glass mirror wall, nine metres long and three and a half metres wide, which contains engravings of the names and addresses (!) of the former Steglitz Jewish citizens who were deported and murdered.[71] The glass memorial (symbolic in its reference to the *Kristallnacht*) reflects the image of the passers-by who stare at themselves through the names and addresses of the victims of the Holocaust – addresses which might as well be their own. In this respect, the memorial is quite similar to another one at the Bayrische Platz, which confronts passers-by with the regulations and prohibitions that, in the 1930s and 1940s, excluded the Jewish population from public life and pushed them to the edge of survival in the very midst of one of the more lively areas of Berlin.[72] In Steglitz, the very idea of a memorial, and a confrontational memorial in particular, encountered serious obstacles during the planning stage. The opposition came partly from the radical right but mostly from well-to-do 'honourable' citizens. For all of them, this memorial was too local, too close to the everyday reality of the citizens of Steglitz, confronting them with a past of which they did not want to be reminded, especially not in such a public space. The Hermann-Ehlers-Platz, where the memorial was to be built, is very distinctly a *German* public sphere. Yet the monument was built and duly dedicated, though it may not have the impact its designers had intended. Designed to confront passers-by in a busy square with a German record of destruction, it has become a piece of public art that blends into the environment.

On the other hand, there was much initial enthusiasm for a private initiative to build a national memorial of the Holocaust on the site of the *Führerbunker*.[73] It was first thought that such a monument was overdue and that it would be a salutary reminder of the Holocaust at a symbolic location. A memorial to the Holocaust at the centre of Nazi power would, indeed, be a remarkable use of this area, or so it seemed. The site is part of the no man's land between East and West that is removed from public life, although it will eventually be adjacent to the future economic and political power centres of the new capital. More suited for obligatory state visits than for the remembrance of the victims of Nazi genocide, its location compromises one of the main tenets of the politics of memory which insisted on the everyday experience of the past and the recognition of the dispersed reality of genocide.

The planning process and design competition for the memorial soon became a full-scale debacle. The problems began with an ugly debate between representatives of the Jewish community and the Roma and Sinti (and various German interlocutors) about who the victims of the Holocaust were. The face-saving solution was to design a main Holocaust memorial for Jews, one for the

Roma and Sinti further down the road. The tendency to split memory into its constituent 'ethnic' parts became uncomfortably evident in this case.

Problems mounted with the artistic competition for the memorial. A sense of disaster and defeat was evident even in the review of the top choices. Even though they have a certain dignity, which could not be said for the vast majority of entries, they entirely lacked a spark of insight into the catastrophe. The design of one of the two top entries led a left Berlin newspaper, *die tageszeitung*, to call it a *Kranzabwurfstelle* (wreath drop site), alluding both to its likely official function and to its main feature, a huge concrete slab with the names of the six million murdered Jews engraved on it. The design echoed various existing memorials including the Vietnam Memorial, but was unable to find a public expression for – for what exactly? The problem was that this was no longer clear, because the more 'the idea' of a Holocaust memorial took shape, the more the fact that Germans had committed mass murder with the intent to annihilate a people got displaced. The critique of the monument became part of this displacement. The design competition and the debate that accompanied it became a public display of an inability artistically to represent the *German* memory of the act of annihilation. Germans came face to face with the difficulties of remembering German genocide.

These difficulties are further marked by the growing irrelevance of the intellectual publics that have mobilized around a politics of memory. One might take the film *Beruf Neonazi* (1993), a much discussed and widely condemned documentary about a young neo-Nazi, as an indication of what has gone wrong with the German politics of memory.[74] The condemnation of this documentary comes mostly in response to the fact that the neo-Nazi under scrutiny is allowed to mouth the 'Auschwitz lie' (or better, Auschwitz denial) without editorial comment. This is a deliberate choice of the filmmaker (whose progressivist pedigree is beyond doubt), because he believes that a *verité* portrayal of the subject matter, a neo-Nazi propounding the Auschwitz denial in Auschwitz, is sufficient to unmask the lie. The director could not even conceive (and still does not concede) the possibility that the documentation of the Auschwitz denial at the very site of Auschwitz adds insult to injury for the victims of Judaeocide. However, in this respect the director is no different from his main critics, who fear that the film will advance the Auschwitz lie, suggesting that the film is incapable of creating its own critical spectator. This uncertainty is most suggestive. For as long as everyone who watches the film can reasonably be expected to oppose the Auschwitz lie (as the director obviously did), the very fact that this lie was delivered in Auschwitz will only enhance the turpitude of the act. If this is no longer the case and if the film can no longer compel this view, *Beruf Neonazi* effectively supports and underwrites the Auschwitz denial.

This is the crux of the matter. The debate on *Beruf Neonazi* suggests that a critical consensus about audiences has broken down.

This interpretation is further supported by the cancellation of the Berlin and Saarbrücken exhibits of photographs, mostly Hitler portraits, by Hitler's photographer Hoffmann. The exhibit, which had originated in Munich, was cancelled in Berlin due to a combination of factors. For one, the director of the Deutsche Historische Museum, Stölzl, had the remarkable idea of opening the exhibit on Hitler's birthday as a publicity stunt – which is not surprising in view of the fact that he had opened a World War II exhibit on the exact anniversary and at the exact time of day of the German invasion of Poland. The more important reason for the cancellation was the protest of the president of the Jewish *Gemeinde* in Berlin, Jerzy Kanal, who argued that the exhibit might attract the wrong crowd and might, thus, become neo-Nazi propaganda. Jerzy Kanal said:

> If one shows a concentrated exhibit of several hundred Hitler-Fotos in the heart of Berlin, there will be people who are not so well introduced into the details and who are unable to decipher these propaganda photos. What has disturbed us in particular is that in this kind of exhibition there are gigantic marches and supplications [*Huldigungen*] shown. And one cannot suddenly argue, now, that in this fashion one unmasks Hitler. It is cheap to say, something has been made out of nothing.[75]

The fear is that Hitler's photos will once again work their magic (presuming that it was, indeed, the 'power of images' that once moved the Germans[76]) and that there is no way of compelling or inducing audiences to be critical. Above and beyond dubious exhibition practices and half-baked documentaries, the very pedagogical project of the politics of memory is at stake in these comments.[77] At issue is the very idea that intellectual or artistic labours can save or salvage a society ravaged by Nazism. Even if the film is not as bad as it is made out to be and even if there is no good reason for banning and censoring it (which is what happened in several states and on national television), there is good enough reason to wonder if the intellectual mission of enlightenment can be accomplished. Incidentally, a young generation of antifascists – present, for example, at the public viewing and subsequent discussion of the film at the (East) Berlin Volksbühne – neither cared for neo-Nazi 'assholes' nor for the 'guilt trips' of West German public opinion.

Even if there still were a ready and self-evident public for a critical culture of memory, what would its politics be? It was and is the firm belief of the politics of memory that the past will not be repeated, if only people remember. But as a politics and culture of memory grew in the 1970s and 1980s, so did a politics and culture of anti-Semitism and racism, as well as a desperate and terrorist identity politics. These were the first indications that there was something wrong with the original argument. The collapse of the Soviet regime and the unification of Germany further advanced these doubts. For the politics of memory proved to be utterly unprepared to face racism and anti-Semitism within Germany and deadly massacres worldwide. This challenge, more than any other, has undercut the politics of memory of the past quarter century. Once, the link between past and present was self-evident, to break the silence of oblivion and to remember also meant the overcoming of evil. Now, however, owning up to one's past no longer opens up a future. How are we to deal with immigrants; accommodate refugees; employ force against murderous regimes; relate to the new multiplicity of cultures in Germany; deal with right-wing radicals and neo-Nazis; judge German films about Israel that focus on the crazy edge of Israeli society; and approach a government-sanctioned Holocaust memory in the United States?

The irrelevance of former commemorative efforts to present conditions is evident in the inability of intellectuals to stem the tide of right radicalism, which has arisen partially in response to the atrocities in former Yugoslavia and particularly in Bosnia. If this were a case of sheer disinterest, or merely of the follies of some initiatives, it would be a relief. But it is not. German intellectuals have been, by and large, very conscientious, very alert, and they have had strong popular support. Germany after all has welcomed the largest group of refugees from former Yugoslavia. But even the best of these efforts does not make a difference – except in individual cases. In this sense, these 'good' Germans have become proverbial Schindlers, saving individuals when the course of events cannot be changed. What is lost is the belief that intellectuals might be able to stitch together alliances that could sway power, whenever the latter is in danger of charting an uncivil course. Only a few years ago the hope of swaying powers through public enlightenment had been the impetus for the postwar German politics of memory.

The Holocaust is the historical event against which current events, as small as they may seem in comparison to the threatened extinction of the European Jews, will need to be read and analysed. For this is the praxis of memory. The context of the popular reception of *Schindler's List* was the uncanny presence of ethnic war and massacres for which there is no end in sight. The reaction in the face of this violence has been panic. During the Gulf War this reaction was already visible when the bombing of Iraq and the Iraqi missile attacks on Israel threw the Germans into extraordinary turmoil. The wars in former Yugoslavia have only further heightened this sense of recognition, which is the 'real' homecoming of memories stirred by so many images of the past.

In the memorial culture of the 1970s and 1980s, Germans burdened themselves with a present that was steeped in the past, only to discover in the

1990s that they would have to engage the world as it moves out of the past into an uncertain future. The alternative to such an engagement is *not* the forgetting of the past, as the new right radicalism and neo-Nazism maintain. Rather, the unhappy alternative is memory without praxis, history without a present, brought about by an intellectual culture without public resonance.

The fact that a new generation is stepping out of the shadow of the Holocaust and the genocidal wars that have ravaged Europe in the first half of the twentieth century is not, in itself, cause for concern. It took the postwar generation of Germans a long time to acknowledge this past and it is ironic that this memory took hold when world events seemed to call for new strategies. But this does not alter the basic fact that the living memory of the past is temporal and that there is nothing in this world – no video recording of witnesses, no written or oral recollection of the pain and suffering, no record of the fact of annihilation – that can keep it alive but the labours of the imagination, or, to use the more appropriate and venerable term, the uses of *Vorstellungskraft*. It would be truly disturbing if this imagination and the praxis it entails were not forthcoming now that they are needed.

Historians, stepping out of the shadows of a murderous past, will do well to remember that, once upon a time, there was a moment when this past could have been averted.

Notes

1. This essay was first presented at a conference entitled 'In Memory: Revisiting Nazi Atrocities in Post-Cold War Europe' in Arezzo, June 1994 and subsequently as a paper 'About the Uses of Shame: The German Reception of *Schindler's List*' at the Society for Cinema Studies Conference in New York, March 1995.
2. Peter Reichel, *Politik mit der Erinnerung: Gedächtnisorte im Streit um die nationalsozialistische Vergangenheit* (Munich and Vienna 1995) uses the notion of 'politics' in a less emphatic sense. He points to the fact that memory is created in the present and that this de/construction is the subject of competing interests. Unfortunately, he leaves it at that.
3. Apart from Michael Geyer and Miriam Hansen, 'German-Jewish Memory and National Consciousness', in Geoffrey Hartmann, ed., *Holocaust Remembrance: The Shapes of Memory* (Oxford and Cambridge, Mass. 1994), pp. 175–90, see especially Elisabeth Domansky, ' "Kristallnacht", the Holocaust and the German Unity: The Meaning of November 9 as an Anniversary in Germany', *History and Memory*, no. 4, 1992, pp. 60–94.
4. Günter Grass, *Deutscher Lastenausgleich – Wider das dumpfe Einheitsgebot – Reden und Gespräche* (Frankfurt 1990; Ulrich Greiner, ' "Die Mauer im Kopf": Toward an Understanding of the 1990 Literary Dispute', *German Politics & Society*, no. 27, 1992, pp. 61–8.
5. Wolfgang Benz, 'Postwar Society and National Socialism: Remembrance, Amnesia, Rejection', *Tel Aviver Jahrbuch für Geschichte*, no. 19, 1990, pp. 1–12; Heinz Bude, *Bilanz der Nachfolge. Die Bundesrepublik und der Nationalsozialismus* (Frankfurt 1992).
6. Peter Steinbach, *Nationalsozialistische Gewaltverbrechen: Die Diskussion in der deutschen Öffentlichkeit* (Berlin 1981).

7. Deutscher Bundestag, ed., *Zur Verjährung nationalsozialistischer Verbrechen. Dokumentation der parlamentarischen Bewältigung des Problems 1960–1979*, 3 vols (Bonn 1980).

8. Bernd Eichmann, *Denkmale deutscher Vergangenheit* (Bad Honnef 1994).

9. Jürgen Habermas, *Eine Art Schadensabwicklung: kleine politische Schriften VI* (Frankfurt 1987).

10. These are undoubtedly extreme cases, but they have gained some notoriety lately after it was discovered that two former Nazis – one having actually been involved in genocide as district commander in former Galicia and the other having been at the margins of medical experiments with concentration camp inmates – changed their names in 1945 and re-emerged as staunch democrats and supporters of a politics of memory.

11. Ulrich Borchhagen, *Nach Nürnberg: Vergangenheitsbewältigung und Westintegration in der Ära Adenauer* (Hamburg 1994).

12. Rainer Maria Lepsius, 'Das Erbe des Nationalsozialismus und die politische Kultur der Nachfolgestaaten des "Großdeutschen Reiches"' in Max Haller et al., eds, *Kultur und Gesellschaft* (Frankfurt-am-Main and New York 1989).

13. Omer Bartov, 'Intellectuals and Auschwitz: Memory, History and Truth', *History and Memory*, no. 5, 1993, pp. 87–129.

14. Filbinger has since retorted with his own defence of a 'vituperated generation'. Hans Filbinger, *Die geschmähte Generation* (Munich 1987).

15. Judith Ryan, *The Uncompleted Past: Postwar German Novels and the Third Reich* (Detroit, Mich. 1983); Rolf Hochhuth, *A German Love Story* (London 1980); Peter Weiss, *The Investigation: Oratorio in 11 Cantos* (London 1966).

16. Alexander and Margarete Mitscherlich, *The Inability to Mourn* (New York 1975).

17. Heinz Bude, *Das Altern einer Generation: Die Jahrgänge 1938–1948* (Frankfurt-am-Main 1995).

18. Matthias Greffrath during a debate with Antje Vollmer at the Literaturhaus Pankow, Berlin, November 1993.

19. On the importance of generational divides in West Germany, see Ulf Preuss-Lausitz et al., *Kriegskinder, Konsumkinder, Krisenkinder: Zur Sozialisationsgeschichte seit dem Zweiten Weltkrieg* (Weinheim, Basel 1988).

20. Peter Reichel, *Politik mit der Erinnerung*, pp. 290–95.

21. On this incident, see Armin Laschet and Heinz Malangré, eds, *Philipp Jenninger. Rede und Reaktion* (Achen, Koblenz, 1989). I follow Domansky's interpretation of this incident in ' "Kristallnacht", the Holocaust and the German Unity'.

22. Michael Schneider, *Demokratie in Gefahr? Der Konflikt um die Notstandsgesetze: Sozialdemokratie, Gewerkschaften und intellektueller Protest, 1958–1968* (Bonn 1986).

23. Antonia Grunenberg, *Antifaschismus. ein deutscher Mythos* (Reinbek 1993); Jürgen Danyel, 'Vom schwierigen Umgang mit der Schuld. Die Deutschen in der DDR und der Nationalsozialismus', *Zeitschrift für Geschichtswissenschaft*, no. 40, 1992, pp. 915–28.

24. Christa Wolf, *The Model Childhood* (London 1983).

25. John Reddick, *The 'Danzig Trilogy' of Gunter Grass: A Study of The Tin Drum, Cat and Mouse, and Dog Years* (New York 1975).

26. Uwe Johnson, *Jahrestage: Aus dem Leben der Gesine Cresspahl*, 4 vols (Frankfurt 1970–83).

27. One of the first was Bernward Vesper, *Die Reise: Romanessay*, edited from the incomplete manuscript by Jörg Schröder and Klaus Behnken (Reinbek 1983).

28. Karl A. Otto, *APO: Außerparlamentarische Opposition in Quellen und Dokumenten, 1960–1970* (Cologne 1988).

29. Conrad Taler, 'Vertanes Erbe: Von der Deformation und der notwendigen Renaissance des Antifaschismus', *Leviathan*, no. 21, 1993, pp. 254–71.

30. Dan Bar-On, *Legacy of Silence: Encounters with Children of the Third Reich* (Cambridge, Mass. 1989).

31. Jillian Becker, *Hitler's Children: The Story of The Baader-Meinhof Terrorist Gang* (Philadelphia 1977).

32. Jürgen Habermas, *The Past as Future: Vergangenheit als Zukunft*, Jürgen Habermas interviewed by Michael Haller (Lincoln, Nebr. 1994).

33. I pick up a discussion that was initiated by Helmuth Lethen, *Verhaltenslehren der Kälte* (Frankfurt 1993).

34. The two sides are demonstrated in Hans-Ulrich Wehler, *Entsorgung der deutschen Vergangenheit? Ein polemischer Essay zum 'Historikerstreit'* (Munich 1988) and his *Deutsche Gesellschaftsgeschichte*, 3 vols (Munich, 1987–95).

35. David Blackbourn and Geoff Eley, *The Peculiarities of the German History: Bourgeois Society and Politics in Nineteenth Century Germany* (New York 1984).

36. Christian Streit, *Keine Kameraden: Die Wehrmacht und die sowjetischen Kriegsgefangenen 1941–1945* (Stuttgart 1978).

37. *Das Deutsche Reich und der Zweite Weltkrieg*, edited by Militärgeschichtliches Forschungsamt, 6 vols (Stuttgart, 1979–).

38 *Bericht über Kurt Waldheim*, edited by an international commission of historians designated to establish the military service of Lt Kurt Waldheim (Vienna 1988); Richard Mitten, *The Politics of Antisemitic Prejudice. The Waldheim Phenomenon in Austria* (Boulder, Colo. 1992).

39. Hannes Heer and Klaus Naumann, eds, *Vernichtungskrieg: Verbrechen der Wehrmacht, 1941–1944* (Hamburg 1995).

40. Lutz Niethammer et al., *Lebensgeschichte und Sozialkultur im Ruhrgebiet 1930 bis 1960*, 3 vols (Berlin, 1983–); Alf Lüdtke, *The History of Everyday Life: Reconstructing Historical Experiences and Ways of Life* (Princeton, N.J. 1995).

41. Ruth Wodak et al., eds, *Die Sprache der Vergangenheiten. Öffentliches Gedenken in österreichischen und deutschen Medien* (Frankfurt 1994); Jürgen Förster, ed., *Stalingrad: Ereignis – Wirkung – Symbol* (Munich, 1992).

42. Anna Rosmus-Wenninger, *Wiederstand und Verfolgung: Am Beispiel Passaus 1933–1939* (Passau 1983).

43. Reinhard Rürup, ed., *Topographie des Terrors. Gestapo, SS und Reichssicherheitshauptamt auf dem 'Prinz-Albrecht-Gelände'. Eine Dokumentation*, 9th ed., (Berlin 1993).

44. Bernd Eichmann, *Versteinert, verharmlost, vergessen. KZ-Gedenkstätten in der Bundesrepublik Deutschland* (Frankfurt 1986); Ulrike Puvogel, *Gedenkstätten für die Opfer des Nationalsozialismus. Eine Dokumentation* (Bonn 1987).

45. Gordon J. Horwitz, *In the Shadow of Death: Living outside the Gates of Mauthausen* (New York 1990).

46. Harold Marcuse, 'Nazi Crimes and Identity in West Germany: Collective Memories of the Dachau Concentration Camp, 1945–1990' (Ph.D. thesis, University of Michigan, Ann Arbor, Mich. 1992).

47. Georg Franz-Willing, *Vergangenheitsbewältigung: Bundesrepublikanischer Nationalmasochismus* (Coburg 1992); Armin Mohler, *Der Nasenring: Die Vergangenheitsbewältigung vor und nach der Mauer* (Munich 1991).

48. Alice Miller, *Breaking Down the Wall of Silence: The Liberating Experience of Facing Painful Truth* (New York 1991); Klaus Theweleit, *Male Phantasies*, 2 vols (Minneapolis, Minn. 1987–89). The likely negative reaction to these books is not entirely made up, because I do recall the outrage on the street after the publication of Tilmann Moser, *Years of Apprenticeship on the Couch: Fragments of My Psychoanalysis* (New York 1977), which detailed the family life of the Moser family, the parents being friends of my family and the younger brothers of Tilmann being my childhood chums.

49. Gita Sereny, *Albert Speer: His Battle with Truth* (New York 1995).

50. Guy Debord, *Society of the Spectacle* (Detroit, Mich. 1977).

51. Gertrud Koch, 'The Angel of Forgetfulness and the Black Box of Facticity: Trauma and Memory in Claude Lanzmann's Film *Shoah*', *History and Memory*, no. 3, 1991, pp. 119–34.

52. Aleida Assmann and Dietrich Harth, eds, *Mnemosyne. Formen und Funktionen der kulturellen Erinnerung* (Frankfurt-am-Main 1991). This approach to (traumatized) memory beyond psychology is worth special attention. It insists that memory is, in the tradition of mnemonics, keyed up with images, and, hence, what one would need to know are the images to which memories are tied.

53. Pierre Nora, ed., *Les Lieux de memoire*, 3 vols (Paris, 1984–92).
54. Michael Cohn, *The Jews in Germany, 1949–1993: The Building of a Minority* (Westport, Conn. 1994).
55. I observed the effects of this 'moral distantiation' after a recent showing of Leni Riefenstahl's most blatant, but extremely seductive Nazi short *Tag der Freiheit – unsere Wehrmacht* (1935) in Leipzig (1995). Several groups of viewers commented that, yes, back then these cuts of high action (the Wehrmacht parade at the Nuremberg party rally in 1935 dissolving into the high drama of a military show-exercise) must have been extremely powerful and moving. The implication was that this is no longer the case, but, in fact, a case of acute fascination was instantly exorcized into the past.
56. Andreas Huyssen, *Twilight Memories: Marking Time in a Culture of Amnesia* (New York 1994).
57. See Domansky, ' "Kristallnacht", the Holocaust and the German Unity'.
58. Ronald Inglehart, *The Silent Revolution: Changing Values and Political Styles among Western Publics* (Princeton, N.J. 1977).
59. Mariam Niroumand, 'Die tiefe Sehnsucht der Regiseure', *die tageszeitung* 20 February 1995, p. 3.
60. Gabriele Taylor, *Pride, Shame, and Guilt: Emotions of Self-Assessment* (Oxford and New York 1985).
61. Alf Lüdtke, ' "Coming to Terms with the Past": Illusions of Remembering, Ways of Forgetting Nazism in West Germany', *Journal of Modern History*, no. 65, 1993, pp. 542–72.
62. Ruth Klüger, *Weiter leben: eine Jugend* (Munich 1994).
63. Alphons Silbermann and Herbert Sallen, *Juden in Westdeutschland: Selbstbildnis und Fremdbild einer Minorität* (Cologne 1992).
64. Frank Stern, *The Whitewashing of the Yellow Badge: Antisemitism and Philosemitism in Postwar Germany* (Oxford and New York 1992).
65. Geoffrey Hartmann, ed., *Bitburg in Moral and Political Perspective* (Bloomington, Ind. 1986).
66. The heated debate is barely reflected in Christoph Stölzl, ed., *Die Neue Wache unter den Linden: Ein deutsches Denkmal im Wandel der Geschichte* (Berlin 1993). But see Akademie der Künste, ed., *Streit um die Neue Wache. Zur Gestaltung einer zentralen Gedenkstätte* (Berlin 1993). As far as I can tell, this was the first substantive debate on 'how-to-remember' the past.
67. Klaus Naumann, 'Dresdener Pietà: Eine Fallstudie zum "Gedenkjahr 1995" ', *Mittelweg*, 36 no. 4, 1995, pp. 67–81.
68. Interview with Steven Spielberg, ' "Die ganze Wahrheit schwarz auf weiß": Regisseur Steven Spielberg über seinen Film Schindlers Liste', *Der Spiegel*, no. 8, 1994, p. 186.
69. This phenomenon is discussed at some length in Bjorn Krondorfer, *Reconciliation and Remembrance: Encounters between Young Jews and Germans* (New Haven, Conn. 1995).
70. I rely on Andrew S. Bergerson, 'In the Shadow of the Towers: An Ethnographic Diary of a German-Israeli Student Exchange Program in Hildesheim, Germany' (ms).
71. Klaus Hartung, 'Spiegelreflexe', *Die Zeit*, vol 20, no. 13, May 1994, p. 18; Johannes Leithäuser, 'Peiliche Enthüllungen, verschleierte Reden', *Frankfurter Allgemeine Zeitung*, no. 131, 8 June 1995, p. 4.
72. Renata Stih and Frieder Schnock, *Arbeitsbuch für ein Denkmal in Berlin. Orte des Erinnerns im Bayerischen Viertel: Ausgrenzung und Entrechtung, Vertreibung, Deportation und Ermordung von Berliner Juden in den Jahren 1933 bis 1945* (Berlin 1993).
73. Jane Kramer, 'The Politics of Memory', *New Yorker*, 14 August 1995, pp. 48–65.
74. Wolf Donner, 'Draufhalten ist nicht genug', *Frankfurter Allgemeine Zeitung*, no. 276, 27 November 1993, p. 27; Mariam Niroumand, 'Den doofen Staatsbürger aufklären', *die tageszeitung*, 8 December 1993, p. 4.
75. *die tageszeitung*, 25 April 1994, p. 23.
76. *Die Macht der Bilder*, dir. Ray Müller (1993) is the title of a documentary on Leni Riefenstahl.

77. What was 'wrong' with the film and the exhibition had been considered 'right' only a short while ago, because one could not possibly conceive of anyone not being moved to revulsion. The director presumed and staged his film for a critical public that no longer exists or can no longer be expected as a matter of course. In fact, the neo-Nazi of the documentary (he has since been tried and convicted for his Auschwitz denial in the film, and was unmasked as an informer for the political police) is a good example of this very change. The grandiloquent young man is not only the child of a 'sixties couple' but he himself grew up engaging in the kind of memory culture (*Aktion Sühnezeichen*) whose consciousness-raising effect the director makes the prerequisite of his film. The neo-Nazi himself is an example of the failure of universal enlightenment through public culture, much as the filmmaker is an example of the historicity of the German politics of memory.

NOTES ON
CONTRIBUTORS

JOAN COPJEC is currently a Fellow at the Society for the Humanities, Cornell University. She teaches at the University of Buffalo and is also Director of the Center for the Study of Psychoanalysis and Culture. The author of *Read My Desire: Lacan against the Historicists*, she is completing a study on ethics and feminism tentatively titled *The Ethics of the Absolute All*.

MICHAEL GEYER is Professor of Contemporary History at the University of Chicago and, currently, Leibnizprofessor at the University of Leipzig. He has written extensively on German history between the First and Second World Wars, and on contemporary German culture. He is completing a book-length study on the stigma of violence in twentieth-century German society.

ANDREW HEWITT is the author of *Fascist Modernism* and *Political Inversions: Homosexuality and Modernism*, which will be published later this year. He is Associate Professor of Comparative Literature at the University of Buffalo.

JULIET FLOWER MACCANNELL is Professor of English and Comparative Literature at the University of California, Irvine and a Fellow at the Headlands Center for the Arts in San Francisco. Her most recent book is *Regime of the Brother: After the Patriarchy*.

JACOB ROGOZINSKI, formerly the Director of Programmes at the College International de Philosophie in Paris, now teaches in the Department of Philosophy, Paris VIII. He has published several studies on Kant, Arendt, Heidegger and contemporary French philosophy. In English, his essays can be found in *Philosophy Today, Research in Phenomenology* and *L'Esprit Createur*.

RENATA SALECL currently teaches at the New School for Social Research in New York and is also a researcher at the Institute for Criminology, Faculty of Law, University of Ljubljana. She is the author of *The Spoils of Freedom: Psychoanalysis and Feminism after the Fall of Socialism*.

GÉRALD SFEZ, Director of Programmes at the Collège International de Philosophie in Paris, is a philosopher who has published extensively on the political writings of Machiavelli.

SLAVOJ ŽIŽEK is still dogged by the epithet 'the Giant of Ljubljana', though this year he is teaching in the US, at Columbia University and Princeton. *The Metastases of Enjoyment* and *Mapping Ideology* (ed.) are the most recent of his numerous books.

ALENKA ZUPANČIČ is a researcher at the Institute for Philosophy, University of Ljubljana. Her book *Die Ethik des Realen: Lacan, Kant* was published in German last year.

INDEX